BOLLINGEN SERIES XLV

The Collected Works of Paul Valéry

Edited by Jackson Mathews

VOLUME 13

PAUL VALÉRY

AESTHETICS

Translated by
Ralph Manheim

With an Introduction by
Herbert Read

BOLLINGEN SERIES XLV · 13

PANTHEON BOOKS

Copyright © 1964 by Bollingen Foundation
Published by Bollingen Foundation, New York, N.Y.
Distributed by Pantheon Books, A Division of
Random House, Inc., New York, N.Y.

THIS IS VOLUME THIRTEEN OF THE
COLLECTED WORKS OF PAUL VALÉRY
CONSTITUTING NUMBER XLV IN BOLLINGEN SERIES
SPONSORED BY BOLLINGEN FOUNDATION.
IT IS THE SIXTH VOLUME OF THE
COLLECTED WORKS TO APPEAR

Library of Congress catalogue card no. 56–9337
Printed in the United States by
Clarke & Way, Inc., New York, N.Y.
DESIGNED BY ANDOR BRAUN

CONTENTS

Introduction

It is possible that Valéry would not have approved a volume in his collected works with the title *Aesthetics*: it would have seemed to him a little too pretentious. Although some of the essays that follow were addressed to academic audiences, he always apologized for his temerity and disclaimed any ambition to compete in their systematic researches. He remained an amateur, and to the French Philosophical Society described his "somewhat adventurous investigations" as "obstinate divagations." "A *system*? Certainly not. The very name terrifies me. At most a body of ideas—or more precisely, a collection of problems. . . ." But one has not to read far in this volume to discover that Valéry had an unerring instinct for the problems that remain unsolved in aesthetics, and that what he left unsaid—the scaffolding of any would-be system —was hardly worth saying by a man of his intelligence.

Valéry approached this subject as a poet, and although he had a lively interest in other arts, notably architecture, painting, and the dance, he generalized from his own creative experiences, and believed, indeed, that such was the only firm basis for generalization. For that reason, perhaps, he rarely brings to his support the observations of other artists or philosophers, though one is constantly aware of the presence of Bergson somewhere in the background, and in one place we find him quoting Wagner with approval: "I composed *Tristan* under the stress of a great passion and *after several months of theoretical meditation*." But no wonder, for in this "brief sentence" Wagner had expressed Valéry's own profoundest conviction—that the use of "a kind of conscious calculation" is not only compatible with the practice of an art, but "indispensable if the artist's action and the work itself are to achieve the highest degree of power and effectiveness."

There is a distinction here between the artist's *action* and the *work of art itself* to which we must return, but we must first elucidate what is in effect the point from which Valéry's obstinate divagations depart: his conviction that the intellect could not be discounted in the creation of a work of art. Our first impression is that such a conviction may be a reaction to the prevailing philosophy of flux, but we then discover that Valéry had his own definition of intellect, one that removes it from the camp of any crude positivism. He describes himself as a man who has never seen a contradiction between intelligence and sensibility. He believed in an intellectual mode of sensibility—in the possibility that "the intelligence, in the exercise of its boundless investigations, aroused emotions which, despite their special tonality, were quite similar to those associated with the impressions we receive from the spectacles of nature, the events of emotional life, and matters of love or faith." The art which might fixate or renew such a rare kind of emotion would inevitably be of limited appeal, but Valéry had "felt the effects of this sensibility violently enough to conceive the ambition of putting some part of it into literature. . . ."

Conscious calculation might be compatible with the practice of an art, and essential for its greatest effectiveness, but Valéry was careful to keep reason in her place—in "some grotto of our mind" from which she appears from time to time to enjoin us to consider the possible consequences of our acts. But the work of the artist, "even the wholly intellectual part of it, cannot be reduced to the operations of a guiding reason." In spite of certain traditional prejudices, which drew him to the side of order and classicism, Valéry's intellectual honesty compelled him to recognize the sensational basis of the arts. "The artist, whether he likes it or not, is absolutely unable to free himself from a sense of the arbitrary. He progresses from the arbitrary toward a certain necessity, and from a certain disorder toward a certain order; and he cannot do without this constant sense of an arbitrariness and disorder that resist the thing which is coming into being beneath his hands and which strikes him as necessary and ordered." Valéry was always aware of the dialectical nature of the creative process, the *drama* of creation, as he called it; and for that reason the possibility of reducing the problems of art to a system of dogmatic aesthetics must be regarded as a vain illusion —the desire to slide from the singular to the universal as a temptation of the dialectical demon. "We must answer the demon with this simple observation: the effect of the Beautiful upon a man is to make him *mute*!"

The effect of the Beautiful: Valéry nowhere admits that the "infinite diversity of concrete and complex impressions" involved in art should be justified by their own vitality— there was no expressionist element in his aesthetics. But it may be suggested that in admitting the accidental or the gratuitous as an element in art he was coming dangerously near to such an unclassical doctrine. "The artist," he said, "lives with *his* arbitrariness and in the expectation of *his* necessity. . . . He awaits an answer that must be *absolutely precise. . .* to a question that is *essentially incomplete.*"

The ideal is completeness, perfection; but it is unattainable. More than that: it is indefinable. All his reflections on the subject of art yield nothing but negative propositions. There is a kind of pleasure to be derived from the work of art, both in its creation and in its active contemplation; but "all men's efforts to define, regularize, regulate, measure, stabilize, or insure this pleasure and its production have thus far been vain and fruitless." Perhaps to give some justification to the activities of the eminent students of aesthetics he was addressing on this occasion, he then admitted that the failure of these efforts has sometimes been curiously creative and fecund.

Nevertheless, Valéry spent much of his time attempting to define the pleasure of art, and since he had come to the conclusion that this particular kind of pleasure (for there are simple pleasures which do not come into the question) is autonomous and indeterminate, extensive description of the phenomenon was the only, though inadequate, way of defining it. Inadequate? One passage at least must be isolated for its wealth of meaning:

A pleasure which sometimes goes so deep as to make us suppose we have a direct understanding of the object that causes it; a pleasure which arouses the intelligence, defies it, and makes it love its defeat; still more, a pleasure that can stimulate the strange need to produce or reproduce the thing, event, object, or state to which it seems attached, and which thus becomes a source of activity *without any definite end*, capable of imposing a discipline, a zeal, a torment on a whole lifetime, and of filling it, sometimes to overflowing—such a pleasure presents a singularly specious enigma, which could scarcely escape the attention or the clutches of the metaphysical hydra. What could have been more worthy of our philosopher's will to power than this order of phenomena in which *to feel, to possess, to will,* and *to make* seemed to be joined in an essential and highly remarkable interaction that defied his Scholastic, not to say Cartesian, efforts to split up the difficulty. The alliance of a form, a material, an idea, an action, and a passion; the absence of any clearly determined aim or of any result that might be expressed in finite terms; a desire and its recompense, each regenerating the other; a desire that creates and hence causes itself; sometimes breaking away from all particular creation and ultimate satisfaction, thus revealing itself to be a desire *to create for the sake of creating*—all this aroused the metaphysical mind: to this problem it devoted the same attention as to all the other problems it habitually invents in exercising its function of reconstructing knowledge in a universal form.

All Valéry's aesthetic theory is but an expansion of this paragraph, but that does not mean the theory is limited: on the contrary, it is, like the work of art itself, a system of indefinite regeneration. What is most characteristic of a work of art is its "unwearied" existence,

> *For ever warm and still to be enjoy'd,*
> *For ever panting, and for ever young. . .*

"*Sensibility*, which is its beginning and its end, abhors a vacuum." "What is most characteristic is the need to see again, to hear again, to experience indefinitely," and in that need lies the germ of the work of art. "We recognize a work of art by the fact that no 'idea' it can arouse in us, no act it suggests to us, can exhaust or put an end to it: however long we may breathe of a flower that accords with our sense of smell, we are never surfeited, for the enjoyment of the perfume revives our need for it; and there is no memory, no thought, no action, that can annul its effect and *wholly* free us from its power."

Lest we should dismiss these observations as mere sensationalism, Valéry hastens to assign a role to intellect. He seems to concede its historical nature. It was preceded by a naïve phase of man's artistic development: then "a kind of calculation" gradually "entered into the work of art. Forms became more complex, the artist tried to make them more interesting." A prejudice in favor of spontaneity remained, and there was much "talk of *inspiration*" (not a reputable faculty in Valéry's aesthetic). At some stage in the evolution of art, the intellect intervened, and to Valéry this was a desirable event, enlarging the scope of art. "The higher the culture, the greater becomes the role of the intellect. It increases with the artist's awareness of the external effect of his work, its effect on the public. It increases also with the physical magnitude of the work: when, like a work of architecture, it is very large and demands considerable time, the co-operation of many men, an advanced technique, the part of the intellect, of knowledge and thought, becomes preponderant." That such a development might, as Collingwood perceived, involve a fatal corruption of consciousness, Valéry does not seem to have realized. He remains "a man who has never seen a contradiction . . . between intelligence and sensibility, conscious reflection and its raw material. . . . " Not only his reflections on art, but the status of his own poetry, depend on this concept of "a kind of intellectual sensibility," on "this strange co-ordination between two modes of vital activity." His ideal was the "felt thought" of the English metaphysical poets.

We return to his notion of art as an active process. Bergson had defined the work of art as an arrest of the process of perception or feeling: as a moment of crystallization in the flux of time. Valéry could not accept such a static notion of art. To him "the process of manufacture is far more interesting than the work itself," and the purpose of a work of art was to set up an analogous process in the spectator or auditor. Art as a *value* depends on the indeterminacy of the act of communication. It is essential that between the producer and the consumer there should be something "irreducible"—"that the work, the medium, should not give the person it affects anything that can be reduced to an idea of the author's person and thinking." This is not merely the classical ideal of objectivity or impersonality: but something much subtler and more profound, which effectively dissociates Valéry from any expressionist theory of art. "All the artist can do," he says, "is to fashion *some thing* that will produce a certain effect on someone else's mind. There will never be any accurate way of comparing what has happened in the two minds; and moreover, if what has happened in the one were communicated directly to the other, all art would collapse, all the effects of art would disappear. The whole effect of art, the *effort* the author's work demands of the consumer, would be impossible without the interposition, between the author and his audience, of a new and impenetrable element capable of acting upon other men's being. *A creator is one who makes others create.*"

There, in that emphatic aphorism, we find the essential aesthetic of Valéry—the "crucial notion" of "things that bear within them something which creates the need for them." Facility has no place in Valéry's art, nor in his aesthetic. Art is a striving, an inner effort of construction. What is constructed is a product of inner necessity, "the indissoluble bond between form and material that are revealed to us by the humblest of shells." It was characteristic of Valéry to take a sea shell as a paradigm for the work of art, and to find in its mysterious and yet mathematical act of formation a parallel for his own incomplete thoughts on the formation of the work of art. Order and fantasy, invention and necessity, law and exception, and above all the fashioning action—all these features of the work of art are exemplified in the shell, as also in a crystal or a flower. And should we for a moment wonder if the image is not too inhuman, Valéry is ready to remind us that it is we who are limited, and should therefore hesitate to compare the best of our creations with a work of Nature.

HERBERT READ

Part I

Man and the Sea Shell

Preface

SINCE *the strangely delicate drawings, woven rather than traced by the fine and sensitive point of Henri Mondor's pencil, have provided an occasion to reprint this little work, I should like to say a few words more on the subject, as though, having taken leave of a friend, I should go back to add a detail or two to our conversation.*

It was chance that made me write about sea shells, very much as though bidding me, by the seashore, to take notice of one of these delightful objects. In taking this marvel as my theme, I did the same as a passer-by who has just picked up a small, curiously formed, calcareous shell in the sand; who examines it and handles it, admiring its mineral convolutions and the arrangement of spots, streaks, spines suggesting the past movement in which they were engendered. I meditated my unexpected theme and raised it closer to the eyes of my mind; I turned it over and over in my thoughts. . . . I knew next to nothing about mollusks, and I took pleasure in illumining, one by one, the facets of my ignorance.

Ignorance is a treasure of infinite price that most men squander, when they should cherish its least fragments; some ruin it by educating themselves, others, unable so much as to conceive of making use of it, let it waste away. Quite on the contrary, we should search for it assiduously in what we think we know best. Leaf through a dictionary or try to make one, and you will find that every word covers and masks a well so bottomless that the questions you toss into it arouse no more than an echo.

In the matter of shells, then, I did my best to define my ignorance, to organize it, and above all to preserve it.

Among the many objects that confront man's mind with questions, some more legitimate than others, he is particularly fascinated by those which, by their form or properties, lead him to reflect on his own powers or tendencies. He is amazed to find objects which, though it is inconceivable to him that they should have been made, he can compare to those he is able to make. In such objects he seems to recognize his own familiar modes of thought, his own types of conscious action: his incorrigible "causality" and "finality"; his geometry; his ingenuity; his need for order and his bursts of inventiveness. As soon as he glimpses an adaptation, a regular functioning, definable forms, an order, in a product of "nature," he cannot help trying to "understand"; that is, the object becomes a problem for him and he begins to consider it as the effect or result of some sort of making, which remains to be defined.

Complete human action, with its own possibility and necessity, its means, its material, its aim, is the inevitable and unique type on which every "explanation" is modeled. What we know of ourselves, our acts, our impulses, of what satisfies our instincts and fits in with our structure, in other words the "forces," the "time," the "space" that suit us, these are the instruments by which we reduce all things to our measure. When we are perplexed, that is, when we have carried our familiar questionnaire too far, an appropriately vague language comes to our aid, masks our helplessness, and enables us (what an admirable thing) to go on arguing indefinitely.

We talk about creation, evolution, chance, *and we endow these terms with precisely everything required in the way of power, disorder, time, and large numbers, to stimulate our minds and, by an odd contradiction, to satisfy them. It is a great mystery to me how opinions on subjects of this kind can differ as much as we know they do.*

But I see that I am gradually slipping from one problem to another, from the formation of shells to the formation of hypotheses, which is perhaps less disheartening to meditate upon. Our intellect is not so rich as it supposes in tenable hypotheses. A man is always at a loss when experience shows him that one phenomenon must be connected with another which seemed unrelated to it. He must own that the connection would never have occurred to him.

Yet mysterious as the genesis of shells may be to the metaphysical eye, an artist, at all events, can examine them as long as he pleases without wasting his time.

Run off by the billions, each different from the rest (though the difference is sometimes imperceptible), they offer an infinite number of solutions to the most delicate problems of art, and of absolutely perfect answers to the questions they suggest to us.

I have indicated in the text of my essay that it was child's play for what we call "living nature" to obtain the relation between form and matter that we take so much pains to attempt or to make some show of achieving. Our hands busy themselves in various acts, all distinct and determinate; with our eyes and our intention we order and supervise this superficial maneuver; but our activity is composite and must always be so; and thus we can never, in our object, arrive at the happy union of substance and shape that is achieved by the inarticulate creature which makes nothing, *but whose work, little by little, is differentiated from its flesh, progressively moving away from the living state as though passing from one state of balance to another.*

In this invincible and one might say flawless progression of form, which involves and develops its whole setting according to the continuous fatality of its convolutions and seems to create its own time, we admire the combination of rhythm, marked by the regular spots or spines, and of indivisible movement. It is like seeing music. The correspondence of ornaments on successive spirals suggests a counterpoint, while the continuity sustains the main theme of the rotation of the surface.

But suddenly an end must come. This strange torsion must cease, the nacre on the inside and the coarser covering must join, and the distinction between the two substances of the shell must vanish or explain itself, while at the same time its form must be completed by some decision that remains to be arrived at.

The problem is very general in kind. Living nature must solve it in all the types it displays, all of which involve extremities to be modeled and cavities or tubes that must be made to reach the outside world. The mind staggers at the mere thought of analyzing the innumerable solutions it has found. We yearn for a profound geometry, a very exact knowledge of what is revealed by dissection and microscopic examination, and an exquisite artistic feeling which, taken together, might enable us to isolate some simple basic principle of natural morphology.

This is a mystery that has always teased my mind, for I can find nothing in the arts that captivates me more than forms or phases of transition, the refinements of modulation. For me, perfect modulation is the crown of art. But in our time little importance is attached

to this ideal of mine. The architect knows only his rule and square.
The musician does pretty much as he pleases. The poet proceeds by
leaps and bounds. But nature has preserved her cautious methods,
the inflection in which she envelops her changes of pace, direction,
or physiological function. She knows how to finish a plant, how to
open nostrils, a mouth, a vulva, how to create a setting for an eyeball;
she thinks suddenly of the sea shell when she has to unfold the
pavilion of an ear, which she seems to fashion the more intricately as
the species is more alert.

If THERE were a poetry of the marvels and emotions of the
intellect (something I have dreamed of all my life), it could
find no subject more delightful and stimulating than the por-
trayal of a mind responding to the appeal of one of those
remarkable natural formations which we observe (or rather
which make us observe them) here and there, among the
innumerable things of indifferent and accidental form that
surround us.

Like a pure sound or a melodic system of pure sounds in
the midst of noises, so a *crystal*, a *flower*, a *sea shell* stand out
from the common disorder of perceptible things. For us they
are privileged objects, more intelligible to the view, although
more mysterious upon reflection, than all those which we
see indiscriminately. They present us with a strange union of
ideas: order and fantasy, invention and necessity, law and
exception. In their appearance we find a kind of *intention* and
action that seem to have fashioned them rather as man might
have done, but at the same time we find evidence of methods
forbidden and inaccessible to us. We can imitate these singular forms; our hands can cut a prism, fashion an imitation
flower, turn or model a shell; we are even able to express their
characteristics of symmetry in a formula, or represent them

quite accurately in a geometric construction. Up to this point we can share with "nature": we can endow her with designs, a sort of mathematics, a certain taste and imagination that are not infinitely different from ours; but then, after we have endowed her with all the human qualities she needs to make herself understood by human beings, she displays all the inhuman qualities needed to disconcert us. . . . We can conceive of the *structure* of these objects, and this is what interests us and holds our attention; but we do not understand their gradual *formation*, and that is what intrigues us. Although we ourselves were formed by imperceptible growth, we do not know how to create anything in that way.

The shell which I hold and turn between my fingers, and which offers me a combined development of the simple themes of the helix and the spiral, involves me in a degree of astonishment and concentration that leads where it may: to superficial remarks and observations, naïve questions, "poetic" comparisons, beginnings of reckless "theories." . . . And my mind vaguely anticipates the entire innate treasure of responses that rise within me in the presence of a thing that arrests and questions me. . . .

First I try to describe this thing to my own satisfaction. It suggests to me the movement we make when we roll a sheet of paper into a cone. One edge of the paper forms an inclined plane that rises toward the tip and ends after a few turns. The mineral cone, however, is formed by a tube and not by a flat sheet. With a tube closed at one end and assumed to be flexible, I not only can reproduce quite well the essential form of a shell, but can also fashion a number of others, some of which, like this one I am examining, might be inscribed in a cone; while the others, obtained by reducing the *pitch* of the conic helix, will end by coiling like the spring of a watch.

Thus the idea of a *tube* and the concept of *torsion* suffice for a first approximation of the form under consideration.

But this simplicity applies only in principle. If I examine a whole collection of shells, I find a marvelous variety. The cone lengthens or flattens, narrows or broadens; the spirals become more pronounced or merge with one another; the surface is incrusted with knobs or spines, sometimes strikingly long, radiating from a center; or it may swell, puffing out into bulbs separated by strangulations or concave gorges where the curved lines meet. Engraved in hard matter, furrows, wrinkles, or ribs follow and accentuate one another, while, aligned on the generatrix, the protuberances, the spines, the little bumps rise in tiers, corresponding from row to row and breaking up the regular intervals of the planes. The alternation of these "ornaments" illustrates, more than it interrupts, the continuity of the general *convolution* of the form. It enriches but does not modify the basic motif of the helical spiral.

Without modifying it, without ceasing to follow and confirm its own unique law, this *idea* of periodic progression exploits all the abstract fecundity of the helix and develops its full capacity for sensuous charm. It beguiles the eye, drawing it into a kind of controlled vertigo. A mathematician, no doubt, would easily read this system of "skew" lines and surfaces and would sum it up in a few signs, a numerical relation, for it is in the nature of the intelligence to do away with the infinite and to abolish repetition. But common language is ill suited to describing forms, and I despair of expressing their whirling grace. Actually, even the mathematician is baffled when in the end the tube suddenly broadens, breaks, curls back, and overflows into uneven lips, often bordered, waved, or fluted, which part as though made of flesh, disclosing in a fold of the softest mother-of-pearl the smoothly inclined starting point of an internal whorl that recedes into darkness.

Helices, spirals, spatial developments of angular relations—the observer who considers them and endeavors to translate them into his own modes of expression and understanding, cannot fail to perceive one essential characteristic of forms of this type. Like a hand, like an ear, one shell cannot be mistaken for another that is its symmetrical counterpart. If we draw two spirals, one the mirror image of the other, no manner of moving these twin curves will enable us to superimpose one on the other. It is the same with two stairways, similar but turning in opposite directions. All shells whose form derives from the rolling of a tube necessarily manifest this *dissymmetry*, to which Pasteur attached so profound an importance, and from which he derived the main idea for the investigations that led him from the study of certain crystals to that of ferments and their living agents.

But despite the dissymmetry of all shells we might, among a thousand specimens, expect the number of those whose spirals turn "clockwise" to be approximately equal to those turning in the opposite direction. This is not the case. Just as there are few left-handed men, there are few shells which viewed from the tip disclose a spiral receding from right to left. Here we have another, quite remarkable sort of statistical dissymmetry. To say that this difference in bias is *accidental* is only to say that it exists. . . .

Thus the mathematician I mentioned a moment ago has been able to make three simple observations in his study of shells.

He first noted that he could describe their general form with the help of very simple notions drawn from his arsenal of definitions and operations. Next, he saw that quite sudden —one might say unforeseen—changes occurred in the forms he was contemplating: the curves and surfaces that made it possible to represent their construction suddenly broke off or degenerated: whereas the cone, the helix, the spiral can well go on "indefinitely," the shell suddenly wearies of following them. *But why not one turn more?*

Lastly, he finds that the statistics of right-handed and left-handed shells marks a strong preference for the former.

We have given a superficial and very general description of a shell chosen at random; and now, if we have time and the inclination to follow the development of our immediate impressions, we might ask ourselves a very naïve question, one of those questions that arise in us before we remember that we are not newborn, but already know something. First of all, we must allow for this; and remember that our knowledge consists largely in "thinking that we know" and in thinking that others know.

We are always refusing to listen to the simple soul within us. We ignore the inner child who always wants to see things for the first time. If he questions, we discourage his curiosity, calling it childish because it is boundless, on the pretext that we have been to school and learned that there is a science of all things, which we might consult if we wished, and that it would be a waste of time to think in our own way and no other about an object that suddenly arrests us and calls for an answer. Perhaps we are too well aware that an enormous stock of facts and theories has been amassed, and that in thumbing through the encyclopedias we may find hundreds of names and words that represent this potential wealth; and we are too sure that we can always find someone somewhere who, if only to impress us, will be glad to enlighten us on any subject whatsoever. And we promptly withdraw our attention from most of the things that begin to arouse it, thinking of the learned men who must have explored or disposed of the event that has just stirred our intelligence. But such caution is sometimes laziness; and moreover, there is no proof that everything has really been examined, and in all its aspects.

So I shall ask my very naïve question. I can easily imagine that I know nothing about shells except what I see on picking this one up; and that I know nothing about this shell's origin, its function, its relations with what I am not considering at this particular moment. I am following the example of the man who one day made *tabula rasa*.

I look *for the first time* at this thing I have found. I note what I have said about its form, and I am perplexed. Then I ask myself the question: *Who made this?*

Who made this? asks the naïve moment.

My first stir of thought has been to think of *making*.

The idea of *making* is the first and most human of ideas. "To explain" is never anything more than to describe a way of *making*: it is merely to remake in thought. The *why* and the *how*, which are only ways of expressing the implications of this idea, inject themselves into every statement, demanding satisfaction at all costs. Metaphysics and science are merely an *unlimited* development of this demand. They may even lead us to pretend not to know what we know, when what we know refuses to be reduced to a clear knowledge of how to make something. . . . This is what we mean by going back to the beginnings of knowledge.

Here then I will introduce the artifice of a doubt: considering this shell, in whose shape I think I can discern a certain "construction" and as it were the work of some hand not acting "at random," I ask myself: *Who made it?*

But soon my question undergoes a transformation. It takes a short step forward along the path of my naïveté, and I begin to inquire by what sign we recognize that a given object is or is not *made by a man?*

It may seem somewhat absurd to pretend not to know that a wheel, a vase, a piece of cloth, or a table has been produced by someone's industry, since we know perfectly well that it has. But what I say is that we do not know this *just by examining these things*. If no one had ever told us, then by what marks, by what signs should we know? What is it that indicates the presence or absence of a human operation? When an anthropologist finds a piece of flint, does he not often hesitate as to whether man or chance fashioned it?

The problem after all is no more futile nor any more naïve than speculation about *who made* a certain fine work in music or poetry; whether it was born of the Muse, or sent by Fortune, or whether it was the fruit of long labor. To say that someone composed it, that his name was Mozart or Virgil, is not to say much; a statement of this sort is lifeless, for the creative spirit in us bears no name; such a remark merely eliminates from our concern all men *but one*, within whose inner mystery the enigma lies hidden, intact. . . .

On the contrary I look at the object and nothing else: nothing could be more deliberately planned, or speak more harmoniously to our feeling for plastic shapes, to the instinct that makes us model with our fingers something we should delight to touch, than this calcareous jewel I am caressing, whose origin and purpose I wish for a time to disregard.

As we say a "sonnet," an "ode," a "sonata," or a "fugue," to designate well-defined forms, so we say a "conch," a "helmet," a "cameo," a "haliotis," a "porcelain"—all of them names of shells; and each one of these words suggests an action that aims to make something beautiful and succeeds.

What can prevent me from concluding that *someone* has made this curiously conceived, curiously turned and ornamented shell that troubles my imagination—and made it perhaps *for someone?*

I found this one in the sand. It attracted me because it was not a formless thing but one whose parts and aspects manifested an interrelation, a sequence and harmony as it were, that enabled me, after a single look, to conceive and foresee the aspects I had not yet examined. Its parts are joined by something more than the cohesion and solidity of matter. If I compare this thing to a stone, I find that the shell has an identity which the stone lacks. If I break them both, the fragments of the shell are not shells; but the fragments of the stone remain stones, just as the stone itself was once no doubt part of a still larger one. Yet even now certain fragments of the shell suggest the fragments that were joined to them; in a measure they engage my imagination and incite me to think further; they call for a *whole.* . . .

My observations thus far concur to make me think it would be *possible* to construct a shell; and that the process would be quite the same as that of making any of the objects I can produce with my hands by choosing some appropriate material, forming the design in my mind, and proceeding, part by part, to carry it out. The unity, the wholeness of the shell's form, force me to conclude that a directing idea presides over the execution; a pre-existing idea, quite separate from the work itself, an idea that maintains itself, supervises and governs, while on the other hand and in *another area* it is put into execution by means of my energies successively applied. I divide myself in order to create.

Then someone made this object. But *of what*? And *why*?

However, if I now attempt to model or chisel out a similar object, I am first of all compelled to seek a suitable way of molding or cutting it; and it turns out that there are only too many possibilities. I am in a quandary. I can think of bronze, clay, stone: in respect to form, the final result of my operation will be independent of the material chosen. Of this material I demand only "sufficient," not strictly "necessary," conditions. According to the material employed, my acts will vary, no doubt; but different as they, and it, may be, I obtain in the end the same desired figure: I have several ways of passing from my idea to its effigy by way of the material.

In any case I am unable to imagine or define a *material* with such precision that the consideration of form will wholly determine my choice.

Moreover, just as I may hesitate in regard to the material, I may hesitate about the dimensions I shall give to my work. I see no necessary dependence between form and size; I can conceive of no form that might not be larger or smaller— it is *as though the idea of a certain figure called forth in my mind an endless number of similar figures.*

Thus I have been able to separate form from matter and both of these from size; and merely by thinking in some detail of my projected action, I have been able to see how it breaks down into stages. The least reflection, the slightest meditation on *how I should go about fashioning a shell*, tells me at once that

I should have to act in several different ways, in several different capacities as it were, for I am not able to carry on all at
once the numerous operations required to form the desired
object. I shall have to connect them as though intervening
from outside; and indeed, it is by a judgment independent of
my action that I shall recognize that my work is "finished,"
that the object is "made," since the object in itself is only one
possible stage, among others, in a series of transformations
that might continue beyond their goal—*indefinitely*.

In reality I do not *make* this object; I only substitute certain
attributes for certain others, and a certain relation that interests me for a certain diversity of forces and properties that
I can only consider and utilize one by one.

I feel, finally, that if I have undertaken to produce one
particular form, it is because I could have chosen to create entirely different ones. This is an absolute condition: if one can
only make a single thing and in a single way, it means that the
thing almost makes itself; therefore, such an action is not
truly human (since thought is not necessary to it), and *we do
not understand it*. What we make in this way really makes *us*
more than we make it. What are we, if not a momentary
balance between a multitude of hidden actions that are not
specifically human? Our life is a tissue of such local acts in
which choice plays no part, and which in some incomprehensible way perform themselves. Man walks, breathes, remembers—but in all this he is in no way different from animals. He
knows neither how he moves, nor how he remembers; and
he has no need to know in order to move or remember, nor
does he need to know *before* doing so. But if he builds a house
or a ship, if he forges a tool or a weapon, a design must first
act upon him and make him into a specialized instrument; an
idea must co-ordinate what he desires, what he can do, what
he knows, what he sees, what he touches and manipulates,

and must organize all this expressly toward a particular and exclusive action, starting from a state in which he was entirely open and free from all intention. Once he is called upon to act, his freedom diminishes, relinquishes its rights, and for a time he accepts a constraint that is the price he must pay if he wishes to impress upon a certain "reality" the configured desire that he carries in his mind.

To sum up: all specifically human production is effected in successive, distinct, limited, enumerable acts. But up to this point certain animals, the builders of hives or nests, are quite like us. Man's specific work becomes unique when the separate, independent acts involved require his deliberate thinking presence to provoke them and adjust their diversity to an aim. Man consciously sustains his mental image and his will. We know only too well how precarious and costly this "presence of mind" is; how quickly the effort wanes, how our attention disintegrates, and that what arouses, assembles, corrects, and revives the efforts of our separate functions is of a nature quite different from them; and this is why our *considered* projects, our *intentional* constructions or fabrications *seem very alien to our underlying organic activity*.

Thus I can make a shell rather like this one I have examined; and I can make it only by means of a composite, sustained action such as I have just described. I can choose the material and the moment; I can take my time, interrupt the work, and return to it; there is no hurry, for my life in no way depends on the outcome but participates only in a revocable, one might say incidental, way; and though my life may spend itself on an object so far removed from its needs, it can equally well refrain from doing so. My life is indispensable to my work, but my work is not indispensable to my life.

All in all, within the limits stated, *I have understood this object.* I have *explained* it to myself by a system of acts that are eminently mine, and I have thereby exhausted my problem: any attempt to go farther would modify it essentially and would lead me to slip from an explanation of the shell into an explanation of myself.

Up to this point, consequently, I can imagine that this shell is a work of man.

Still, one element of a human work is lacking. I do not see the *utility* of this thing; it calls to mind no need which it satisfies. It has intrigued me; it delights my eyes and fingers; I stop to look at it as I would stop to listen to a melody; and unconsciously I consign it to oblivion, for we unthinkingly withhold the future from whatever is of no use to us. . . . And I find but one answer to the question that comes to my mind: *Why was this object made?* But what, I ask myself, is the use of the things that artists produce? What they make is of a strange kind: there is no vital need for it. *It does not result from any necessity,* which as a matter of fact would determine its whole character; *still less can it be attributed to "chance."*

So far I have purposely ignored the true origin of sea shells, and attempted in my reasoning—or raving—to stick as close as possible to this feigned ignorance.

In this I have been imitating the philosopher, who makes every effort to know *just as little* about the well-known origin of well-defined things as is known about the origin of the "world" and the beginnings of "life."

Doesn't philosophy after all consist in pretending not to know what one does know, and to know what one does not? It doubts existence, but speaks seriously of the "Universe." . . .

If I have dwelt at some length on the act of a man who might apply himself to making a sea shell, it is because in my opinion one should never lose an opportunity to compare, in some detail, our way of making things with the work performed by what we call *nature*. Nature: that is to say, the genetrix, the *producer*. Whenever we run across something we do not know how to *make* but that appears to be *made*, we say that nature produced it. Yet there are certain special cases where we can compete with nature, and attain by our own methods what it accomplishes in its way. We are able to make heavy bodies swim or fly and to construct certain "organic" molecules. . . .

All the rest—everything that we can assign neither to thinking man nor to nature's power of generation—we attribute to "chance." The word is an excellent invention. It is very convenient to have a word which enables us to say that a *remarkable* thing (remarkable in itself or in its immediate effects) is brought about *in exactly the same way as something else* that is not remarkable. But to say that a thing is *remarkable* is to bring in a *man*—a person who is particularly sensitive to it, and it is this person who supplies everything that is remarkable about it. What difference does it make to me, if I have no lottery ticket, whether one number or another is picked out of the urn? I have not been "sensitized" to the event. For me there is no "chance" in the drawing, no contrast between the uniform way in which these numbers are drawn and the inequality of the consequences. Take away man and his expectation, and everything comes out the same, sea shell or stone; but chance *makes* nothing in this world, apart from making us take notice of it. . . .

But now it is time for me to stop pretending and come back to the area of certainty, to the surface of common experience.

A sea shell emanates from a mollusk. To *emanate* strikes

me as the only term close enough to the truth since its proper meaning is: to *exude*. A grotto emanates stalactites; a mollusk emanates its shell. As to the elementary process of this emanation scientists tell us many things that they have seen under the microscope. They add a number of other things which I think they have not seen: some are inconceivable, though that scarcely precludes discoursing about them; others would require observation over hundreds of millions of years, for that much time is needed to change anything into anything. Others insist that some extremely favorable accident occurred at one point or another. . . .

Such an accident, according to science, is what enabled the mollusk to spin out so skillfully the charming object that holds our attention.

Beginning in the germ, we are told, this mollusk, the maker of our shell, suffered a strange limitation of its growth, an atrophy of no less than half its organism. In most mollusks the right (and in the others the left) half has been sacrificed, while, on the other side, the visceral mass bent itself into a semicircle and then twisted. We are told that the nervous system, whose first intention it was to form two parallel networks, crisscrossed strangely and inverted its central ganglia. On the outside, the shell was exuded, and solidified. . . .

More than one hypothesis has been suggested to explain why certain mollusks (and not certain others that are very much like them) develop this strange predilection for one side of their organism; and—as is inevitable in the realm of supposition—what one supposes is deduced from what one needs to suppose: the question is human, the answer too human. This is the whole basis of our famous Principle of Causality. It leads us to *imagine*, that is, to substitute our own machinations for the gaps in our knowledge. But in general the greatest and most precious discoveries are quite unexpected. They demolish, more often than they confirm, the products of our preferences: they consist in facts that are not yet *humanized*, that no imagination could have foreseen.

As for me, I am perfectly willing to admit that I do not know certain things, and that all genuine knowledge reduces itself to what one sees and what one has power over. If the hypothesis is seductive and the theory is attractive, I take pleasure in them without worrying about whether they are true. . . .

If then we disregard our intellectual inventions, sometimes naïve and often wholly verbal, we are obliged to recognize that our knowledge of living things is insignificant beside our knowledge of the inorganic world. This is tantamount to saying that we possess incomparably greater power over inorganic than over organic things, for I see no way to measure knowledge except by the real power it confers. *I know only what I know how to handle.* For it is strange, and deserving of some attention, that despite so much effort, despite our marvelously subtle tools and methods, we should have so little power over this living nature, *which is ours.* On closer scrutiny we should find, no doubt, that our mind is baffled by everything that is born, reproduces, and dies on our planet, because the mind is strictly limited, in its representation of things, to its awareness of its means of *external action* and of the form this action—*of whose mechanics it need know nothing*—will take.

This type of action, it seems to me, is the only model we can follow in trying to resolve a phenomenon into imaginary and voluntary operations that will at last enable us either to reproduce at will or to foresee a development with some degree of accuracy. Everything that diverges too much from this type defies our intellect (as may be seen in the most recent physics). If we attempt to force this barrier, we are faced at once with all sorts of contradictions, linguistic illusions, sentimental falsifications; and it sometimes happens that these mythical products occupy and even delight the minds of men for many years to come.

The little problem of the sea shell suffices to illustrate this quite well, and to throw light on our limitations. Since man is not the maker of this object and chance is not responsible for it, we are reduced to inventing something we have called *living nature*. There seems to be no other way of defining it except by the difference between its work and ours; and that is why I have been impelled to say something about our way of doing things. I have said that we undertake our works on the basis of several kinds of *freedom*: freedom with respect to *material*, with respect to *size and shape*, with respect to *time*; the mollusk seems deprived of all these—a creature that can only recite its lesson, which is hardly distinguishable from its very existence. Full of fancy as it may seem (so much so that we borrow certain of our ornamental motifs from it), the mollusk's work, never retouched, unmarred by changes or reservations, is a fancy that repeats itself indefinitely; we cannot even see why certain eccentrics among the gastropods should work leftward where others work to the right. Still less do we understand the oddly shaped complexities that some shells disclose; or those spines and spots of color, to which we vaguely ascribe some utility that escapes us, without even stopping to think that, *outside of man's little intellectual sphere, our idea of the useful has no meaning*. These oddities add to our perplexity, for a *machine* produces no such deviations; a *mind* would have chosen them with some intention; *chance* would have equalized the possibilities. Neither machine, nor inten-

tion, nor chance. . . . All our methods have been rejected.
Machine and chance, these are the two methods of our physics; as for intention, it can intervene only if man himself is
involved, explicitly or in disguise.

But the making of the shell is lived, not calculated: nothing
could be more contrary to our organized action preceded by
an aim and operating as a cause.

Nevertheless, let us try to gain an idea of this mysterious act
of formation. Let us leaf through some learned works, with
no intention of getting to the bottom of them, and without
in the least forgoing the advantages of ignorance or of the
caprices of error.

I observe first of all that living nature is unable to work
directly with solids. In the solid state neither stone nor metal
is of any use to it. When nature wishes to turn out a hard
article of set shape, a support, a lever, a brace, an armor plate;
or when it aims to produce a tree trunk, a femur, a tooth or a
tusk, a skull or a sea shell, it works in the same indirect way:
it takes the liquids or fluids from which all organic matter is
made, and slowly separates out the solid substances it needs.
Everything that lives or has lived results from the properties
and modifications of a few liquids. And every present solid
has passed through the liquid phase, molten or in solution.
But living nature does not tolerate the high temperatures
that enable us to work with the "elements," to shape molten
glass, bronze, or iron into the forms we desire, which will set
in cooling. In molding solid organs life has only solutions,
suspensions, or emulsions.

I have read that the animal we are examining draws food
containing calcium salts from its environment, and that the
calcium is extracted and digested by the liver, whence it

23

passes into the blood stream. This is the raw material for the mineral part of the shell—it will feed the activity of a strange organ specialized in the craft of secreting the elements of the solid body to be constructed and of putting them in place.

This organ, a muscular mass that encloses the animal's viscera and extends to the foot on which it stands and moves, is called the *mantle*, and performs a dual function. Through its *epithelium*, the edge exudes the outer coating of the shell, which covers a layer of very curiously and subtly shaped calcareous prisms.

This gives us the outside of the shell. But it grows in thickness, and this growth involves very different material, structure, tools. Protected by the solid rampart that the edge of the mantle has built, the rest of this admirable organ fashions the refinements of the inner wall, the water-smooth lining of the animal's home. There is nothing too precious or delicate for the meditations of a life so much of which is spent at home; successive layers of mucus spread a coating as thin as a soap bubble over the deep, twisted cavity into which the solitary creature withdraws in concentration. But never will it become aware of the beauty of this retreat it has made. After its death the exquisite substance it has formed by depositing alternately the organic product of its mucus cells and the calcite from its nacre cells will see the light; it will break the sun's rays into their wave lengths, and will enchant our eyes with the tender richness of its iridescent bands.

This, we are told, is how nature builds the dwelling and mobile refuge of this strange animal clothed in a muscle cloaked in a shell. But I must own that my curiosity is not satisfied. Microscopic analysis is a fine thing. But while I am occupied with cells, making the acquaintance of blastomeres and chromosomes, I lose sight of my mollusk. And if I concern myself with all this detail in the hope that it will ultimately enlighten me about the formation of the whole, a certain disappointment is in store for me. . . . But this perhaps is an essential difficulty—that is, a difficulty arising from the very nature of our senses and of our mind.

In order to imagine this formative process, we must first dispose of an obstacle, and in so doing we automatically sacrifice the inner consistency of our image. For actually *we*—who cannot even perceive our own growth—*are unable to visualize a movement so slow that a perceptible result springs from an imperceptible change.* We can imagine the living process only by lending it a rhythm which is specifically ours and has no connection with *what happens in the creature we are observing.* . . .

Indeed, it seems quite probable that in the growth of the mollusk and its shell according to the ineluctable theme of the spiral, all the components which the no less ineluctable form of the human act has taught us to consider and define *separately*, are *indistinct and indivisible*: the *energy*, the *time*, the *material*, the *connections*, and the different "orders of magnitude" between which our senses compel us to distinguish. Life passes continuously from the molecule to the micelle, from the micelle to the perceptible mass, without concern for the compartments of our sciences, that is to say, for our means of action.

Without the slightest effort life creates a very "generalized" relativity.

It does not separate its geometry from its physics but endows each species with all the axioms and more or less "differential" *invariants* it needs to maintain a satisfactory harmony between the individual and the world around it. . . .

Clearly the rather secretive individual, addicted to asymmetry and torsion, who fashions a shell, has long abandoned the postulates that were Euclid's idols. Euclid believed that a stick keeps its length under any circumstances; that one can toss it up to the moon or twirl it about, and that neither distance, movement, nor change of orientation will detract from its clear conscience as an infallible unit of measurement. Euclid worked on a sheet of papyrus and traced figures that *to him seemed similar*; he saw no other obstacle to the growth of his triangles than the size of his papyrus. He was very far— two thousand light-years—from imagining that one day a certain Mr. Einstein would develop an octopus capable of ensnaring and devouring all geometry; and not only geometry, but time, matter, and gravitation, and a good many other things unsuspected by the Greeks, which, ground up and digested together, provide a dainty dish for the all-powerful *Mollusk of Reference*. This monstrous cephalopod need only count its tentacles and the suckers on each tentacle to feel that it is "master of itself and of the Universe."

But millions of years before Euclid and the illustrious Einstein, our hero, who is only a simple gastropod and has no tentacles, was himself obliged to solve some rather knotty problems. He had his shell to make—and his living. These are very different activities. Spinoza made spectacles. More than one poet has been an excellent civil servant. And possibly two trades practiced by one and the same individual can be kept reasonably separate. After all, what do we mean by *the same*? But we are speaking of a mollusk and we know nothing of his inner unity.

What are our findings? The internal construction is organized in a mysterious way. The secretory cells of the mantle and its edge operate in *rhythm*: the turns of the spiral progress; the walls are built; the nacre is deposited on them. But the microscope does not show what creates the harmony between the different points and different moments in this simultaneous progress of the whole periphery. The pattern of the colored furrows or bands that curve round the shell, and of the bands that intersect them, reminds us of "geodesic lines" and suggests the existence of some sort of "field of force" which we are unable to discern, but whose action would give the growth of the shell the irresistible torsion and rhythmic progress we observe in the finished product. Nothing we know of our own actions enables us to imagine what it may be that so gracefully modulates these surfaces, element by element, row by row, without other tools than those contained in the thing that is being fashioned; what it may be that so miraculously harmonizes and adjusts the curves, and finishes the work with a boldness, an ease, a precision which the most graceful creations of the potter or bronze founder are far from equaling. Our artists do not derive the material of their works from their own substance, and the form for which they strive springs from a specialized application of their mind, which can be *completely* disengaged from their being. Perhaps what we call *perfection* in art (which all do not strive for and some disdain) is only a sense of desiring or finding in a human work the sureness of execution, the inner necessity, the indissoluble bond between form and material that are revealed to us by the humblest of shells.

But our mollusk has other things to do besides this rhythmic distillation of his marvelous covering. He must supply the mantle which constructs the durable shell with energy and mineral salts; from the resources of his environment he must gather what perhaps, some day in the future, will be a frag-

27

ment of the foundations of a continent. Thus he must sometimes forsake his secret, subtle work of emanation and venture
out into the world, bearing his dwelling, his den, his fortress,
his masterpiece, like a wondrous tiara or turban. At once he is
involved in an entirely new set of circumstances. Here we
are tempted to credit him with a genius of the first order, for
he must confront two utterly different realities accordingly
as he closets himself in laborious, concentrated aloofness to
co-ordinate the efforts of his mantle, or as he ventures out
into the vast world and explores it, his eyes groping, his
feelers questioning, his firm *foot* with its broad viscous sole
supporting the majestic traveler and his sanctuary, rocking
them to and fro. How is he to combine, under a single set
of principles and laws, the two kinds of consciousness, the
two forms of space and time, the two geometries, and the
two systems of mechanics with which these two modes of
existence and experience alternately confront him? Perhaps
when he is all inside, he takes his spiral arc for his "straight
line," just as we take for ours a little arc of a meridian, or,
unaware that its trajectory is relative, a ray of light. And
perhaps he measures his private "time" by the sensation of
secreting a little prism of calcite and putting it in place. But
once he leaves his shelter and takes up his outside life, heaven
only knows what hypotheses or conventional rule of thumb
he lives by! . . . The mobility of the feelers; the touch, sight,
and movement associated with the exquisite elasticity of the
wonderfully sensitive shafts by which they are oriented, the
perfect retractility of the body of which the whole shell is an
appendage, the binding obligation to skip over nothing, to
adhere strictly to his path—all this is bound to move a gifted
mollusk, when he withdraws from the world and buttons up
once more in his case of nacre, to profound meditations and

radical synthetic abstractions. He will need what Laplace rather pompously called "the resources of the most sublime analysis" if he is to adjust the experience of his worldly life to that of his private life. He will have to reason profoundly if he is to discover "the unity of nature" underlying the two so different aspects between which his organization compels him to alternate.

But do we not, ourselves, fluctuate between "the world of bodies" and that of the "mind"; and all our philosophy, is it not an eternal quest for the formula that will efface the difference between them and reconcile two divergent orders, two systems of time, two modes of transformation, two types of "forces," in short, two frames of reference which thus far have seemed, the more closely we examine them, to become more and more distinct, though concomitantly more interwoven?

In a more immediate order of things, far from all metaphysics, do we not make ourselves at home amid the most irreconcilable disparity of sensory experience; do we not, for example, accustom ourselves to a visual and an auditory world which resemble each other in no way and which, if we thought about it, would give us a perpetual impression of perfect incoherence? Of course we say that such an impression is effaced, fused as it were, by custom and habit, and that the parts join to form a single "reality." . . . But with this we are not saying very much.

I shall throw away this thing that I have found as one throws away a cigarette stub. This sea shell has *served* me, suggesting by turns what I am, what I know, and what I do not know. . . . Just as Hamlet, picking up a skull in the rich earth and bringing it close to his living face, finds a gruesome image of himself, and enters upon a meditation without issue, bounded on all sides by a circle of consternation, so beneath the human eye, this little, hollow, spiral-shaped calcareous body summons up a number of thoughts, all inconclusive. . . .

Some Simple Reflections on the Body

On the Blood and Us

1. How we can kill the living creature by giving it *gratis* (and in the best quality) what is ordinarily supplied by its organism and by its own acts in its environment.

2. When I look at a living thing, what I see and what first occupies my attention is this mass, all of a piece, which moves, bends, runs, jumps, flies, or swims; which howls, speaks, sings, performs its many acts, takes on many appearances, assumes a multiplicity of selves, wreaks its havoc, does its work, in an environment which accepts it and from which it is inseparable.

This thing, with its discontinuous activity, its spontaneous movements springing suddenly from a state of immobility to which they always return, is curiously contrived: we note that the visible organs of propulsion, legs, feet, wings, occupy a considerable part of the creature's total bulk; and we discover later on that the rest of its volume is made up of organs of internal work, some of whose outward effects we have witnessed. It would seem as though the creature's whole life span were the effect of this work, as though its entire production, visible or not, were expended in feeding the insatiable consumer of matter that the creature itself is.

AESTHETICS

3. But I also know that what the system of implements which is almost the whole animal is continuously looking for or manufacturing might be provided by other means than his own. If his blood were supplied directly, from the outside, with the substances whose preparation now requires so many co-ordinated industries and so elaborate a directing apparatus, if all this equipment and its functioning, now useless, were eliminated, it seems likely that life might still be sustained, perhaps more efficiently and reliably than it is by the natural mechanisms. An artificial mode of conservation would first do away with the organs of relation: the senses, the muscles, the instincts, the "psyche"; and then with the grinders, mixers, conveyors, filters, tubes, burners, and radiators, in short, the whole production line that is put to work when the senses give the signal.

4. The whole organism has no other function than the renewal of its blood—except perhaps the maintenance and service of the reproductive equipment, a very special, almost lateral function, which is often suppressed without vital damage.

But the blood itself has no other use than to restore to the apparatus which regenerates it what that apparatus needs in order to function. *The body makes blood that makes body that makes blood.* . . . Actually all the body's acts are cyclic in relation to the body itself, for they break down into comings and goings, contractions and decontractions, while the blood itself pursues its cyclic journey round its world of flesh, the continuous circumnavigation wherein life consists.

5. There is something absurd about this monotonous system of mutual conservation. It shocks the mind, which abhors

repetition and even ceases to understand or to pay attention once it has grasped what it calls a "law"; for a *law* is what does away with "eternal returns." . . .

6. Yet we observe two escapes from the body's life cycle: on the one hand, the body inevitably *wears out*; on the other hand, *it reproduces itself.*

7. To go back for a moment: if we suppose that the blood is regenerated directly from the outside, that the creature is preserved as today we preserve bits of tissue, in an appropriate medium and temperature, in this case the animal will be reduced to nothing, or perhaps to a single "cell," endowed with some sort of elementary life. Once what we call sensibility and action have been done away with, the mind must disappear along with what permits and compels it to emerge, for it has no other function indispensable to life than to cope with the variety, uncertainty, unexpectedness of circumstances. It devises actions which respond to the formless or the multiform. But where unconscious operations or reflex (that is, uniform) responses suffice, the mind is superfluous. At most it will disturb or prevent the proper functioning of the organism. This it does not fail to do, and there are famous examples to show that it is sometimes quite proud of the fact.

8. Accordingly, such products of life as memory, thought, feeling, invention, etc., with all the quality of the marvelous we attribute to them, are inevitably reduced to the rank of accessories. All our intellectual passions, our superfluous actions, our strivings to know or to create, amount to developments, *impossible to calculate in advance*, of a function that tended originally to do no more than compensate for the

inadequacy or ambiguity of our immediate perceptions and to relieve the resulting indeterminateness.

The great variety of species, the amazing diversity of the forms and instruments they manifest, their resources, their many different solutions to the problem of living, suggest that sensibility and conscious thought might have been replaced by entirely different properties rendering the same services.

What one species obtains by trial and error, by a kind of statistical method, another achieves with the help of a *sense* that the first does not possess; or else . . . by some internal process akin to "reasoning."

9. I note that our senses provide us with only a bare minimum of hints, which transpose into forms of sensibility only an infinitesimal part of the probable variety and variations of a "world" we can neither conceive nor imagine.

10. To sum up what I have said above: if we divest what we call *our life* of everything we have considered as replaceable— if its organs, forms, functions are replaced by artificial devices and so relegated to the rank of useless accessories (we are reminded of the cases of atrophy that have occurred in the course of evolution)—life is reduced to nothing or next to nothing; then sensation, feeling, thought, are not essential to it, but mere accidents.

There is an example of this: life reduced to nothing but life gives us the embryo, such a paltry thing at the beginning of its career, and sprung from next to nothing—from a germ.

11. And now one last reflection in the form of a question: In what way is the mind's peculiar activity indispensable to the

preservation of life, under circumstances that offer a man the possibility of action? I think it would be interesting to look into this. We should be led no doubt to define the mind as the "power of transforming" its own formations, a power such that, in the face of a situation that cannot be met by simple automatisms and reflexes and therefore calls for the exercise of that power, it seeks to provide the corresponding idea and impulses to action which will ultimately restore the living system to a state in which its resources are again available to it—the state one might call "freedom." Whatever internal combinations, creations, modifications have occurred—the process as a whole will always tend to restore the system to a state of free possibility.

The Problem of the Three Bodies

In common usage the word "body" responds to several very different needs of expression. One might say that each of us in his thought has *Three Bodies—at least*. Let me explain.

The first is the privileged object of which, at each instant, we find ourselves in possession, although our knowledge of it —like everything that is inseparable from the instant—may be extremely variable and subject to illusions. Each of us calls this object *My Body*; but we give it no name *in ourselves*, that is to say, *in it*. We speak of it to others as of a thing that belongs to us; but for us it is not entirely a thing; and it belongs to us a little less than we belong to it. . . .

It is for each of us, in essence, the most important object in the world, standing in opposition to the world, on which, however, it knows itself to be closely dependent. We can say that the world is based on it and exists in reference to it; or just as accurately, with a simple change in the *adjustment* of our intellectual vision, that the selfsame body is only an infinitely negligible, unstable event in the world.

But neither the word "object" that I have just used nor the word "event" is appropriate. There is no name to designate our sense of the substance of our presence, our actions and feelings, not only in their actuality, but also in an imminent, deferred, or purely potential state—something more remote and yet less intimate than our secret thoughts: we find in ourselves a capacity for modifications almost as varied as the circumstances surrounding us. This *My Body* obeys or disobeys, favors or obstructs our designs; it engenders surprising strengths and weaknesses connected wholly or in part with its perceptible mass, which at times takes on a sudden charge of impulsive energies that make it "act" in response to some interior mystery, and at other times seems to become the most crushing and immovable weight. . . .

The thing itself is formless: all we know of it by sight is the few mobile parts that are capable of coming within the conspicuous zone of the space which makes up this *My Body*, a strange, asymmetrical space in which distances are exceptional relations. I have no idea of the spatial relations between "My Forehead" and "My Foot," between "My Knee" and "My Back." . . . This gives rise to strange discoveries. My right hand is generally unaware of my left. To take one hand in the other is to take hold of an object that is *not-I*. These oddities must play a part in sleep and, *if such things as dreams exist*, must provide them with infinite combinations.

This thing that is so much mine and yet so mysteriously and sometimes—always, in the end—our most redoubtable antagonist, is the most urgent, the most constant and the most variable thing imaginable: for it carries within it all constancy and all variation. Nothing moves before us unless this *My Body* traces a corresponding modification that follows or imitates the movement perceived; and nothing ceases to move unless some part of it is immobilized.

It has no past. The word "past" has no meaning for this *My Body* which is the present itself, wholly made up of events and impending events. Sometimes certain of its parts or regions make themselves felt, light up, take on an importance before which everything else ceases to be; they dominate the moment with their incomparable pleasure or pain.

Our *Second Body* is the one which others see, and an approximation of which confronts us in the mirror or in portraits. It is the body which has a form and is apprehended by the arts, the body on which materials, ornaments, armor sit, which love sees or wants to see, and yearns to touch. It knows no pain, for it reduces pain to a mere grimace.

This is the body that was so dear to Narcissus, but that drives many to despair, and is a source of gloom to almost all of us once the time comes when we cannot help admitting that the aged creature in the glass, whom we do not accept, stands in some terribly close though incomprehensible relation to ourselves. How can we admit that we are that wreck of a man? . . .

But our knowledge of our *Second Body* goes little farther than the view of a surface. One can live without ever having seen oneself, without knowing the color of one's skin; that is the fate of the blind. But life compels none of us to know what is under the relatively unbroken skin of our *Second Body*. It is worthy of note that the living, thinking, acting man is without knowledge of his inner organization. He is not equipped to know it. Nothing leads him to suspect that he has a liver, a brain, kidneys, and the rest: in any event such information would be useless, for under normal conditions he has no means of acting on these organs. All his faculties of action are turned toward the "outside world," so much so that the "outside world" might be defined as what can be affected by our means of action. Everything I *see*, for example, can be transformed by *my movement*; I act upon my environment, but by what mechanisms I do not know.

Thus there is a Third Body. But it has unity only in our thought, since we know it only for having dissected and dismembered it. To know it is to have reduced it to parts and pieces. It gives off scarlet or whitish liquids, or hyalines, some of them quite viscous. We remove elements of varying sizes, fashioned so as to fit quite exactly in place: sponges, vessels, tubes, fibers, articulated rods. . . . Reduced to thin slices or tiny drops, our specimens reveal under the microscope corpuscular shapes that resemble nothing at all. We try to decipher these histological cryptograms. We wonder how this fiber produced motive force? And in what way these little asterisms with their fine radicles could have been related to sensation and thought? But what would a Descartes, a Newton, ignorant as they would be of our electromagnetism, make of induction and all the other phenomena discovered since their day, if without explanation we gave them a dynamo to examine, merely describing its effects? They would proceed as we do with a brain: they would take the machine apart, unroll the spools, note the presence of copper, carbons, steel, and in the end admit defeat, acknowledging their inability to guess the workings of this machine which, we have told them, effects the transformations familiar to us all.

These *Three Bodies* which I have just claimed for us are necessarily related in a number of ways that it would be highly interesting, though rather arduous, to explore. I prefer at this point to resort to a kind of fantasy.

I suggest that each of us has a *Fourth Body* which I might call the *Real Body* or equally well the *Imaginary Body*.

Let us consider this body as indivisible from the unknown and unknowable medium intimated by the physicists when they torture the perceptible world and, proceeding by the indirect means of *relays within relays*, disclose phenomena whose origin they situate far below or above the scope of our senses, our imagination, and ultimately of our intellection itself.

From this inconceivable medium my *Fourth Body* is neither more nor less distinct than is a whirlpool from the liquid in which it is formed. (I am entitled, it seems to me, to dispose of the inconceivable as I please.)

It is not one of the Three other Bodies, for it is not the *My Body*, nor the *Third* which is that of the scientists, since it is made of what they know nothing about. . . . And moreover, the mind's knowledge is a product of what this *Fourth Body is not*. Necessarily and irrevocably *everything that is* masks for us *something that might be*. . . .

But why bring up this utterly fruitless notion here? Simply because an idea, even if thoroughly absurd, is never entirely without value; and an expression, an empty sign, never fails to goad the mind in some way. Where did I get this idea of a *Fourth Body*?

As I was reflecting on the notion of "body" in general, and on my *Three Bodies* that we have just been discussing, the famous problems that have been raised by these themes arose

39

dimly in the half-darkness of my thoughts. I own that I ordinarily banish them from the most sensitive and urgent point of my attention. I seldom speculate on the origin of life and the species; I seldom ask myself whether death is a simple change of climate, costume, and habits, whether or not the mind is a by-product of the organism; whether our acts can ever be what we call *free* (though no one has ever managed to say exactly what we mean by that); and so on.

It was against this background of timeworn difficulties that my absurd and luminous idea emerged: "I give the name of *Fourth Body*," I said to myself, "to the unknowable object, *knowledge of which would solve all these problems at one stroke, for it is what they imply.*"

And as a protest arose within me, the Voice of the Absurd added: "Think carefully: where do you expect to find answers to these philosophical questions? Your images, your abstractions, derive only from the properties and experiences of your *Three Bodies*. But the first offers you nothing but moments; the second a few visions; and the third, at the cost of ruthless dissections and complicated preparations, a mass of figures more indecipherable than Etruscan texts. Your mind, with its language, pulverizes, mixes, and rearranges all this and from it, by the abuse, if you will, of its habitual questionnaire, evolves its notorious problems; but it can give them a shadow of meaning only by tacitly presupposing a certain Nonexistence—of which my *Fourth Body* is a kind of incarnation."

Aesthetics

Gentlemen:

EVIDENTLY your Committee is not afraid of paradoxes since
it has decided—as though introducing a grand opera with a
comic overture—to invite a mere amateur (who feels very
much at a loss) to address this gathering of the world's most
eminent authorities on Aesthetics.

But though it may seem rather astonishing at first sight,
perhaps this sovereign act of your organizers can be explained
by a consideration which I shall submit to you and which may
enable us to transform the paradox of my speaking here, at
the formal opening of this Congress, into a gesture of rather
profound significance.

I have often thought that it might sometimes be useful
and almost always interesting for those engaged in any established science already far removed from its beginnings to call
on a mortal among mortals, to consult a man who is sufficiently a stranger to this science, and to ask him whether he has
any idea of the subject matter, the methods, the findings, and
the possible applications of a discipline which, I grant you, may
be known to him by name. Strictly speaking, his reply would
be without importance; yet I feel sure that these questions, addressed to a man who has nothing in his favor but his simplicity and good faith, might in some measure be mirrored in his

naïveté and might, thus returning to the learned men who had questioned him, revive for them certain elementary problems or initial conventions of a kind that tend to be effaced from the mind and forgotten as one advances into the intricacies and subtleties of an investigation pursued with passion.

One person might say to another (and in the present case my second person is a science): *What are you doing? What are you looking for? What is your aim? What are you expecting to accomplish? And in sum who are you?* Such questions no doubt would oblige the interrogated individual to return, as it were—and such a return is bound to be fruitful—to his first intentions and ultimate ends, to the root and motive of his curiosity, and finally, to the very substance of his knowledge. And this perhaps would not be without interest.

If, gentlemen, it is indeed for the role of *ingénu* that the Committee has selected me, I shall feel perfectly at ease. Then I know what I have come here to do: I have come to be ignorant out loud.

To begin with, I must tell you that the mere name of Aesthetics has always filled me with wonderment and that I am still dazzled, not to say intimidated, by it. It makes me hesitate between the strangely seductive idea of a "Science of the Beautiful"—which on the one hand would enable us to distinguish *with certainty* what we must love or hate, acclaim or destroy; and which, on the other hand, would teach us to produce, *without fail*, works of art whose value cannot be contested—and the idea of a "Science of Sensations," which seems no less seductive, or perhaps even more so. If I had to choose between the destiny of a man who knows how and why a certain thing is what we call "beautiful," and the privilege of knowing what it means to *feel*, I believe I should choose the second, with the idea that if such knowledge were possible (and I rather fear that it is not even conceivable) it would soon lead me to all the secrets of art.

But I am saved from my perplexity by the thought of a perfectly Cartesian method (for this year we must honor and obey Descartes) which, building on pure observation, will give me a precise and flawless notion of Aesthetics.

I shall undertake a "complete enumeration" and a very general review, as the *Discourse on Method* recommends. I put myself (but I am there already) outside of the precinct where Aesthetics is made, and observe what comes out. What comes out is a great many products of a great many minds. I diligently note the subjects; I try to classify them. I shall judge that I have enough observations for my purpose when I see that there is no longer any need to set up new classes. Then I shall decree for my own benefit that, on such and such a date, Aesthetics is the sum of findings thus assembled and arranged. Can it actually be anything else; and could I devise any wiser or more reliable method? But what is wise and reliable is not always clear and convenient, and at this point it occurs to me that if I am to construct a notion of Aesthetics that will be of any use to me, I must attempt to sum up in a few words what all these products of the mind have in common. My task is to digest this vast material. . . . And so I leaf through books; I investigate. . . . And what do I find? As luck would have it, the first book I take up is devoted to pure geometry; the next falls under the head of biological morphology. I run across a great number of history books. And neither anatomy, nor physiology, nor crystallography, nor acoustics is missing from the collection: one supplies a chapter, another a paragraph, but there is virtually no science that does not pay some tribute.

And I am far from the end of my pains . . . . Next I come to techniques innumerable as the sands of the sea. From stone-cutting to ballet exercises, from the secrets of stained glass to the mystery of violin varnishes, from canons and fugues to the lost-wax process, from poetic diction to encaustic painting, to dress design, marquetry, the laying out of gardens—how many treatises, albums, theses, works of all dimensions, ages, and formats ! . . . In the face of this prodigious diversity, where *manual skill* rubs shoulders with the *golden section*, our Cartesian enumeration becomes illusory. There seems to be no limit to this proliferation of studies, processes, contributions, all of which however bear some relation to the common aim of which I am thinking and trying to form a clear idea. Half discouraged, I abandon the literature on all these techniques. . . . What works remain to be consulted? Two piles of unequal size: one, it seems to me, consists of works in which ethics plays a large part. Suspecting that they speak of the intermittent relations between Art and the Good, I lose no time in turning away from this pile, attracted as I am by another that is far more imposing. Something tells me that my last hope of forging a sound and succinct definition of Aesthetics lies in this one. . . .

And so I gather my wits and attack this last lot, a pyramid of metaphysical works.

It is here, gentlemen, that I hope to find the germ and first word of your science. All your investigations, in so far as they may be grouped together, stem from an initial act of philosophical curiosity. Aesthetics was born one day of some philosopher's observation and appetite. The event was by no means an accident. In his undertaking, which consisted in a general attack on all things and a systematic transformation of whatever came to mind, our philosopher, proceeding from question to answer, endeavoring to assimilate the whole span of knowledge and reduce it to a coherent type of expression that he found within himself, almost inevitably encountered certain questions which could be assigned neither to the realm of pure understanding, nor to the sphere of pure sensibility, nor to the domain of men's ordinary actions; but which partook of these diverse modes and combined them so closely that it was necessary, willy-nilly, to consider them apart from all other objects of study, to impute an irreducible value and meaning to them, hence to give them a destiny of their own, and to find a justification for them before the authority of reason, a purpose and a necessity within a satisfactory system of the world.

At first and for quite some time, the Aesthetics thus established developed abstractly in the area of pure thought; it was built up in stages from the raw materials of the common language by the strange and industrious dialectical animal who separates these materials to the best of his ability, isolates the elements he regards as simple, and endeavors, by matching and contrasting intelligible propositions, to build a home for the speculative life.

At the root of the problems it had taken for its own, the newborn Aesthetics discovered a certain kind of *pleasure*.

Pleasure and pain (I consider them in one breath only by way of conforming to rhetorical usage; *if there is any relation* between them, it must be far more subtle than that of "going in pairs"), pleasure and pain, then, are always troublesome elements in an intellectual construction. They are indefinable, incommensurable, or, in any case, incomparable. They perfectly typify the confusion or interdependence between the observer and the thing observed, which is driving theoretical physicists to despair.

Even so, the common kind of pleasure, the purely sensory fact, was readily accorded a certain function, limited if you will, but honorable: it was assigned a useful role in the mechanism of self-preservation, and an intimate one in the propagation of the race—I have nothing to say against that. In brief, the phenomenon of *pleasure* was saved in the eyes of reason by teleological arguments which were formerly quite solid. . . .

But there is pleasure and pleasure. All pleasures are not so readily assigned to a well-defined place in a sound order of things. There are some which serve no purpose in the economy of life and yet on the other hand cannot be regarded as simple aberrations of a sensory faculty necessary to the living creature. They are explained neither by use nor misuse. And that is not all. This kind of pleasure is inseparable from developments that go beyond the sensibility and connect it with the kinds of modified feeling which are prolonged and enriched in the channels of the intellect and sometimes lead to outward actions—on matter, on the senses, and on the minds of others—requiring the combined exercise of all the human powers.

There you have it. A pleasure which sometimes goes so deep as to make us suppose we have a direct understanding of the object that causes it; a pleasure which arouses the intelligence, defies it, and makes it love its defeat; still more, a pleasure that can stimulate the strange need to produce or reproduce the thing, event, object, or state to which it seems attached, and which thus becomes a source of activity *without any definite end*, capable of imposing a discipline, a zeal, a torment on a whole lifetime, and of filling it, sometimes to overflowing—such a pleasure presents a singularly specious enigma, which could scarcely escape the attention or the clutches of the metaphysical hydra. What could have been more worthy of our philosopher's will to power than this order of phenomena in which *to feel, to possess, to will*, and *to make* seemed to be joined in an essential and highly remarkable interaction that defied his Scholastic, not to say Cartesian, efforts to split up the difficulty. The alliance of a form, a material, an idea, an action, and a passion; the absence of any clearly determined aim or of any result that might be expressed in finite terms; a desire and its recompense, each regenerating the other; a desire that creates and hence causes itself; sometimes breaking away from all particular creation and ultimate satisfaction, thus revealing itself to be a desire *to create for the sake of creating*—all this aroused the metaphysical mind: to this problem it devoted the same attention as to all the other problems it habitually invents in exercising its function of reconstructing knowledge in a universal form.

But a philosopher who aspires to such sublime heights, where he hopes to reign supreme, actually fashions the world while purporting only to represent it. His mind is far too powerful to see only what can be seen. He is led to deviate imperceptibly from his model, rejecting its true face which offers him only chaos, the immediate disorder of perceptible things: he is tempted to neglect the singularities and irregularities which are awkward to express and which interfere with the distributive uniformity of method. He applies logical analysis to what men say. He puts their words to the question, and even from his adversary draws thoughts that the other never suspected he had. He shows him an invisible *substance* behind the visible, which is a mere *accident*; changes his reality into *appearance*; delights in creating the names that are needed to satisfy the formal balance of propositions but were lacking in the language; if a *subject* is lacking, he derives it from an *attribute*; if contradiction threatens, he slips in the subtle distinction which saves the game. . . .

All this is well and good—up to a certain point.

Thus, in the presence of that mysterious pleasure of which I am speaking, the philosopher, justly concerned with giving it a categorical place, a universal meaning, an intelligible function; fascinated by, yet curious about the combination he has found here of sensuality, fecundity, and an energy quite comparable to that which springs from love; unable, in this new object of his attention, to separate necessity from the arbitrary, contemplation from action, matter from mind—the philosopher, I say, kept trying to apply his usual methods of reduction by exhaustion and progressive division to this monster of the Fable of Intellect, this sphinx or griffin, siren or centaur, in which sensation, action, dream, instinct, reflection, rhythm, and excess are as closely intermingled as chemical elements in living bodies; this strange thing which nature sometimes offers us, but as though by chance, and which at other times is formed, at the cost of immense efforts, by man, who puts into it every bit of his mind, time, determination, in short, his life.

Ardently pursuing this marvelous prey, Dialectic harassed it, tracked it down, cornered it in the thicket of Pure Ideas.

There it captured the *Idea of the Beautiful*.

But the dialectical hunt is a magical hunt. When poets repair to the enchanted forest of Language it is with the express purpose of getting lost; far gone in bewilderment, they seek crossroads of meaning, unexpected echoes, strange encounters; they fear neither detours, surprises, nor darkness; but the huntsman who ventures into this forest in hot pursuit of the "truth," who sticks to a single continuous path, from which he cannot deviate for a moment on pain of losing the scent or imperiling the progress he has already made, runs the risk of capturing nothing but his shadow. Sometimes the shadow is enormous, but a shadow it remains.

It was inevitable, no doubt, that the application of dialectical analysis to problems which are not restricted to a clearly defined realm and are not expressed in exact terms, should produce mere conventional "truths" without validity beyond the limits of a given doctrine, and that beautiful but recalcitrant realities should always be turning up to trouble Ideal Beauty in its sovereignty and disturb the serenity of its definition.

I do not deny that the discovery of the *Idea of the Beautiful* was an extraordinary event with important positive consequences. The whole history of Western art for more than twenty centuries is a record of our debt to it, in regard both to styles and to great works. Abstract thought has proved no less fertile in this realm than in the development of science. And yet the Idea of the Beautiful carried within it the original and inevitable blemish to which I have just alluded.

In this realm the virtues of purity, universality, strictness, and logic engendered a number of paradoxes, the most startling of which is this: the Aesthetics of the metaphysicians decreed a cleavage between the *Beautiful* and *beautiful things*! . . .

Now though it is true that there is no science of the particular, it is equally true that there is no action or production which is not essentially particular, and there is no sensation that lives in the realm of the universal. Reality rejects the order and unity that thought strives to inflict on it. The unity of nature is manifested only in the systems of signs fashioned expressly to this end, and the universe is only a more or less convenient invention.

Pleasure exists only in the moment and there is nothing

more individual, more uncertain, more incommunicable. Men's judgments concerning it provide no basis for reasoning, for far from analyzing their subject, they merely add an *attribute of indeterminateness*: to say that an object is *beautiful* is to make an enigma of it.

But there is no longer any need to speak of a beautiful object, since we have isolated the *Beautiful*, abstracted it from *beautiful things*. I doubt whether sufficient attention has been paid to this astonishing consequence of a *Metaphysical Aesthetic*: by substituting an intellectual knowledge for the immediate and singular effect of phenomena and their specific resonance, it tends to absolve us from the experience of the *Beautiful* as encountered in the sensory world. Once the essence of beauty has been extracted, once its general formulas have been noted, and nature along with art has been exhausted, surmounted, replaced by principles whose implications can be derived with certainty—all the works and aspects that delighted us might just as well vanish, or at most continue to serve as provisional examples or teaching aids.

This consequence is not acknowledged—small wonder, since it is scarcely the kind of thing one can acknowledge. None of our dialecticians of Aesthetics will agree that his eyes or ears have become superfluous except for the needs of practical life. Much less will any of them claim that, thanks to his formulas, he might for his own amusement turn out—or at least give exact specifications for—unmistakable masterpieces, without contributing any more of himself than the mental effort of performing a kind of calculation.

Actually such a supposition is not entirely imaginary. We know that dreams of this sort have haunted more than one mind, and not among the least gifted; and we know on the other hand to what degree critics, in appraising works of art, have in the past both used and abused the authority conferred, as they thought, by their infallible precepts. For there is no greater temptation than to hand down sovereign decisions in matters of uncertainty.

The very idea of a "Science of the Beautiful" was bound to be shattered by the diversity of the beauties that have been produced or accepted in different times and places. Where pleasure is involved, there can only be questions of fact. Individuals take their pleasure where and as they can; and the wiles of sensibility are infinite. It outwits the soundest counsels, even those based on the shrewdest observation and the most subtle reasoning.

What, for example, is so sound and satisfying to the mind as the famous rule of the three unities, so appropriate to the requirements of attention and so favorable to the solidity and density of dramatic action?

But Shakespeare, among others, ignores it and triumphs. Here I shall take the liberty of bringing up an idea which has just occurred to me and which I pass on just as it came to me, as a tenuous fancy: Shakespeare, so free in his plays, also wrote some famous sonnets, fashioned according to the rules and obviously polished with great care. Who knows whether the great man may not have set more store by these studied poems than by the tragedies and comedies that he improvised for a random audience and even modified in the course of performance?

Yet, though the classical rule ultimately succumbed to contempt or neglect, this does not mean that the precepts it embodies are devoid of value, but only that they had been endowed with an imaginary value, as absolute prerequisites for works producing the *most desirable effect*. By "most desirable effect" I mean (my definition is improvised) the effect attained when there is a minimum of discrepancy between our immediate impression of a work, our initial shock as it were, and our mature judgment of it after we have had time to reflect and to scrutinize its form and structure; when, on the contrary, these two aspects concur, analysis and study confirming and increasing the satisfaction supplied by the first contact.

There are a good many works (and indeed this is the modest aim of certain arts) which yield no more than primary effects. If we stop to think about them, we find that they owe their existence to some inconsistency, impossibility, or sleight of hand, which a prolonged look, an indiscreet question, a little too much curiosity would endanger. Certain monuments of architecture have been inspired solely by a desire to set up an impressive piece of scenery that could be admired from a selected spot; such temptation has often led the builder to sacrifice certain qualities, the absence of which is evident once we move a few steps away from the favorable vantage point. Too often the public confuses the limited art of scene painting—the character of which is determined by a strictly defined and limited space, a unique perspective, and a particular lighting—with the complete art in which the dominant structure, the relations between material, forms, and forces have been brought out in such a way as to be discernible from all directions, and somehow communicate to the eye a sense of mass, static power, muscular effort and stress, that identifies us with the building as though by an awareness permeating our whole body.

Forgive the digression. I now come back to that Metaphysical Aesthetic which, as I was saying, has almost as often as not been contradicted by the event whenever it aspired to dictate taste, to pass definitive judgment on the merit of works of art, to impose itself on artists as well as the public, in short, to make people love what they did not love and hate what they loved.

But only its pretensions were shattered. The Aesthetic itself was sounder than its dream. Its mistake, to my way of thinking, related only to itself and its true nature; to its true value and function. It thought itself universal; but on the contrary, it was marvelously itself, that is to say, original. What could be more original than to set itself up against the greater part of the existing or possible tendencies, tastes, and productions, to condemn India and China, the "Gothic" and the Moorish, to repudiate almost all the wealth of the world, in order to will and to produce *something different*: an object of sensuous delight that would be in perfect harmony with the scruples and judgments of reason, a harmony between the instant and what time reveals at leisure?

In the days (which are not yet ended) when poets were engaged in a great controversy, some advocating what has been called "free" verse, others standing for traditional verse subject to various conventional rules, I sometimes told myself that the supposed boldness of the former and the supposed servitude of the latter were a simple matter of chronology, that if up to that time there had only been free prosody and then suddenly a group of eccentrics had invented rhyme and the strict Alexandrine, we should have heard cries of madness and mystification. . . . It is not difficult, in the arts, to conceive of an inversion between the classics and the moderns, to think of Racine as coming a century after Victor Hugo. . . .

And so our rigorously pure Aesthetic strikes me as an invention unaware that it is one, taking itself for an infallible deduction of a few self-evident principles. Boileau thought he was following reason, and was impervious to the oddness and particularity of his precepts. What could be more capricious than forbidding the hiatus? What could be more far-fetched than his justification of the advantages of rhyme?

Let us bear in mind that it is perfectly natural and perhaps inevitable that we should regard what seems simple, evident, and general as something more than the specific result of personal reflection. Every idea that takes itself to be universal is actually particular. Every universe we form relates to a single point in which it imprisons us.

But far from underestimating the importance of rational Aesthetics, I reserve a positive role for it, and a role of the greatest practical importance. An Aesthetic which springs from reflection and from a consistent desire to understand the aims of art, carrying its pretensions even to the point of forbidding certain methods or of imposing certain conditions on the enjoyment or production of works of art, can render, and in fact has rendered, immense services to certain artists or groups of artists by proving useful in their work, providing formulas for some particular art (not for all art). It supplies laws under which it is possible to subsume the numerous conventions, and from which one can derive the detailed decisions that are assembled and co-ordinated in a work of art. In certain cases such formulas can exert a creative power; they can suggest a good many ideas that would not have arisen without them. Restriction has been inventive at least as often as a superabundance of freedom. I shall not go so far as to say, with Joseph de Maistre, that whatever restricts a man strengthens him. Perhaps de Maistre forgot that shoes can be too tight. But speaking of the arts, he would no doubt reply that tight shoes would make us invent new dances.

It is clear by now that I regard what is called classic art, an art attuned to the Idea of the Beautiful, as a singularity and not as the purest and most general form of art. I do not deny that such an art is in accord with my personal taste; but the only value I impute to my preference is that of being my own.

To my mind the term *bias* that I have used signifies that the precepts worked out by the theoretician, the work of conceptual analysis he has done with a view to progressing from dispersed to ordered judgment, from fact to law, from the relative to the absolute, and to establishing himself in dogmatic possession of the loftiest consciousness of the Beautiful, can be useful in the practice of art as a convention chosen among others that are equally possible. Such a choice is not obligatory—it does not result from an ineluctable intellectual necessity that we cannot evade once we have understood it.

For what constrains reason never constrains reason alone.

Reason is a goddess we think of as watchful, but who is really asleep in some grotto of our mind; now and then she appears to us, enjoining us to calculate the various probabilities of the consequences of our acts. From time to time (for the law governing these apparitions of reason to our consciousness is quite irrational) she invites us to pretend that our judgments are equal, that one forecast is as good as another and that we have no secret preferences, that all arguments are impressively balanced; and all this demands of us what is most repugnant to our nature—*our absence*. Reason in her majesty would like us to identify ourselves with reality in order to dominate it, *imperare parendo*; but we ourselves are real (or nothing is), and particularly so when we act, for action requires a tendency, that is to say, an imbalance, a kind of injustice, that springs almost inevitably from our person, which is singular and different from all others—and this is contrary to reason. Reason ignores or assimilates individuals, who

55

sometimes repay her in kind. Reason is concerned only with types and systematic comparisons, with ideal hierarchies of values, the enumeration of symmetrical hypotheses; and all these structures, which define reason, occur in thought and nowhere else.

But the labor of the artist, even the wholly intellectual part of it, cannot be reduced to the operations of a guiding reason. When it comes to producing a work, the material, the methods, even the moment, and a host of accidents (which at least for the nonphilosopher characterize reality) not only introduce unforeseen and indeterminate elements into the drama of creation, but moreover conspire to make it inconceivable in terms of reason, for they carry it into the realm of things, where it becomes a *thing*; it ceases to be an object of thought and becomes an object of sensibility.

On the other hand, the artist, whether he likes it or not, is absolutely unable to free himself from a sense of the arbitrary. He progresses from the arbitrary toward a certain necessity, and from a certain disorder toward a certain order; and he cannot do without this constant sense of an arbitrariness and disorder that resist the thing which is coming into being beneath his hands and which strikes him as necessary and ordered. It is this contrast that makes him feel that he is creating, since he cannot deduce what is coming to him from what he has.

Consequently his necessity is quite different from that of the logician. It rests entirely in this moment of contrast, and derives its strength from this moment of resolution which the artist will subsequently try to recapture or transpose or prolong, *secundum artem*.

The logician's necessity results from the impossibility of thinking a contradiction: it is based on a rigorous adherence to the conventions of notation—to *definitions* and postulates. But this excludes from the dialectical realm everything that cannot be defined (or properly defined), everything that is not essentially *language* or reducible to linguistic expression. There is no contradiction without *diction*, that is to say, *outside of discourse*. Thus for the metaphysician discourse is an end, while for the man who wishes to act, it is only a means. The metaphysician's first preoccupation has been the *True*, to which he is devoted heart and soul and which he recognizes by its freedom from contradictions. Hence when, in the course of time, he discovers the *Idea of the Beautiful* and tries to develop its nature and consequences, he is bound to remember the quest for *his* Truth. Under the name of the *Beautiful*, he begins to pursue some *Truth* of a "second" kind and, without suspecting it, he invents the *Truth of the Beautiful*. Thereby, as I have said, he separates the *Beautiful* from moments and things, including beautiful moments and beautiful things. . . .

When he returns to works of art, he is tempted to judge them according to principles, for his mind is trained to look for conformity. First of all he must translate his impression into words; he will base his judgments on words, and speculate about unity, variety, and other concepts. Thus he posits the existence of a Truth in the order of pleasure, a Truth that everyone can know and recognize: he decrees that all men are equal in the presence of pleasure, declares that there are true pleasures and false pleasures, and that judges can be trained to decide infallibly between them.

I am not exaggerating. There is no doubt that a stanch belief in the possibility of solving the problem of subjective judgments in the realm of art and taste has been pretty well ingrained in the minds of all those who have imagined or tried, successfully or not, to build up systems of dogmatic

Aesthetics. We may as well admit, gentlemen, that none of us is immune to such temptation, that all of us quite frequently slide from the personal to the universal, fascinated by the promises of the dialectical demon. The seducer beguiles us with the hope that everything will reduce itself to categoric terms and so achieve completion, that everything will culminate in the *Word*. But we must answer the demon with this simple observation: the effect of the Beautiful upon a man is to make him *mute*.

Mute, at first; but we shall soon observe another effect that is quite remarkable: if, without the least intention of judging, we try to describe our immediate impressions of what has just taken place in our sensibility, we shall find that we cannot avoid contradiction. The event compels us to employ such scandalous expressions as *the necessity of the arbitrary* or *necessity by way of the arbitrary*.

Let us put ourselves into the requisite state: the state into which we are transported by one of those works which make us desire them the more, the more we possess them (I trust that we have only to consult our memory to recall such a state). We shall find within ourselves a curious mixture, or rather a curious alternation, of nascent feelings, the presence and contrasting nature of which I believe to be characteristic.

We feel on the one hand that the source or object of our will is so appropriate to us that we cannot conceive of its being otherwise. Even in certain cases of supreme contentment we feel that by some profound process we are being transformed into the man whose general sensibility is capable of such an extreme or fullness of delight.

But we feel no less strongly, as though by another sense, that the phenomenon which is inducing and developing this state in us, which is inflicting its invisible power on us, *might not have been*, or even that it *should not have been*, that it belongs to the realm of the improbable. Our enjoyment or joy has the force of fact, yet the existence and formation of the means, the instrument, that has engendered these feelings strike us as *accidental*, the result of a great stroke of luck, a gratuitous gift of fortune. And in this respect, it seems worth mentioning, we note a distinct analogy between the effect of a work of art and that of an aspect of nature resulting from some geological accident, or perhaps from a passing combination of light and mist in the sky.

Sometimes it seems inconceivable that a man like ourselves can be the author of so extraordinary a blessing, and the praise we give him is an expression of our inability to conceive such a thing.

Now the artist has these contradictory feelings in the highest degree: they are a condition of every work of art. The artist lives with *his* arbitrariness and in the expectation of *his* necessity. He is always looking for his necessity and he obtains it from the most unforeseen and insignificant circumstances; there is no proportion, no uniform relation of magnitude, between the effect and the cause. He awaits an answer that must be *absolutely precise* (since it must engender an act of execution) to a question that is *essentially incomplete*: he yearns for the effect that will be produced in him by what is to be born of him. Sometimes the gift precedes the asking, comes as an overwhelming surprise, and finds him unprepared. It is such instances of sudden grace that most strikingly reveal the contrast we just mentioned between the two sensations that accompany one and the same phenomenon; what, as far as we can tell, *might not have been* takes hold of us with the same power as *what had to be* and *had to be as it is.*

I confess, gentlemen, that I have never been able to go any further in my reflections on these problems without venturing beyond the observations that I can make on myself. If I have gone to some length in describing the nature of strictly philosophical Aesthetics, it is because it offers us the very type of an abstract development applied to, or inflicted upon, an infinite diversity of concrete and complex impressions. The consequence is that it does not speak of what it thinks it is speaking of, something, incidentally, of which no one has ever proved that it is possible to *speak*. In any case there is no doubt that this philosophical Aesthetics has been creative. Whether it dealt with the rules of the theater or of poetry, the canons of architecture, the golden section, the effort to devise a science of art or at least to prescribe methods, to put order as it were into a field already mastered or believed to have been mastered, it has attracted the greatest philosophers. This explains why I have occasionally confused these two races of men—and been roundly taken to task for it. I thought I discerned a thinker in Leonardo and a kind of poet or architect in Spinoza. I was no doubt mistaken. And yet it seemed to me that a man's external mode of expression might sometimes be less important than the quality of his desire and the structure of his ideas.

Be that as it may, there is no need to add that I did not find the definition I was looking for. I am not dismayed at this negative result. If I had found the perfect definition, I might have been tempted to deny the existence of an object corresponding to it and to claim that Aesthetics did not exist. As far as I know, no one has ever claimed to define mathematics, yet no one doubts its existence. Some men have tried to define life; their efforts have always been rather futile, but life is there just the same.

Aesthetics exists; and there are even aestheticians. In conclusion I should like to suggest to them a few ideas which they are perfectly free to regard as products of ignorance or naïveté, or as a happy combination of the two.

Let us go back to the pile of books, treatises, and theses I was discussing a little while ago, in which, as you doubtless recall, I found a certain diversity. I should like to suggest a way of classifying them.

I should call my first group *Esthesics*. Into it I should put everything related to the study of sensations; but most particularly works dealing with the sensory excitations and reactions that *have no uniform, well-defined physiological function*. For our wealth consists in all those sensory modifications that the living creature can do without (though *rarely* we may run across useful or even indispensable sensations among them). From these infinite resources all the luxury of our arts is derived.

Another pile would comprise all the writing that deals with the actual production of works. I should call this second group *Poetics* or rather *Poietics*; and an over-all conception of *the complete human act*, from its psychic and physiological roots to its attempts to affect matter or individuals, would serve as a basis for subdividing it. On the one hand, we should have the study of invention and composition, the role of chance, reflection, and imitation, of education and environment; and on the other hand, the examination and analysis of the techniques, methods, instruments, materials, means, and conditions of action.

The classification is rather crude. It is also inadequate. We shall require at least one more pile comprising works treating of problems in which my *Esthesics* and my *Poietics* overlap.

But this last observation suggests that my idea may be illusory, and I suspect that every last one of the papers read at this Congress will demonstrate its absurdity.

In that case what have I gained from my little attempt at aesthetic thinking? Shall I at least, for want of a definite idea, a solution, be able to sum up my multifarious gropings?

A review of my reflections gives me nothing but negative propositions. But that in itself is worth noting. Are there not numbers which analysis can define only by way of negations?

Here, then, is what I tell myself:

There is a form of pleasure which cannot be explained; which cannot be circumscribed; which is not limited to the sense organ from which it springs, nor even to the realm of the sensibility; which differs in its nature or its causes, in its intensity, its scope, and its consequences, according to the person, his age, his circumstances, the era in which he lives, his culture and environment; which incites to actions without universally valid causes, directed toward uncertain ends, and committed by individuals who seem to be scattered at random among a people; and these actions result in products of different kinds, whose use value and exchange value depend very little on what they are. And here is our final negative statement: all men's efforts to define, regularize, regulate, measure, stabilize, or insure this pleasure and its production have thus far been vain and fruitless; but since everything in this realm is, and is bound to be, impossible to circumscribe, they have been only imperfectly vain, and their failure has sometimes been curiously creative and fertile.

I shall not go so far as to say that Aesthetics is the study of a system of negations, though there would be a grain of truth in it. If we look the problems in the face, if we really come to grips with such problems as pleasure and the power to produce pleasure, we find any positive solution, or even a satisfactory formulation of the problems to be quite beyond us.

On the other hand, I should like to express a very different thought, namely, that I see a wonderfully vast and luminous future in store for your investigations.

Just think: today all the most highly developed sciences appeal, even in their techniques, to the considerations or insights that it is your calling to study. The mathematicians are forever speaking of the structural beauty of their inferences and demonstrations. Their discoveries are developed through the perception of formal analogies. At the end of a lecture at the Institut Poincaré, Einstein once said that in order to complete his ideal construction of symbols, he had been obliged "to introduce certain perspectives derived from architecture." . . .

Physics, on the other hand, is facing a crisis in its imagery. From time immemorial it had represented matter and motion as wholly distinct and considered space and time to be perfectly discernible and measurable by any scale whatsoever; it had drawn considerable advantage from the notions of continuity and similarity. But today its powers of action have exceeded all predictions; they have outgrown all our means of symbolic representation and are even shattering our venerable categories. Yet fundamentally the object of physics is to be sought in our sensations and perceptions. Nevertheless, it considers them as the substance of an outward universe over which we have some power of action, and it repudiates or disregards those of our immediate impressions for which it cannot find a corresponding operation making it possible to reproduce them under "measurable" conditions, that is, conditions related to the permanence we attribute to solid bodies. To the physicist, color, for example, is only an accessory circumstance; he derives from it nothing more than a rough indication of frequency. As to the effects of color contrast, complementary colors, and other phenomena of the same order, he simply dismisses them. This brings us to an interesting observation: while for the physicist an impression of color is an accident connected with such and such a value of an indefinitely increasing series of numbers, the same scientist's eye offers him a closed and limited set of sensations that correspond in pairs; if one is given with a certain intensity and duration, it is immediately followed by the production of the other. If someone had never seen *green*, he would come to know it by merely looking at *red*.

I have sometimes wondered, in thinking about the recent perplexities in physics, about all the rather uncertain conceptions, the quasi entities it is each day compelled to produce and deal with, whether, after all, the retina might not have its own opinions about photons and its own theory of light; whether the tactile bodies, the muscle fibers and nerves with their miraculous qualities, might not have a great deal to do with the manufacture of time, space, and matter? And then physics would have to go back to the study of sensation and its organs.

But is all this not *Esthesics*? And if we introduce certain inequalities and certain relations into *Esthesics*, shall we not come very close to our indefinable *Aesthetics*?

I have just mentioned the phenomenon of complementary colors, which in the simplest and most readily observable way shows us a veritable creation. An organ fatigued by a sensation seems to get away from it by producing another, symmetrical sensation. And we might find any number of spontaneous productions that come to us as complements of a system of impressions felt to be inadequate. We cannot see constellations in the sky without tracing imaginary lines between their stars, and we cannot hear sounds that are relatively close together without conceiving of them as a sequence,

64

having an action within our muscular apparatus which, for the plurality of these distinct events, substitutes a rather complicated process of generation.

All these are elementary *works of art*. Perhaps art consists merely in a combination of such elements. The need to complete, to *respond* by producing either the symmetrical or the similar, the need to fill an empty time or space, to satisfy an expectation, or to hide the ungainly present beneath gratifying images—are they not all manifestations of a power which, increased by the transformations effected by the intellect with its multitude of methods and techniques borrowed from our experience of practical action, has thus become capable of those great works by a few individuals, who from time to time achieve the highest degree of *necessity* that human nature, as though in response to the variety and indeterminateness of all the possibilities within us, can obtain from its ability to make use of the *arbitrary*?

Aesthetic Invention

In so far as "creation" is defined by "order," disorder is essential to it.

The creation of order involves on the one hand *spontaneous formations* comparable to the symmetries or shapes—"intelligible" in themselves—of certain natural objects; and on the other hand, a *conscious act* (that is to say, an act whose *end* and *means* can be distinguished and expressed separately).

In a work of art, in sum, two kinds of constituents are always present: first, those whose origin we cannot conceive, which cannot be expressed by means of acts, although they can be modified by acts later on; second, those which are *articulate*, and thus may be the result of thought.

In every work these constituents are mingled in a certain proportion, and that proportion plays a considerable role in art. Epochs and schools are distinguished by the predominance of one or the other factor. In general, the successive reactions that mark the history of any art with a continuous tradition amount to no more than modifications of this proportion; reflection and spontaneity alternate in the dominant character of the works. But the two factors are always present.

Musical composition, for example, demands a translation into *signs* standing for *acts* (that will result in sounds), of melodic or rhythmic ideas drawn from the "universe of sound" considered as disorder—or rather as a virtual aggregate of all possible orders, though in itself this notion is beyond our powers of representation. The case of music is particularly important—for it is music that shows, in the purest state, the interplay of spontaneous formations and conscious constructions combined. Music is characterized by a whole world of choice—that of *sounds* chosen and clearly distinguished from the aggregate of *noises*, then classified and gauged with the help of instruments that can be made to reproduce them exactly *by means of acts*. Once the universe of sound is thus defined and organized, the musician's mind is situated, as it were, in a single system of possibilities: the musical state. If a spontaneous formation appears, it immediately establishes a system of relations with the whole world of sound—and these are the data he will work upon, to which he will apply his conscious acts, exploiting their diverse relations with the realm to which their elements belong.

The first idea occurs of itself. If it arouses a need or desire for embodiment, the artist sets himself a goal, which is the work; his consciousness of that end summons up his whole panoply of means and methods and takes the form of the complete human act. Deliberations, decisions, gropings, all make their appearance in this phase, which I have called "articulate." Similarly, the notions of "beginning" and "end," *which are alien to spontaneous production*, make themselves felt only at the moment when aesthetic creation has to assume the character of a construction.

In poetry the problem is far more complex. Let me sum up the difficulties it presents:

A. Poetry is an art of language. Language is a combination of heterogeneous functions, co-ordinated in reflexes acquired by a usage that consists in endless gropings. Motor, auditory, visual, mnemonic elements form relatively stable groups; the conditions controlling their production and communication, and the effects produced by their reception vary appreciably with individuals. Pronunciation, the tone and rhythm of the voice, the choice of words, and, on the other hand, the psychic reactions aroused, the state of the person to whom we speak—all these are independent variables, indeterminate factors. One kind of discourse takes no account of euphony, another of logical sequence; still another of plausibility . . . etc.

B. Language is a practical instrument; moreover, it is so closely attached to the "self," expressing all the self's changing states so directly, that its own aesthetic virtues (sound, rhythm, the resonance of its images, etc.) are constantly slighted and obscured. They are coming to be considered very much as friction is considered in mechanics (one symptom is the disappearance of the art of calligraphy).

C. Poetry, an art of language, is thus obliged to struggle against its practical uses and the modern acceleration of its practical use. It will emphasize everything that distinguishes it from prose.

D. Thus, quite unlike the musician and less fortunate, the poet is compelled, in each of his creations, to create the *universe of poetry*—that is to say, he is compelled to create the psychological and emotional state in which language can fulfill a role quite different from that of signifying what is or was or will be. And whereas practical language is destroyed, nullified, once its aim (comprehension) is attained, poetic language must aim at the preservation of form.

E. Thus, for the poet, signification is not the essential, nor ultimately the only, element of language, but merely one of its constituents. The poet operates with the complex value of

words—that is, by composing *sound* and *sense* (I am simpli-
fying . . .)—very much as algebra operates with complex
numbers. I apologize for this comparison.

F. Accordingly, the simple notion of word meanings does
not suffice for poetry: I have just spoken, figuratively, of
resonance. I wished to allude to the psychic effects produced,
independently of syntactical connections, by groups of words
and their physiognomies, and by the reciprocal (that is, non-
syntactical) influences resulting from their proximity.

G. Finally, poetic effects, like all aesthetic or for that matter sensory effects, are momentary.

Poetry, you see, is essentially "*in actu.*" A poem exists only
at the moment when it is spoken, and its *true value* is inseparable from performance. Which shows how absurd it is to
teach poetry in total disregard of pronunciation and diction.

From all this it follows that poetic creation is a very special
category of artistic creation, and this because of the nature of
language. A consequence of the complexity of language is
that the nascent state of poems can vary greatly: sometimes a
certain subject, sometimes a group of words, sometimes a
simple rhythm, sometimes (even) a diagram of prosodic form,
may serve as germs and develop into an organized poem.

It is important to remember that one germ may be as good
as another. Among those I have cited I forgot to include the
most startling: a sheet of white paper, an idle moment, a slip
of the tongue, a misreading, a pen that is pleasant to hold.

I shall not go into the matter of the conscious effort of
composition, or the question of breaking it down into *acts*. I
have only wished to give a very summary idea of poetic invention in the strict sense, which should not be confused, as
it constantly is, with imagination, unqualified and without
substance.

The Idea of Art

I. ORIGINALLY the word Art meant simply *way of doing*. This unrestricted sense has gone out of use.

II. Then, little by little, the word was limited to mean the *ways of doing* that involve voluntary action or action initiated by the will. It implied that there was more than one way of obtaining a desired result and it presupposed some sort of preparation, training, or at least concentrated attention in the agent. Medicine is said to be an art, and we say the same of hunting, horsemanship, reasoning, or the conduct of life. There is an art of walking, of breathing: there is even an art of silence.

Since diverse modes of operation tending toward the same goal are not, as a rule, equally effective or economical; and since, on the other hand, they are not equally available to a given operator, the notion of quality or value enters quite naturally into the meaning of our word. We say: *Titian's Art*.

But this manner of speaking confuses two characteristics that we attribute to the author of the action: one of them is his singular, native aptitude, his inalienable personal gift; the other consists in what he has learned or acquired by experience, which can be put into words and passed on to others. In so far as the distinction is applicable, we conclude that *every art can be learned*, but not *the whole art*. However, a confusion

70

between these two characteristics is almost inevitable, for the distinction between them is easier to state than to discern in observing the particular case. To learn anything requires at least a certain gift for learning, while the most marked, most firmly implanted individual aptitude can remain unproductive, unappreciated by others—and may even remain unknown to its possessor, unless it is awakened by certain outward circumstances or some favorable environment, or fed from the wellsprings of a culture.

To sum up: Art, in this sense, is that quality of the *way of doing* (whatever its object may be) which is due to *dissimilarity in the modes of operation* and hence in the results—arising from the *dissimilarity of the agents*.

III. To this notion of Art we must now join certain new considerations that will explain how it came to designate the production and enjoyment of a certain species of works. Today we distinguish between a *work of skill* (*œuvre de l'art*) which may be a production or operation of any ordinary kind and with a practical aim, and a *work of art* (*œuvre d'art*). It is the essential characteristics of the latter that we shall here try to ascertain. We shall seek an answer to the question: How do we know that an object is a *work of art*, or that a system of acts is performed with a view to *art*?

IV. The most evident characteristic of a *work of art* may be termed *uselessness*, but only if we take the following considerations into account:

Most of the impressions and perceptions we receive from our senses play no part in the functioning of the mechanisms essential to the preservation of life. Sometimes, either by their direct intensity or by serving as *signs* that release an action or

71

call forth an emotion, they provoke certain disturbances or changes of regimen; but it is easy to observe that of the innumerable sensory stimuli which perpetually assail us only a very small, an almost infinitesimal part is necessary or useful to our purely physiological existence. The dog's eye sees the stars; but the dog makes nothing of the visual image: he annuls it at once. The dog's ear perceives a sound that makes him look up in alarm; but of this sound he absorbs only as much as he needs in order to replace it by an immediate and completely determined action. He does not dwell on the perception.

Thus most of our sensations are useless as far as our essential functions are concerned, and those that do serve some purpose are purely transitory, exchanged as soon as possible for representations or decisions or acts.

v. On the other hand, the consideration of our possible acts leads us to juxtapose (if not join) the idea of *uselessness* as explained above to another idea, that of the *arbitrary*. Just as we receive more sensations than necessary, we can also make of our motor organs and their actions more combinations than we really need. We can trace a circle, give play to our facial muscles, walk in cadence, etc. In particular, we can employ our energies to fashion something without any practical purpose, and then drop or toss away the object we have made; and as far as our vital necessities are concerned, the making and the throwing away will be equally irrelevant.

vi. In the life of every individual we can thus circumscribe a peculiar realm constituted by the sum of his "useless sensations" and "arbitrary acts." *Art* originated in the attempt to endow these sensations with a kind of *utility* and these acts with a kind of *necessity*.

But this utility and this necessity are by no means as self-evident or universal as the vital necessities of which we have spoken above. Each individual feels and judges them as his nature allows, and judges or deals with them as he will.

VII. But among our useless impressions there are some that may take hold of us and make us wish to prolong or renew them. Or they may lead us to expect other sensations of the same order, that will satisfy a kind of need they have created.

Sight, touch, smell, hearing, movement lead us, then, from time to time, to dwell on sensation, to act in such a way as to increase the intensity or duration of the impression they make. Such action, having sensibility as its origin and its goal, and guided by sensibility even in the choice of its means, is thus clearly distinguished from actions of a practical order. For the latter respond to needs and impulses that are extinguished by satisfaction. The sensation of hunger dies in a man who has eaten his fill, and the images that illustrated his need are dispelled. But it is quite different in the sphere of exclusive sensibility that we have been discussing: here *satisfaction* resuscitates *desire*; *response* regenerates *demand*; *possession* engenders a mounting *appetite* for the thing possessed: in a word, *sensation* heightens and reproduces the *expectation of sensation*, and there is no distinct end, no definite limit, no conclusive action that can directly halt this process of reciprocal stimulation.

To organize a system of perceptible things possessing this property of perpetual stimulation, that is the essential problem of Art; its necessary, but far from sufficient, condition.

VIII. It will be worth our while to put a certain stress on the last point; its importance will be made clear if we reflect for a moment on a special phenomenon arising from the sensibility of the retina. The retina responds to a strong color impression by the "subjective" production of another color, which we term complementary to the first; wholly determined by the original color, the complementary gives way in turn to a repetition of its predecessor, *and so on.* This oscillation would go on indefinitely if the organ's fatigue did not put an end to it. The phenomenon shows that localized sensibility can act as a *self-sufficient producer* of corresponding impressions, each of which seems necessarily to engender its "antidote." Yet, on the one hand, this local faculty plays no part in "useful vision"—but on the contrary can only obscure it. "Useful vision" retains only as much of any impression as is needed to make us think of something else, to arouse an "idea" or provoke an act. On the other hand, the uniform correspondence of colors in pairs of complementaries defines a system of relations, since to each actual color there corresponds a virtual color, to each color sensation a definite response. But these relations and others like them, which play no part in "useful vision," play an essential part in organizing perceptible things, and in the attempt to confer a kind of higher necessity or higher utility upon sensations that are without value for the vital processes, but are fundamental, as we said above, to the notion of art.

IX. If, from this elementary property of the excited retina, we pass to the properties of the parts of the body, particularly the most mobile among them; and if we observe these possibilities of movement and effort that have nothing to do with utility, we find that this particular group of possibilities includes any number of associations between tactile sensations and muscular ones which fulfill the conditions we have spoken of: reciprocal correspondence, resumption, or indefinite prolongation. To *feel of an object* is merely to seek with our hand a certain *ordered group of contacts*; if, whether or not we recognize the object (and in any case disregarding what our mind tells us about it), *we are compelled or induced to repeat our enveloping maneuver indefinitely*, we gradually lose our sense of the *arbitrary* character of our act, and a certain sense of its *necessity* is born in us. Our need to begin the movement all over again and to perfect our local knowledge of the object tells us that its form is *better suited than another* to maintain this repeated action. Its favorable form is distinguished from all other possible forms, for it tempts us singularly to pursue an exchange between motor sensations and sensations of contact and effort, which, because of its form, become in a manner of speaking *complementary*, each movement or pressure of the hand provoking another. If we then try to fashion, in an appropriate material, a form satisfying the same condition, we shall be making a *work of art*. All this may be expressed roughly by speaking of "creative sensibility"; but that is merely an ambitious expression promising more than it can deliver.

x. To sum up: there is a whole sphere of human activity that is quite negligible from the standpoint of the immediate preservation of the individual. Moreover it is opposed to intellectual activity proper, since it consists in a development of sensations tending to repeat or prolong what the intellect tends to eliminate or transcend—just as the intellect tends to abolish the auditive substance and structure of a discourse in order to arrive at its meaning.

xi. But, on the other hand, this activity is opposed, in and of itself, to vacant idleness. *Sensibility*, which is its beginning and its end, *abhors a vacuum*. It reacts spontaneously against a short-age of stimuli. Whenever a lapse of time without occupation or preoccupation is imposed on a man, he undergoes a change of state marked by a kind of productivity that tends to bring back regular exchanges between *potentiality* and *activity* in the sensibility. The tracing of a design on a surface that is too bare, the birth of a song in a silence felt too keenly: these are only re-sponses, complements to counterbalance the absence of exci-tation—as though this *absence*, which we express by a simple negation, had a *positive effect* on us.

Here we capture the production of a work of art in its very germ. We recognize a work of art by the fact that no "idea" it can arouse in us, no act it suggests to us, can exhaust or put an end to it: however long we may breathe of a flower that accords with our sense of smell, we are never surfeited, for the enjoyment of the perfume revives our need for it; and there is no memory, no thought, no action, that can annul its effect and *wholly* free us from its power. That is what the man who sets out to make a *work of art* is striving for.

XII. This analysis of elementary and essential facts concerning Art leads us to modify quite profoundly the usual notion of sensibility. As a rule, it is taken to be merely receptive or transi-tional, but we have seen that it must also be credited with powers of production. That is why we have insisted on the complementaries. If someone were ignorant of the color *green*, having never seen it, he would merely have to stare for some time at a *red* object to produce the unknown sensation in himself.

We have also seen that sensibility is not limited to re-sponding, but sometimes demands and then responds to itself.

All this is not limited to sensations. If we carefully observe the production, the effects, and the curious cyclic substitutions of *mental images*, we find the same relations of contrast and symmetry, and above all the same system of indefinitely repeated regeneration that we have noted in the areas of specialized sensibility. These images may be complex, may develop over a considerable period of time, may resemble the accidents of the outside world, or at times actually combine with practical needs—yet they behave in the ways we have described in speaking of pure sensation. What is most characteristic is the need to see again, to hear again, to experience indefinitely. The lover of form never wearies of caressing the bronze or stone that excites his sense of touch. The music lover cries "encore" or hums the tune that has delighted him. The child wants the story repeated: "Tell it over again! . . ."

xiii. From these elementary properties of our sensibility man's industry has derived prodigious results. The innumerable works of art produced over the ages, the diversity of means and methods, the variety of types represented by these instruments of the sensory and affective life, are wonderful to conceive. *But this immense development was possible only because of the contribution made by those of our faculties in which sensibility plays but a secondary part.* Those of our abilities which are not useless, but indispensable or at least useful to our existence, have been cultivated and given greater force or precision by man. Man's control over matter has become continuously stronger and more accurate. Art has benefited from these advantages, and the various techniques created for the needs of practical life have given artists their tools and methods. On the other hand, the intellect and its abstract instruments (logic, method, classification, analysis of data, criticism, which are sometimes opposed to sensibility since, unlike it, they always

progress toward a limit, pursue a determinate aim—a formula, a definition, a law—and tend to exhaust all sensory experience or replace it by signs) have brought to Art the help,
beneficial or otherwise, of repeated and critically formed
thought, constituting distinct, conscious operations, rich in
forms and notations of admirable generality and power.
Among other consequences, the intervention of the intellect
has given rise to Aesthetics, or rather to the various systems
of Aesthetics, which have treated Art as a problem of knowledge, and thus tried to reduce it to ideas. Apart from Aesthetics in the strict sense, which is a matter for philosophers and
scholars, the role of the intellect in Art deserves a thorough
investigation. Here we can only suggest such a project and
content ourselves with an allusion to the innumerable
"theories," schools, and doctrines conceived or followed by
so many modern artists, and to the endless wrangling among
the eternal and identical characters of this *commedia dell' arte*:
Nature, Tradition, Novelty, Style, the True, the Beautiful, etc.

XIV. Art, considered as an activity at the present time, has been
forced to submit to the conditions of our standardized social
life. It has taken its place in the world economy. The production and consumption of works of art are no longer wholly
independent of each other, but tend to be organized together.
The career of the artist is becoming once again what it was in
the day when he was looked upon as a practitioner, that is to
say, a member of a recognized profession. In many countries
the State is trying to administer the arts; it does what it can to
"encourage" artists and takes charge of preserving their
works. Under certain political regimes, the State tries to enlist
the arts in its propaganda activities, thus imitating what has
always been the practice of all the religions. The legislator has

given Art a statute which defines the conditions under which it may be practiced, establishes the ownership of an artist's works, and consecrates the paradox whereby a limited term is assigned to a right that is better founded than most of those the law perpetuates. Art has its press, its domestic and foreign policy, its schools, its markets, and its stock markets; it even has its great savings banks, the museums, libraries, etc., which accumulate the enormous *capital* produced from century to century by the efforts of the "creative sensibility."

Thus Art takes its place side by side with utilitarian Industry. On the other hand, the amazing technological developments which make all prediction impossible in all fields are bound to exert an increasing effect on the destinies of Art, by creating unheard-of new methods of employing the sensibility. Already the inventions of photography and cinematography are transforming our notion of the plastic arts. It is by no means impossible that the extremely minute analysis of sensations which certain means of observation or recording (such as the cathode-ray oscillograph) seem to foreshadow, will lead to methods of playing on the senses compared to which even music, even electronic music, will seem mechanically complicated and obsolete in its aims. The most astonishing relations will perhaps be established between the "photon" and the "nerve cell."

Yet certain indications may justify the fear that the increase in intensity and precision, and the state of permanent disorder engendered in man's thoughts and perceptions by the stupendous novelties that have transformed his life, may gradually dull his sensibility and make his intelligence less supple than it was.

The "Aesthetic Infinite"

OUR perceptions generally arouse in us, when they arouse anything at all, something that annuls or tends to annul them. Sometimes by an act (that may or may not be a reflex), sometimes by a kind of indifference (natural or acquired), we do away with them or try to. We have an unfailing tendency, with regard to our perceptions, to get back as quickly as possible to the state we were in before they occurred to us. It would seem as though the main business of our life consisted in turning some sort of index of our sensibility back to *zero*, and in finding the shortest way to restore a *maximum* of freedom or availability to our senses.

Our reactions that tend to abolish our sensations are as varied as the sensations themselves. Yet we may subsume them under a common name and say that all those reactions that have a *finite aim* constitute the *practical order*.

But there are other reactions which quite to the contrary arouse desires, needs, and changes of state that tend to preserve, recapture, or reproduce the initial sensations.

If a man is hungry, his hunger will make him do whatever must be done to annul it as quickly as possible; but if he finds the food delectable, his delight will *strive in him* to endure, to perpetuate itself, or to be reborn. Hunger impels us to cut the sensation short; pleasure to develop another; and these two tendencies will become so independent of one another that the man soon learns to indulge in delicacies and to eat when he is not hungry.

What I have said about hunger can easily be extended to the need for love; and indeed to all kinds of sensation, to every mode of sensibility in which conscious action can interfere to restore, prolong, or increase what reflex action in itself seems made to annul.

Sight, touch, smell, hearing, movement, speech may from time to time cause us to dwell on the impressions they induce —to sustain or renew them.

Taken together, all those reactions I have singled out as tending to perpetuate themselves might be said to constitute the *aesthetic order*.

To justify the word *infinite* and give it a precise meaning, we need only recall that in the aesthetic order *satisfaction* revives *need*, *response* renews *demand*, *presence* generates *absence*, and *possession* gives rise to *desire*.

Whereas, in the order that I have called *practical*, attainment of the aim dispels the sensory motives of the act (which vanish completely, or at most leave behind them a dim, abstract memory), quite the contrary is true in the *aesthetic order*.

In the "universe of sensibility," there is a kind of reciprocity between sensation and its anticipation; endlessly one calls for the other, just as in the "universe of colors," complementaries alternately replace one another, starting from a powerful impression on the retina.

This oscillation, as we might call it, does not cease of its own accord: it is exhausted or interrupted only by some extraneous circumstance—such as *fatigue*—which halts it and prevents or defers its recurrence.

Fatigue (by way of an example) is accompanied by a lessening of sensibility toward the thing which at first meant pleasure or desire: a new object is needed.

Change becomes desirable in itself: *variety* is sought as complementary to the duration of sensation and as a remedy for the satiety resulting from the exhaustion of the finite resources of our organism as it responds to a local and particular but endless tendency. In this sense, we are a system of *intersecting functions*, and one constant feature of the system is the periodic interruption of each partial activity.

If we are to keep on desiring, we must desire something else; and the need for change becomes a mark of our *desire to desire*, or of our desire for anything whatever that will arouse our longing.

But if no such thing appears, if the surroundings we live in do not offer us quickly enough an object worthy of infinite development, our sensibility provokes itself to produce images of what it wants, just as thirst brings visions of marvelously cooling drinks. . . .

These very simple considerations will help to differentiate or define with some clarity the realm—sprung from our perceptions and composed entirely of the internal relations and variations proper to our sensibility—that I have called the *aesthetic order*. But the order of finite aims, the practical order, which is the order of action, combines with it in many ways. In particular, what we called a "work of art" is the result of an action whose *finite aim* is to call forth *infinite* developments in someone. From this we may infer that the artist is a "double man" for he applies the laws and instrumentalities of the world of action in order to produce an effect in the universe of sensory resonance. Many attempts have been made to reduce the two tendencies to one or the other: Aesthetics has no other object. But the problem remains unsolved.

On the Teaching of *Poetics* at the
Collège de France

RECENT YEARS have seen a great increase of interest in the History of Literature, and today a good many courses are devoted to it. It seems strange by contrast that the form of intellectual activity which engenders the works themselves should be studied hardly at all, or taken up only incidentally and with insufficient precision. It is no less worthy of note that the strictness of method applied to the criticism and philological interpretation of texts is seldom to be met with in the analysis of the positive phenomena that characterize the production and consumption of works of the mind.

If some precision could be achieved in this field, the first result would be to rid the History of Literature of countless accessories, details, and byplay which bear only the most arbitrary and inconsequential relation to the essential problems of art. There is a great temptation to neglect the study of these extremely subtle problems in favor of circumstances or events which, interesting as they may be in themselves, do not, by and large, help us to appreciate a work more fully, or to form a sounder and more profitable idea of its structure. We know very little about Homer; yet this does not detract from the marine beauty of the *Odyssey*; and as for Shakespeare, we are not even sure whether his name should really be put to *King Lear*.

A serious History of Literature should then be conceived

not as a history of authors and the incidents of their lives, not as a history of their works, but as *a history of the mind in so far as it produces or consumes "literature,"* and one might even write a history of this kind without so much as mentioning the name of any writer. We can study the poetic form of the Book of Job or the Song of Songs without any help from the biographies of their authors, who are quite unknown.

But such a history presupposes or requires, by way of preamble or preparation, a study whose purpose it would be to provide as exact as possible an idea of the conditions of the existence and development of literature, an analysis of its modes of action, its methods, and the diversity of its forms. It seems inconceivable that anyone would take up the history of painting or mathematics (for example) without previously acquiring a considerable knowledge of these disciplines and their techniques. But because of the apparent ease with which literature is produced (since its substance and instrument is the common language, and since it works entirely with ideas that are not specifically elaborated), it seems, both for its practice and enjoyment, to require no special preparation. We do not deny that the preparation may *seem* to be negligible; indeed, it is commonly supposed that to become a writer one needs nothing more than a pen, a notebook, and a certain natural gift.

This was not the feeling of the ancients nor of our own most eminent authors. Even those who believed that their works sprang simply from their desire and the direct exercise of their talents, had, without suspecting it, formed a whole system of habits and ideas resulting from their experience, and these habits and ideas took effect in their production. Even if they never dreamed of all the definitions and conventions,

84

the logic and "combinatorial analysis" that composition pre-supposes, even if they thought they owed everything to the present moment, their work inevitably involved the whole gamut of modes and methods without which the mind cannot function. The revisions, the retouching, the erasures, and above all the progress we note from one work to another, show that the part played by the arbitrary, the unforeseen, the emotional, or even by present intention, is preponderant only in appearance. Normally, when our hand writes, it does not reveal the amazing complexity of its mechanism and of the diverse forces combined in its action. But what the hand writes is surely no less complicated; and, like all complex, unique acts, every sentence we form must be appropriate to some circumstance that is never repeated; it calls for a co-ordination of present perceptions, momentary impulses and images, with a whole "stock" of reflexes, memories, and habits. All this must be apparent from the slightest observation of language "in action."

But an equally simple reflection leads us to believe that *literature is and can be nothing else than a kind of extension and application of certain properties of language.*

For example, it employs, for its own ends, the phonic properties and rhythmic possibilities of language, which are neglected in ordinary speech. It even classifies them, organizes them, and sometimes makes a systematic, strictly defined use of them. Sometimes it even develops the effects that may arise from the affinities or contrasts between terms; it devises contractions or employs substitutions that impel the mind to produce more vivid images than those which suffice for the understanding of the ordinary language. This is the realm of the "figures of speech" with which ancient "rhetoric" concerned itself, a field virtually neglected in modern education.

85

Regrettably so. The formation of such figures is inseparable from that of language itself, whose "abstract" terms are all obtained by some abuse or transference of a word's meaning, while the original sense is forgotten. Thus a poet who makes repeated use of figurative speech is only rediscovering, within himself, the *nascent state* of language. Indeed, if we look at things at a sufficient remove, may we not consider language itself as the masterpiece of literary masterpieces, since all creation in this field amounts to a combination of the potentialities of a given vocabulary in accordance with forms established once and for all?

In short, the study of which we were speaking would aim to define and develop the search for specifically literary effects in language; it would investigate the expressive and suggestive inventions purporting to increase the power and penetration of the word, and the restrictions that have sometimes been imposed with a view to distinguishing the language of imagination from the language of everyday use, etc.

These few suggestions show what a vast number of problems, what an immense range of subject matter a theory of literature as we conceive it will give us to think about. The name of *Poetics* seems appropriate to such a study if we take the word in its etymological sense, that is, as a name for everything that bears on the creation or composition of works having language at once as their substance and as their instrument —and not in the restricted sense of a collection of aesthetic rules or precepts relating to poetry.

Thus of all the arts it is the literary art, derived from language and influencing it in turn, in which convention plays the greatest part; in which memory takes a hand at every moment, in every *word*; which acts largely by *relays* and not by direct sensation; and which works simultaneously and even concurrently with the abstract intellectual faculties, the emotions, and the sensibility. Of all the arts it is that which involves and utilizes the greatest number of independent factors (*sound, meaning, syntatical forms, concepts, images* . . .). The study of literature taken in this sense is obviously very difficult to carry on or even to organize, because basically it is nothing more nor less than an analysis of the mind, directed by a special intention, and because there is no order in the mind itself: it finds an order in things or puts one into them, but finds none in itself that is either necessary or more fruitful than its own incessantly renewed "disorder."

But *Poetics* is less concerned with solving problems than with stating them. Here, as in all higher learning, teaching should go hand in hand with investigation; and furthermore we should approach this study on a high plane of generality. For it is impossible to give a true and complete idea of literature unless we try to situate it as accurately as possible, by exploring the entire field of the expression of ideas and emotions; unless we examine the conditions under which literature can exist, both in the author's inward endeavor and in the reader's inward reaction; and unless, on the other hand, we consider the cultural environments in which it develops. This last consideration brings us (among other consequences) to an important distinction: the distinction between works *which are in a way created by their audience* (whose expectation they fulfill, so that they might almost be said to be determined by an awareness of this expectation) and those which, on the contrary, *tend to create their audience*. All the questions and controversies born of conflict between innovation and tradition, all the arguments about conventions, the comparisons between the "élite" and the "general public," the changing trends in criticism, the destinies of works in time and the changes in their value, etc., may be treated on the basis of this distinction.

Yet the essential part of a doctrine of *Poetics* should consist in a comparative analysis of the mechanics (that is, of what might *figuratively* be so called) of the writer's act and of the other less clearly defined conditions that it seems to call for ("inspiration," "sensibility," etc.).

Personal observation and even introspection play a very important part, provided that we do our utmost to express them precisely. It must be admitted that the terminology of the arts, and particularly of the literary art, is exceedingly vague: *form*, *style*, *rhythm*, *influences*, *inspiration*, *composition*, etc., are terms which can be understood, no doubt; but which are understood only to the extent that the persons who use them and exchange them understand each other. As a matter of fact, words as "elementary" as *phrase* or *verse* or even *consonant* are still very ill defined.

To sum up: a possible course in Poetics at the Collège de France, far from substituting itself for or setting itself up against the History of Literature, would aim to provide it with an introduction, a direction, and a purpose.

The Opening Lecture of the
Course in *Poetics*

Mr. Minister,
Mr. Rector,
Ladies and Gentlemen:

I FEEL strangely moved at finding myself in this chair, taking up an entirely new career at an age when a man might have every reason to withdraw from active life.

And you, members of the Faculty, I wish to thank you for the honor you have done me by receiving me in your midst, and for the confidence you have shown, not only in the proposal that you should inaugurate a course in *Poetics*, but also in the man who put it forward.

It may have seemed to you that certain matters which are not strictly speaking objects of scientific knowledge and never can be, because they are too inward and too much a part of the individuals who cultivate them, might nevertheless, perhaps not be taught, but at least in some sense be communicated as the fruit of the personal experience of a whole lifetime; and accordingly that, in this rather special case, advanced age might justifiably be regarded as a kind of qualification.

I should also like to express my gratitude to my colleagues of the French Academy who have joined you in proposing my candidacy.

And lastly I wish to thank the Minister of National Education for approving the change in the subject of this course and for proposing my appointment to the President of the Republic.

Gentlemen, I should not like to begin the explanation of my undertaking without first expressing my gratitude, respect, and admiration for my illustrious friend, M. Joseph Bédier. There is no need to remind this audience of the glory and unique merit of Bédier the scholar and author, the pride of French letters, nor need I speak of his gentle and persuasive authority as an administrator. But what I do want to mention is that it was he, conjointly with several of you members of the Faculty, who first had the idea that is being implemented here today. It was he who won me over to the charms of your House, which he was on the point of leaving, and persuaded me that I might possibly fill this post, which I had not so much as dreamed of. And it was in conversation with him, as we were exchanging questions and reflections, that the title of this course emerged.

First of all let me explain the term "Poetics," to which I have restored its original meaning, very different from the one in current use. It struck me as the only appropriate name for the kind of study that I plan to develop in this course.

Ordinarily the term is applied to any exposition or collection of rules, conventions, or precepts concerning the composition of lyric or dramatic poems or the construction of verse. But perhaps this use of the word—along with the practices it describes—has aged so much that the time has come to give it another.

Until quite recently all the arts lent themselves, each in its own way, to certain definite forms or modes which were imposed on all works of the same genre, and which had to be learned as we learn the syntax of a language. However powerful, however apt it may have been, the effect produced by a work was not thought to be a sufficient justification of that work, or a guarantee of its universal value. What counted was not so much the fact as the principle. It had been recognized almost from the beginning that there were, in each of the arts, certain commendable practices, certain observances and restrictions which favored the success of the artist's undertaking and which it was in his interest to know and respect.

But little by little, on the authority of very great men, a certain notion of legality came to replace the empirical recommendations of former times. Reason stepped in and the rules became rigid. Criticism armed itself with exact formulas. And the paradoxical consequence was that what had served as a discipline in the arts by putting rational barriers in the path of the artist's impulses gained wide and lasting favor, because the possibility of referring works to a well-defined code or canon made it so much easier to judge and classify them.

These formal rules also made things easier for those who wished to produce. Restrictions—even severe ones—relieve the artist of a good many extremely difficult decisions and responsibilities in matters of form, while at the same time they often encourage inventions that would never have resulted from complete freedom.

But whether we welcome the fact or deplore it, the days of authority in the arts ended quite some time ago, and today the word "Poetics" suggests little more than the idea of troublesome and obsolete rules. Consequently I have thought fitting to revive the term in a sense consonant with its etymology, though I shall not go so far as to pronounce it "Poietics," as the physiologists do when they speak of hematopoietic or galactopoietic functions. Actually all I wish to express is the very simple notion of *making*. The making, the *poiein*, that I mean to consider is that which culminates in *a work*, or more precisely, as I shall soon make clear, in that class of works generally called *works of the mind*, that is to say, those works which the mind decides to make for its own use, employing in the process all the physical means at its disposal.

Like the simple act of which I have spoken, any work may or may not lead us to meditate on its production, and may or may not give rise to an attitude of questioning, sometimes clear and urgent, sometimes less so, which turns it into a problem.

A study of this sort is no necessity. We may judge it to be futile and may even think the very idea is an illusion. More than that: certain minds will find such an investigation not only futile but actually harmful; and perhaps they owe it to themselves to think so. It is conceivable, for example, that a poet may be justifiably afraid of damaging his original gifts, his spontaneous powers of production, by analyzing them. He instinctively refuses to explore them otherwise than by the exercise of his art or to master them more fully by means of demonstrative reason. For it seems likely that our simplest act, our most familiar gesture, would be impossible to perform, and the least of our faculties would become paralyzed, if in order to exercise them we had to think about them and really know them.

Achilles cannot outrun the tortoise if he thinks of space and time.

Yet, on the other hand, one may take so keen an interest in this curiosity and attach so high an importance to pursuing it that in the end, perhaps, one will look with greater pleasure and even passion upon *the act of making* than upon *the thing made*.

It is on this point, ladies and gentlemen, that my task must necessarily be distinguished from that of literary history or textual and literary criticism.

The History of Literature looks for the outwardly attested circumstances under which the works were composed, under which they appeared and produced their effects. It informs us about the authors, the vicissitudes of their lives and their work, considered as visible things which left traces that can be detected, collated, and interpreted. It studies traditions and collects documents.

I need not remind you with how much learning and originality this kind of teaching was dispensed in these very halls by your eminent colleague Abel Lefranc. But the knowledge of authors and their times, the study of successive literary phenomena, can only lead us to *conjecture* what may have gone on *inside* those men who did what was necessary to have their names inscribed in the annals of the History of Letters. If they succeeded, it was by a concurrence of two requirements that should be regarded as separate: one, of course, is the actual production of the work; the other is the production of a certain *value* attaching to the work, by those who have known and savored it, who have made its reputation and seen to its transmission, conservation, and survival.

I have just used the words "value" and "production." Let me speak of them for a moment.

In exploring the domain of the creative mind, we must not be afraid to start from the most general considerations.

They will enable us to advance without having to turn back too often, and moreover they will offer us the greatest number of analogies, that is to say, of approximate expressions for facts and ideas which often, by their very nature, evade any attempt at direct definition. This brings me to the words I have borrowed from economics. It seems to me that it might be convenient to group the various activities and persons we shall be discussing under the heads of *production* and *producer* when we wish, not to distinguish their different species, but to speak of what they have in common. And rather than specify a reader or listener or spectator, it will be no less convenient to lump all these votaries of literature of every kind together under the economic term *consumer*.

As to the notion of value, we know that in the realm of the mind it enjoys a primary position comparable to its position in the economic world, though spiritual value is much subtler than the economic variety, because it relates to infinitely more varied needs which cannot, like those of physical existence, be enumerated. If the *Iliad* is still known, and if after all these centuries gold has remained a (relatively) simple but quite remarkable and generally venerated substance, it is because rarity, inimitability, and certain other properties distinguish gold and the *Iliad*, making them privileged objects, standards of *value*.

Though I do not wish to overdo my economic comparison, it is clear that the idea of work, the idea of the creation and accumulation of wealth, of supply and demand, comes quite naturally to mind in the field with which we are concerned.

As much by their similarity as by their different applications, these notions of like name remind us that two realms which seem far removed from one another may both raise the problems involved in the relation of individuals to their social

environment. And indeed, just as there is an economic analogy, and for the same reasons, there is also a political analogy
between the phenomena of organized intellectual life and
those of public life. There is a whole politics of intellectual
power, an internal politics (very internal, mind you) and an
external politics. The latter falls within the scope of literary
history and should be one of its main concerns.

Politics and economics, then, taken in this very general
sense, are notions that suggest themselves at our very first
glance into the world of the mind; and even in its productive
phase, when the mind might reasonably be regarded as a completely isolated system, considerations of politics and economics seem to be profoundly present in most of its creations,
and always hovering in the background of the creative act.

Deep within his thought, the scholar or artist most ab-
sorbed in his pursuits, who seems most withdrawn into his
own sphere, alone with his most impersonal *self*, has a certain
indefinable presentiment of the reactions that the work in
progress will provoke in others: it is hard for man to be alone.

We may be perfectly sure that such a presentiment is there;
though it may enter into such subtle combination with other
factors in the work, and sometimes disguises itself so well that
we can scarcely isolate it.

Yet we know that the real aim of this or that choice, this
or that effort on the part of a creator, often lies beyond the
creation itself, and is the result of a more or less conscious
concern for the effect that will be produced and its consequences for the producer. In the course of his work, his mind
passes incessantly from himself to another; he modifies the
product of his most inward being according to his private
sense of the judgment of others. Thus, in our reflections
on a work, we may take one or the other of these mutually

exclusive attitudes. If we wish to proceed by the strictest methods that such a subject allows, we must be extremely careful to separate our research into *the production of a work* from our study of *the production of its value*, that is, of the effects it may engender here or there, in this or that mind, at this or that time.

To demonstrate this it suffices to remark that what we can really know or think in any field is only what we ourselves can either *observe* or *make*, and that it is impossible to encompass in one reaction, in one act of attention, the mind that produces the work and the mind that produces the value of the work. No eye is capable of observing these two functions at once; producer and consumer are two essentially separate systems. For one the work is the *end*, for the other it is the *origin*, of developments that may be quite unrelated to one another.

We are bound to conclude that any judgment which expresses a triangular relation between producer, work, and consumer—and judgments of this kind are not rare in criticism —is a delusion that a moment's reflection will dissipate. We can consider only the relation of the work to its producer or else the relation of the work to someone who is affected by it once it is completed. The action of the first and the reaction of the second are not to be confused. Their ideas of the work are incompatible.

This often leads to surprises, some of which are beneficial. There are creative misunderstandings. And there are many effects—sometimes tremendous—which depend on the absence of any direct relation between the two activities in question. A certain work, for example, is the outcome of long effort; it embodies innumerable trials, fresh starts, a long process of elimination and selection. It has required months or years of reflection, and it may have drawn upon the experience and acquirements of a whole lifetime. But the effect of this work makes itself felt in a few moments. At a glance we can take in an imposing monument of architecture, feel the impact of it. In two hours all the calculations of the dramatic poet, all the labor he has put into organizing his play, into shaping his lines, one by one; all the composer's combinations of harmony and orchestration; or all the philosopher's meditations, the years during which he has held his ideas in check, waiting until he could discern and accept their final order; all these acts of faith and choice, all these mental transactions converge at last in the finished work, to strike, astonish, dazzle, or disconcert the mind of *Another*, who is suddenly subjected to this enormous charge of intellectual effort. It is an *incommensurate* act.

The effect might be compared (very roughly, of course) to that produced in a few seconds by the fall of a mass that has been raised bit by bit to the top of a tower, without concern for the time or the number of trips involved.

We thus obtain an impression of superhuman power— though, as you know, this effect is not always achieved; in this exercise in intellectual mechanics the tower may prove to be too high, the mass too great, and the result nil or negative.

But let us suppose that the great effect has been obtained. Those who have experienced it, who have been overwhelmed as it were by the power, the perfections, the strokes of genius, the many fine surprises, cannot and *must* not conceive of the mental effort, the sifting of possibilities, the painstaking selection of appropriate elements, the close reasoning whose conclusions take on an appearance of divination; in a word, they must not suspect how much inner life has been treated by that chemist the producing mind, or sorted out from the mental chaos by a kind of Maxwell's demon. They tend to imagine a human being endowed with immense powers, capable of creating these prodigies with no more effort than it takes to turn out something perfectly ordinary.

What the work produces in us at such a time is incommensurable with our own faculties of instantaneous production. And certain elements of the work, which came to its author by some happy accident, will be attributed to a singular power of his mind. Thus the consumer becomes a producer in his turn: a producer, first, of the work's value; and then, by a direct application of the principle of causality (which, basically, is no more than a naïve expression of one mode of the mind's production), he becomes a producer of the value of the imaginary being who has made what he admires.

Perhaps if great men were as conscious as they are great, no man would be great in his own eyes.

Thus our example, though very particular, shows—and this is what I was coming to—that the mutual independence of the producer and the consumer, their ignorance of each other's thoughts and needs, is almost essential to the effect of a work. In this realm the secrecy and surprise recommended by tacticians are perfectly natural.

To sum up: when we speak of works of the mind, we mean either the end of a certain activity or else the beginning of a certain other activity: two incommunicable orders of inner transformation, each requiring a special adjustment that is incompatible with the other.

There remains the work itself as a perceptible thing. Here we have a third consideration very different from the other two.

In this case we regard a work as an *object*, as pure object, that is to say, we put into it no more of ourselves than may be applied indiscriminately to any object—an attitude that is adequately characterized by the absence of any production of value.

What power have we over this object which, regarded in this way, has no power over us? But we do have power over it. We can measure it in space and time; we can count the words of a text or the syllables in a line of poetry; we can note that a certain book appeared at a certain time; that a certain element in a painting is copied from some other painting; that there is a hemistich in Lamartine that can be found in Thomas, and that a certain page in Victor Hugo was written as early as 1645 by some obscure Père François. We can point out that a certain piece of reasoning is a paralogism; that this sonnet is incorrect in form; that the drawing of that arm defies anatomy, and that a certain use of words is not customary. All these conclusions result from a kind of mechanical operation which amounts to superimposing the work, or parts of it, on a particular model.

This way of dealing with works of the mind makes no distinction between them and all the other possible kinds of works. By giving them a *definable* existence, it ranks them with things. This is the point to remember:

Everything that can be defined is ipso facto *dissociated from the producing mind and set off against it.* By defining it the mind turns it into raw material on which it can operate, or an instrument with which it can work.

Thus the mind puts what it has defined out of its own reach, thereby showing that it knows itself and trusts only what is other than itself.

These different ways of looking at a work, these distinctions, based not on any striving for subtlety but on the simplest and most immediate observation, are an attempt to bring out an idea that will serve to introduce my analysis of the production of works of the mind.

Everything I have said so far may be summed up in these few words: *a work of the mind exists only in action.* Outside of its action nothing is left but an object that presents no particular relation to the mind. Transport a statue you admire to a country sufficiently different from ours, and it turns into a meaningless stone; a Parthenon into nothing more than a small marble quarry. And when a piece of poetry is used as a collection of grammatical difficulties or illustrations of rules, it ceases immediately to be a *work of the mind*, since the use that is made of it is utterly alien to the conditions under which it came into being, while at the same time it is denied the consumption value that gives it meaning.

A poem on paper is nothing but a piece of writing, subject to all the uses to which such writing can be put. But among all its possibilities there is one, and only one, that creates the conditions under which it will take on the force and form of action. A poem is a discourse that demands and induces a continuous connection between the *voice that is* and the *voice that is coming* and *must come*. And this voice must be such as to command a hearing, and call forth an emotional state of which the text is the sole verbal expression. Take away the voice—the right voice—and the whole thing becomes arbitrary. The poem becomes a sequence of signs, connected only in the sense that they are traced one after the other.

For these reasons I shall never cease to condemn the abominable practice of misusing the works best suited to creating and developing a feeling for poetry in young people, of treating poems as things, dismembering them as though there were no such thing as structure, and tolerating, or even insisting on, the kind of recitation with which we are all familiar, which makes poems into tests of memory or spelling; the practice, in a word, of disregarding the essence of such works, of ignoring what makes them what they are and not entirely different, what gives them their peculiar virtue and necessity.

The poem is in the reading. Without this performance its sequences of curiously assembled words are inexplicable fabrications.

Works of the mind, poems and all the rest, relate only to *that which creates what created them,* and to absolutely nothing else. Divergencies can arise, of course, between poetic interpretations of a poem, between impressions and meanings, or rather between the resonances that the work's action provokes in one man or another. On reflection, however, this banal observation takes on an importance of the first order: the potential diversity in the legitimate effects of a work is the very hallmark of the mind. Moreover, it corresponds to the different paths that opened up to the author in the course of his productive work. For every act of the mind is accompanied as it were by a certain more or less perceptible atmosphere of indeterminateness.

Forgive this way of putting it. I can find no better.

Let us put ourselves in the state of mind that a work of art induces in us, one of those works which make us desire them the more, the more we possess them (or they us). At such times we find ourselves divided between nascent sentiments which alternate and contrast in an extremely remarkable way. On the one hand we feel that the work which is acting upon us is so intimately appropriate to us that we cannot conceive of its being different from what it is. Even in certain cases of supreme contentment we feel that we are undergoing some profound transformation that is turning us into the man whose sensibility is capable of creating such fullness of delight and immediate understanding. But we feel no less strongly, and as though by an entirely different sense, that the phenomenon which causes this state and develops it in us, which inflicts its power on us, might not have been and even ought not to have been—in fact, that it is improbable.

While our enjoyment or joy is powerful, having the force of fact, the existence and formation of the instrument, the work that has engendered these feelings, strike us as accidental. The existence of the work seems to be the effect of some extraordinary accident, some lavish gift of fortune, and it is here (as we should not forget to note) that we discover a close analogy between the effect of a work of art and that produced by certain aspects of nature: a geological accident, a fleeting combination of light and mist in the evening sky.

Sometimes it is inconceivable to us that a man like ourselves could be the author of so extraordinary a blessing, and the praise we give him is an expression of our inability to conceive such a thing.

But regardless of the speculations or struggles that take place in the producer, the whole process must end in the visible work, and for this very reason take on an absolute determinateness. This end is the culmination of a sequence of inner modifications which may be as disordered as you please, but which, once the hand acts, must resolve into a single command, that may or may not be a good one. Whether successfully or not, the hand, the outward action, must resolve the state of indeterminateness of which I was speaking. The producing mind seems to be elsewhere, seeking to mark its work with characteristics directly opposed to its own. In fashioning a work it seems to shun the instability, incoherence, inconsistency of which it knows itself to be capable and which constitute its habitual way of life. And so it resists the influences from all directions and of all kinds to which it is perpetually exposed. It assimilates the innumerable incidents of its own life; it rejects all the indifferent images, sensations, impulses, and ideas that traverse, and try to substitute themselves for, its other ideas. It struggles against what it is obliged to accept, to produce, or to emit; and, in sum, against its own nature and its accidental, momentary activity.

During its meditations the mind buzzes round its own point of reference. Just about anything can distract its attention. "*Odoratus impedit cogitationem,*" said St. Bernard. Even in the soundest mind contradiction is the rule; straight reasoning is the exception. And straight thinking itself is a logician's artifice which, like all the artifices the mind devises against itself, consists in materializing the elements of thought, what logic calls the "concepts," in organizing them into spheres or fields, and in endowing these intellectual objects with a stability independent of the vicissitudes of the mind, for logic after all is only a speculation on the permanence of notations.

But here we encounter a startling circumstance: this ever-impending dispersion is almost as important as concentration and contributes almost as much to the production of the work. The mind at work, struggling against its own mobility, against its constitutional restlessness and characteristic diversity, against the natural dissipation or degeneration that threatens any specialized attitude, finds incomparable resources in the very condition it is combating. The instability, incoherence, inconsistency which I have mentioned and which are obstacles and limits to the mind's project of building or composing a consistent whole, are at the same time treasure houses of possibility, which the mind senses almost as soon as it begins to look within. They are storerooms where it may expect to find anything it needs, reasons for hoping that the missing solution, signal, image, or word is closer than it seems. In its inner twilight the mind can always find a presentiment of the truth or decision it is looking for, knowing that it may be revealed by the merest trifle, by the selfsame futile distraction that seemed to be carrying one away from it endlessly.

Sometimes what we are trying to find in our thoughts (even if it is only a simple memory) is like a precious object which we hold and feel of through an enveloping tissue that hides it from view. It both is and is not ours, and the slightest incident may uncover it. Sometimes, by setting up conditions, we define what ought to be there. We look for it in a conglomeration of elements, all equally present, but none of them standing out singly to meet our requirement. We implore our mind for some sign of a distinction. We bring our desire to it as one might apply a magnet to a composite powder, from which it suddenly disengages a grain of iron. In mental questions of this kind there seem to be very mysterious relations *between the desire and the event.* I should not go so far as to say that the mind's desire sets up a kind of field, far more complex than a magnetic field, endowed with the power of bringing forth whatever we need. The image is only a way of expressing an observed fact of which I shall have more to say later on. But regardless of the clarity, evidence, force, beauty of the mental event which puts an end to our expectancy, which completes our thought or dispels our doubt, nothing is irrevocable so far. The following moment still has absolute power over the product of the one before it. For the mind reduced to its own substance cannot do anything finite and is absolutely unable to tie itself down.

When we say that our opinion on a certain point is final,

we say so to make it so: we appeal to others. The sound of our voice gives us far more assurance than the resolute inward statement we claim to be making. When we suppose that we have completed a certain thought, we never feel really sure that if we went back to it we might not improve it or spoil it. Thus the mind is divided against itself the moment it sets out to produce a work. Every work requires voluntary acts (although it always involves a number of factors that have nothing to do with what we call *will*). But when our will, our overt power, turns upon our mind and demands to be obeyed, all it can do is bring the mind to a pause, either maintaining or renewing certain conditions.

Indeed, our only means of direct action on our mental system is to curtail its freedom. But as for the rest, the modifications and substitutions that still operate despite restrictions, all we can do is wait for our desideratum to turn up. *We have no way of finding within ourselves exactly what we want.*

For the desire and the desideratum are of the same mental substance, and in operating at the same time they may well get in each other's way. We know that quite often a solution comes to us only after we have lost interest in the problem for a time—as a reward, so to speak, for restoring our mind's freedom.

What I have just said applies most particularly to the producer, but the same process may be noted in the consumer of the work. His production of value—for example, his understanding, the interest aroused in him, the effort he makes to possess the work more fully—might give rise to similar observations.

Whether I chain myself to the page I wish to write or to the page I wish to understand, in either case I am entering upon a phase of reduced freedom. But in both cases the limitation of my freedom may take two opposite forms. Sometimes the task itself incites me to pursue it, and far from feeling it to be a burden, a deviation from the more natural ways of my mind, I abandon myself to it and advance so eagerly along the path laid out by my intention that my sense of fatigue is diminished—up to the moment when it suddenly beclouds my thoughts, muddles my ideas, brings back the disorder of normal short-term exchanges, and restores a state of dispersive, restful indifference.

But sometimes the constraint is the main thing; I force myself to maintain a direction that becomes increasingly painful; I am more aware of the effort than of its effect, the means fight the end, and I am compelled to preserve the tension of my mind by more and more precarious expedients, having less and less to do with the ideal object whose power and action must be maintained at the expense of a fatigue that soon becomes unbearable. Here we have a striking contrast between two ways in which the mind may operate. It will help me to show that the care I have taken to specify that works should only be considered in the act either of production or consumption is entirely in keeping with observation; and it will also enable us to draw a very important distinction between different kinds of works of the mind.

Among these last, usage has created a category known as works of art. It is not an easy term to define—if there is any need to define it. To begin with, I find nothing about the *process of producing* a work of art that definitely obliges me to set up such works as a category. In all men's minds, more or less, I find attention, fumbling and groping, unexpected clarity and dark night, improvisations and experiments, urgent new beginnings. Every hearth of the spirit contains both fire and ashes; good and bad judgment; method and disorder;

and a thousand forms of chance. In regard to the components of this strange life of the mind, artists, scholars, and other thinkers are all very much alike. We may say that at any particular moment no functional difference between minds in labor is discernible. But if we look at the *effects* of works already produced, we discover in certain works a special quality that sets them off as a group and distinguishes them from all others. Some particular work we have singled out divides into parts, each complete in itself, each containing what is needed to arouse a desire and to satisfy it. In each of these parts the work offers us both *food* and *appetite*. It continually creates in us both thirst and the water to quench it. In return for a share of our freedom, it gives us a love for the captivity it imposes and a delicious sort of sense of immediate knowledge. And *to our infinite contentment*, it does all this by expending our own energy, which it calls forth in a way so wonderfully compatible with the most efficient use of our organic resources that even our sense of effort is intoxicating and, magnificently possessed, we feel like possessors.

The more we give at such times, the more we wish to give, though it seems to us that we are receiving. We are kindled by an illusion of acting, expressing, discovering, understanding, solving, conquering.

All these effects, which sometimes verge on the miraculous, are instantaneous—like everything that partakes of sensibility. They attack, by the shortest route, the strategic points that command our emotional life, and through the latter they constrain our intellectual freedom; they quicken, suspend, or sometimes even regularize the various functions whose harmony or dissonance is what finally determines our sense of being alive, in all its modulations from flat calm to tempest.

The mere sound of the cello exerts an almost visceral

power over some people. There are words whose frequent occurrence in a writer's work shows that for him they are endowed with incomparably greater resonance and hence creative power than for most men. This is an example of the personal evaluations, the *great values-for-one-individual*, which assuredly play an outstanding part in artistic production, where originality is all-important.

These considerations may help us to throw a little light on the nature of poetry, which is rather mysterious. It is strange that men should try so hard to fashion a kind of discourse that must simultaneously take account of such utterly heterogeneous considerations as the *musical*, the *rational*, the *semantic*, the *suggestive*, which necessitate a continuous or sustained relation between rhythm and syntax, *sound* and *sense*.

Between these elements no connection is conceivable. We must create the illusion that there is a profound bond between them. *What is the use of all this?* The observance of rhythms, rhymes, verbal melody hampers the direct movement of my thought; it prevents me from saying what I want to say. . . . But *just what is it that I want to say?* That is the question.

The answer is that I must want what is required in order that thought, language, and its conventions borrowed from external life may harmonize with the rhythm and tones of the voice which flow directly from the inner being. And this harmony exacts mutual sacrifices, the most noteworthy of which is the sacrifice that *thought* must consent to.

I shall explain one day how this compromise affects the language of poets, and how there is a poetic language whose words are not the words of unhampered practical use. Their association is not governed by the same attractions; and they are charged with two equally important values which are

brought to bear simultaneously: their sound and their immediate psychological effect. They remind us of the mathematician's complex numbers, and the coupling of the *phonetic
variable* with the *semantic variable* gives rise to problems of extension and convergence which the poets have to solve blind-
fold—but solve them they do (that is the essential), from time
to time.... *From time to time*—there's the rub! There we have
all the uncertainty, all the difference between moments and
between individuals. This is our central question. We shall
consider it at length later on, for all art, poetic or otherwise,
is an act of self-defense against this difference of the moment.

All I have touched on in this brief inquiry into the general
notion of the creative work must lead me finally to indicate
the point of departure I have chosen, from which to explore
our vast field, the production of works of the mind. I have
tried to give you in a brief span an idea of the complexity of
these questions, in which everything may be said to happen
at once, and in which what is most profound in man is combined with a good many external factors.

To put it briefly: in the production of a given work, action
comes to grips with the indefinable.

A voluntary action which in any of the arts is compounded
of many elements—which may demand protracted effort,
the most abstract attention, the most precise knowledge—
must in the artistic process be adapted to an intrinsically irreducible state of being, to a finite expression referring to no
object that can be localized, defined, or apprehended by a
system of uniformly determined acts. And all this culminates
in a work the effect of which must be to reconstitute in someone a state *analogous*—I do not say identical (for we can never
know)—to the original state of the producer.

Thus we have on the one hand the *indefinable* and on the

other an *action* which is necessarily finite; on the one hand a *state*, sometimes a single sensation, productive of value and impulse, a state which (and this is its only definite characteristic) does not correspond to any finite term of our experience; and on the other hand an *act*, that is to say, the very essence of finiteness, since an act is a miraculous escape from the closed world of the possible into the universe of fact. And this act is often produced in opposition to the mind and all its plans; it springs from the unstable element as Minerva sprang fully armed from the mind of Jupiter—an ancient image still full of meaning.

It sometimes happens—and this is the most favorable case —that a single internal impulse gives the artist, all at once and indistinguishably, the motive, the immediate external objective, and the technical means of action. Generally a productive regimen is established, in which an exchange, of varying intensity, takes place between the requirements, the knowledge, the intentions, the means, in short, between the *mental* and the *instrumental* factors. All these are the elements of an action whose stimulus is not situated in the same world as the aims of *ordinary* action and consequently does not lead to foreseeing any program of acts by which one is sure to attain its aim.

It was reflection on this fact—so remarkable, it seems to me, though so little remarked—the *performance of an act* as culmination, issue, ultimate definition, of a state which is inexpressible in finite terms (which, in other words, exactly negates the sensation that is its cause)—that led me to take the most general possible type of human action as the general form of this course. It seemed necessary to establish a simple line, a sort of geodesic, by which to get our bearings among the observations and ideas which arise in connection with a subject that does not lend itself to enumeration. In a study of this kind, which to my knowledge has never before been undertaken, it would be illusory to look for an intrinsic order, a development free from repetition, that might enable us to arrange the problems according to the progression of a variable, for such a variable does not exist.

To raise the question of the mind is to call everything into question; all is disorder and every reaction against disorder is itself disorder. But this disorder is the condition and promise of the mind's fecundity, which depends on the unexpected rather than the expected, on what we do not know (and because we do not know it) rather than on what we know. How could it be otherwise? The field I am attempting to survey is unlimited, but everything takes on human proportions once we resolve to stick to our own experience, to observations we ourselves have made, to methods we ourselves have tested. I always try to keep it in mind that each man is the measure of all things.

My "Poetics"

AGE BIDS me to step down from a chair to which I was appointed five years ago. I was astonished at the time to find myself occupying it, and intimidated at the thought of speaking in this imposing place: here was an elderly poet metamorphosed into a young professor, on the initiative of my deeply regretted friends Joseph Bédier and Alexandre Moret. They had taken it into their heads one day that I might teach something and in the end they made me believe it. The Collège de France agreed to accept a candidate without the usual diplomas, for freedom was the founding principle of this distinguished old house of the "royal readers." It appoints whom it pleases, regardless of university degrees; it does not prepare students for any examination; there is no program; only professorships, whose title is determined by the specialty of the incumbent and may disappear with him. Finally, the lectures are public: all who wish may attend.

The proposal that I should teach "Poetics" was then submitted to the Faculty, who passed on it, and was finally decreed by the government. It was generally supposed (nothing seemed more likely) that I would talk about the art of poetry. Perhaps I had a certain experience of the matter; but this very experience had led me to such a wide range of reflections that I could not think of restricting the exposition of my ideas and investigations to a study of the more or less "technical" question of versification. Moreover, I was only too well aware that in matters of art, opinion nowadays is repelled by any semblance of doctrine, rejects all the old precepts, models, and rules, and expects the artist to draw from within himself, by immediate personal revelation, the means of communicating to others the fervor and vibration of the lyric state. In any case, I could not flatter myself that I should turn out poets—the only result that could justify a course in Poetics in the usual sense of the term. Instead, taking the word in all the simplicity of its original meaning, I ventured, on the basis of my personal experience and speculations, to deal, to the best of my ability and at my own risk, with the *fabrication* of "works of the mind" in general: I mean those works which the mind produces for its own use, and which indicate and encourage its own growth. Perhaps, in order to avoid any misapprehension, I ought to have said, and written, *Poietics* instead of Poetics, after the manner of physiology with its hematopoietic and galactopoietic functions; but I must own that I did not dare. Be that as it may, what I intended to express was the quite elementary notion of *making*, or fabricating.

But first of all I was obliged to point out the obvious characteristics that make it possible to distinguish succinctly the various *fabrications of the mind for the mind* from all the other kinds of production that man may undertake for any purpose whatsoever. I noted first that these particular works of the mind, in whatever genre, may be regarded as perfectly and equally useless, since they respond to no common vital need and since the vast majority of people manage without them, or at least could do so. Furthermore, works of this useless kind are produced by acts that spring from no outward necessity.

So, just as we are open to numerous impressions and perceptions that are of no use to us, we are capable of a variety of actions that have no definite organic purpose. All this *useless* and *arbitrary* activity stores up within us a treasure of stimulated energies and free possibilities with which we can either do nothing, or else construct the works in which our arts, our letters, and our pure sciences have their being.

Useless and arbitrary as they are, these works of our hands figure nonetheless among the various exchanges that make up our social life. They are created and supplied by one group; acquired or needed by another. Such a relationship implies *production* and *consumption*, *supply* and *demand*—which immediately suggests the notion of a *poetic* or *poietic economy*, playing the same role in the "universe of the mind" as the notion of political economy in the realm of practical things. It seemed to me natural and convenient to adopt this analogy, to give the name of *producers* indiscriminately to painters, writers, musicians, mathematicians, etc. . . . in order to designate their activities as a whole, in contrast to *useful* activities. It is this whole which, by the accumulation of works, constitutes a sort of *capital*, the creation, enjoyment, and increase of which are the proper function of what we call a "civilization." The production of such works would therefore tend to create *utility of a second kind*, a variety of needs that must be both aroused and satisfied at once, while the producer seeks to communicate to his work a kind of *necessity* capable of imposing itself on some *consumer*. (We say that a work succeeds or not, according as it does or does not make us feel this necessity of the sensibility or intellect.) Thus there arises the notion of *value*, which is just as important in our poetic universe as in the other, but infinitely more subtle. My analogy, which, it seems to me, serves quite well to represent the outward aspect of aesthetic or speculative life, loses its meaning once we turn to the inner process itself by which works are created. While ordinary economic facts merge and fall into groups, so lending themselves to statistical considerations and the computation of averages, the facts I am concerned with are essentially individual. I have tried nevertheless, on the basis of my personal experience, to study them by looking into the inner workings of the producer's mind, and at least to define the more general conditions of this inner production in so far as the producer himself can be aware of them.

I cannot attempt to sum up here all that I have projected in these few years of teaching—which have no doubt been more instructive to me than to my faithful audience. Indeed, I made no secret of the fact that my ambition was not to solve problems, but to pose them and to propose many more; and I own that I was rather pleased with myself whenever my mind encountered its own resistances and defied me to express before an audience what it had just been easily contemplating in its commerce with itself. All in all, what I have attempted was to organize in a general form a kind of theory of my own mind, and this precisely is the failing of all who cultivate the useless and the arbitrary features of their thought; but I have made every effort, nonetheless, to put forward nothing that each one of my listeners, with a little reflection, might not easily find in himself and by himself; and to show that there is nothing that may not be new, nothing that may not recover its pristine freshness in our consciousness, provided we take care not to be misled by the facility of language or by the illusion of understanding which we derive from the use of abstract terms. . . .

I now see what I might have done, which is not what I have done. That is a natural reaction which, it seems to me, any work laid aside must arouse. Perhaps it is always too late to do better.

The Creation of Art

Gentlemen, and even Ladies:

I AM DISCONCERTED and honored to be summoned to appear before the members of the French Philosophical Society.

Indeed, it is an intimidating honor: I feel terribly inhibited at the thought of speaking—or trying to speak—in your presence.

First of all, I should like to thank M. Xavier Léon, who has addressed me in terms that are far too flattering. What could be more formidable, what could be more difficult to hear without trepidation, than so gracious an introduction? M. Xavier Léon wishes at all costs to make me a philosopher. . . . I shall try for a few moments to become one of you.

The truth of the matter—since some sort of public confession seems inescapable—is that my intellectual life falls into two parts that have sometimes come together, one devoted wholly to the impassioned, persistent study of a few questions which, as I later found out, may have been philosophical; the other consecrated to literary production (in the form of poetry)—to the very intermittent practice of an art.

Now it happens that in my case these two modes of activity have been related in a special way and that, even while I was engaging in various investigations that were in no way literary, the demon or, if you prefer, the feeling, of art was lurking in the back of my mind; but afterward, when circumstances led me, or led me back, to *writing*, when I began once more to compose poems—it turned out that the ideas, the methods, the system of thought which had become essential to me, could not help making themselves felt in my work as a writer. This, I believe, is noticeable. Too much so, perhaps! . . .

There was nothing essential about this combination of activities. A thinker and an artist can live unbeknownst to each other in the same person; just as science and faith, so I am told, stand as distinct modes of evaluation in certain minds.

Since, as I see it, I have come here, not to solve any problems at all, but to raise certain problems, let me suggest this one, which follows quite naturally from what I have just said:

What part, indeed, can general, theoretical ideas—a conception of the "world," for example, an idea of man, or of the human mind—play in the artist; what effect can they have on the practice of his art?

It is quite a delicate problem, difficult to formulate clearly. It is a problem not of aesthetics but rather of psychology, and what I have in mind is not the theories of art that sometimes become the doctrines of schools; such theories are generally devised on the basis of art and with a view to art. No, I wish to speak of conceptions which are general but personal (that is, which are not only *acquired* but also profoundly *felt*), which can moreover be reflected in a work of art and may be said to form—though not explicitly—the very substance of an artistic creation . . . or more precisely, if I may risk a highly adventurous expression, which provide the specialized acts of the artist with a kind of *metaphysical field* which orients them in such a way that movement in certain directions is facilitated and furthered, while in others it is obstructed and hindered. . . .

It is possible, I believe, to wonder whether artistic creation is compatible with any individual's profound and *uncommon* view of the essence of things.

I purposely employ the word *essence* in order to distinguish clearly the abstract, theoretical vision with which I am concerned, from the intense, original view of objects and beings which is obviously indispensable to the artist.

In a moment I shall quote a statement that moved me deeply in this connection.

I say "moved," for one can be moved by purely "intellectual" considerations. Some of us, you will agree I am sure, have a kind of intellectual sensibility. At certain moments in my life I have felt the effects of this sensibility violently enough to conceive the ambition of putting some part of it into literature, although the literary art, like all others, appeals chiefly to emotions of a sensory, social, or sentimental kind. I have wondered whether the efforts of the isolated intellect, its peculiar events, its joys and sorrows, its splendors and miseries, its grandeurs and servitudes, might not be represented through the medium of art. Up to now, when art has taken intellectual life as a subject, it has considered and portrayed the intellectual, the thinker, more than the intellect itself. But it seemed to me that the intelligence, in the exercise of its boundless investigations, aroused emotions which, despite their special tonality, were quite similar to those associated with the impressions we receive from the spectacles of nature, the events of emotional life, and matters of love or faith. This intellectual emotion is obviously less frequent than the other kinds. The art which captures and reproduces it can have only a limited appeal. . . .

I am coming to the statement whose importance I wished to point out to you. I cannot guarantee that my quotation of it is altogether faithful, for I have been unable to find the text.

But here is the gist of it. Writing to someone in connection with the composition of *Tristan and Isolde*, Richard Wagner said roughly this. As you know, Wagner conceived *Tristan* at a time when he was passionately in love; so far nothing unusual, this has been true of a good many works of art, some of them quite mediocre. But Wagner adds:

"I composed *Tristan* under the stress of a great passion and *after several months of theoretical meditation*."

Consider, gentlemen, these two conditions, or rather, the one *and* the other, for they cannot be added together. They form a kind of antinomy.

Nothing has given me more food for thought than this brief sentence, which responded to some sort of expectation and conviction within me. . . . What, I wondered, could be more rare and enviable than this strange co-ordination between two modes of vital activity that are generally regarded as independent if not incompatible? on the one hand, a profound agitation of "feeling," an overpowering emotional turmoil, the sensual exaltation of a psychological *idol*; on the other hand, a complex *theoretical meditation*, compounded of technique and metaphysics and combining new solutions to the problems of harmony with ideas about man and the universe, drawn from Schopenhauer but intensely refelt and rethought by a prodigious artist.

I found in these words a high intellectual excitement. I found an almost intoxicating justification of what I had so often thought about the role of *theoretical meditation*, that is to say, a closely reasoned, penetrating analysis, employing even the resources of an abstract symbolism, of organized notations, in sum, all the implements of the scientific mind applied to an order of facts that seem at first sight to exist only in the realm of emotional, intuitive life.

Thus it becomes evident—and Wagner provides a particularly striking example—not only that the use of the abstract faculties, of a kind of conscious calculation, can be compatible with the practice of an art, that is, with the production or creation of poetic values, but moreover that such calculation is indispensable if the artist's action and the work itself are to achieve the highest degree of power and effectiveness.

Just as the sciences provide means of action upon nature far surpassing the immediate power of man, so in the realm of the arts a well-wrought theoretical analysis can make possible such combinations of means, such *precision* in their use, such a deployment of complex resources—can serve, in short, to give the works an emotional power so intense and sustained— that the spellbound spectator or listener may be tempted to attribute the creation to some superhuman being. A few signs traced on a staff will unleash organic powers which engender within us the immense universe of sound—and this illusory universe, in turn, will give us the more profound and meaningful illusion of a total universe or of "infinite" complexity. By writing a few symbols we succeed in *representing* numbers which, whether by their magnitude or by their structure, defy all intuition, but with which we can speculate and operate precisely and usefully *without conceiving them*; and that is what the composer does when by an abstract and external method he maneuvers, stimulates, exalts, binds and unbinds our inner powers—and through them arouses the entire system of our ideas.

Is what applies to music true also of literature? An infinitely delicate problem. It must never be forgotten that literature, while definitely an art, is an art based on language, which is a practical implement of collective and statistical origin. But art is an action and an affirmation made by *someone*, and because it is personal it takes a direction contrary to that of the haphazard action of men in general. . . . Moreover, to pursue the same line of reasoning, language involves a body of conventions that may be classified under the heads of vocabulary and syntax. I have called them *conventions*, that is to say, relations that might be otherwise. But these conventions are imprecise; a good many of them are all but indefinable. The literary art takes advantage of the possibilities provided by this lack of strictness, but at its own risk, profiting or losing by the misunderstandings, the different values and effects that words have for different people.

Thus it is through little else than rhythm and the sensuous qualities of the word that literature can address a reader's organic being, with some hope that the results will conform to the intention, etc.

I shall not pursue this sort of analysis. All I have been trying to do, gentlemen, is to give you an idea of the questions I used to think about—whenever I happened to think of literature—during that long part of my life spent happily in not writing. From 1892 to 1912 I worked only for myself, without thought of publication. My literary career set in very late and was molded by circumstances independent of my will.

Yet despite the work, the occupations or obligations that now clutter up my days, I have not lost sight of what was the main object of my curiosity and my perhaps somewhat adventurous investigations. This has been the guiding thread of my attention throughout the varied accidents of my life. Always I come back to the same problems, to those that I believe to be fundamental or that my type of mind keeps bringing back to me as such. From time to time, I must own, it has even occurred to me that I might develop these obstinate divagations into one of those stout green volumes whose format and aspect make us assign them forthwith to the philosophy shelves. A *system*? Certainly not. The very name terrifies me. At most a body of ideas—or more precisely, a collection of problems—some of which no doubt would be formulated in several different ways. But I always put this volume infinitely far off from the moment when I think of it. It would be hard for me to give you an idea of so remote a work. I should not know how to approach what I hold to be unapproachable. . . . And there you have a definition of sorts!

Fortunately, we have a more definable subject. We have agreed that the subject or pretext for this meeting would be "The Creation of Art." M. Brunschvicg wished me to speak of creation pure and simple. But as I have no intuition or experience of that phenomenon, I thought it preferable to limit the project by an adjective and reduce it to an examination of things and facts concerning which we can have a more positive knowledge.

The problem of artistic creation is already vast and difficult enough. . . . How shall I approach it? Forgive me if in your presence I indulge a kind of quirk to which I am addicted. When a problem of this sort springs up in my mind, all I see at the start is what I call a *verbal situation*. I find myself confronted by a *system of words* corresponding to a body, or realm, of confused notions and disorganized or incomplete relations. In the beginning is confusion, even if one is unaware of it. Only too often investigation begins with this state, leaping at solutions without having *cleared the mental field* or transposed the problems into the language of our actual thinking. Blindly we hasten to follow a spontaneous questionnaire formulated in a language that has not been tested.

This is why we find so much confusion, so much misunderstanding, in the order of aesthetic philosophy. One of the most frequent and noteworthy mistakes one can make in speculating on the questions of art is to consider *works* as clearly defined entities. The consequence is that the aesthetician, eager to reconstruct the genesis of a work, supposes that he can rise from the work to the author by a direct and, in a manner of speaking, *linear* operation. Thus, without suspecting it, he moves away from *truth* and *reality*. From truth, because a work can be considered only *through*, or *in relation to* a definite observer, and never in itself. From reality, because the execution of the work is made up of innumerable inward incidents and outward accidents, whose effects accumulate and combine in the *substance* of the work, which in the long run, especially if it has been much reworked and reconsidered, may become a work without a definable author, which *no author* could have produced in one breath, without digressions and revisions.

In questions of art there are three main factors to distinguish: a creator or author; a concrete object which is the work; and a recipient—a reader, spectator, or listener.

We must never lose sight of this simple distinction, and never confuse what pertains to one with what relates to the other. We must distrust judgments that effect unconscious or implicit syntheses of these three concepts. Such judgments are meaningless.

When we speak of a work of art, let us not forget that a work in itself is only a thing, that its life is just as latent as that of a phonograph record when the machine is not running. . . .

But this image suggests a very real example of the kind of error I have in mind.

A few years ago someone devised a phonetic method of criticizing poems, based on the analysis of recordings. The use of voice recordings is perfectly legitimate when it comes to fixing and characterizing the *facts*. But aesthetic judgments cannot be deduced from them. The interposed machine, which gives an illusion of objectivity, simply registers in its way the voice of the person who has recited for it, whose diction may be good or bad. We all of us know that nothing is simpler than to transform a poem by reading it aloud, to make the good bad and the bad bearable. In a word, the recording, by developing and amplifying the voice, can enable us to note every detail of a recitation at our leisure. It cannot choose between one recitation and another. The selection must be made by someone's ear or according to some preconceived theory.

We see by this example how difficult it is to isolate the notion of a work as such.

Let us return to the author. . . . Permit me to repeat the paradox I stated a moment ago: that an author—even the most perspicacious and critical of authors—is in the worst possible position to know what others call his work. We may say that authors do not know what they are doing. As I said before, the truth of this proposition increases with the scope of the work, the time and effort needed to produce it. Each of us is usually far removed from the point to which sustained effort sometimes leads him. May we not, in this light, say that to work is to force oneself to differ from oneself ? . . . And when the author reviews his work, his idea of it is always mingled with his memory of the circumstances of composition. It is next to impossible for him to see it without at the same time seeing a whole *context* of incidents, hesitations, parts that have been deleted or never executed, makeshifts and surprises. (It is possible, for example, that an idea which came to me suddenly and incidentally may take its place at once in my work and strike the reader as having come quite *naturally* and necessarily, as though produced without effort by what precedes it in the text.)

Thus it is difficult for an author to perceive the effect of a whole work as a finished, isolated construction. He has passed through all the stages of creation, hesitated at a good many crossroads; he knows that certain parts came to him without effort, that others were hard to produce; he is aware both of what he has had to leave out, and of his unexpected developments. Sometimes the solution that is decisive for the whole outward existence of the work comes to him when he is on the point of giving up, and in a few seconds the work as originally conceived is utterly modified. The impossible becomes possible, the obstacle becomes a means, etc.

Here we might mention a singular problem that sometimes confronts an author: *How can he know that his work is finished?* He has to make a decision.

But the decision that writes finis to a work can only be extraneous, alien to the work itself. Time, the required dimensions, the date on which he must deliver his work, boredom, fatigue, or surfeit, for that matter—these are what tell the author to break off his effort. But in fact the completion of a work is no more than a surrender, a halt that may always be regarded as fortuitous, in a development that might have continued indefinitely.

Here again we see that the work, as a finite and clearly delimited thing, may always be thought of by the author as a kind of fragment accidentally cut away from his inner wholeness, a transitional form; while to the reader it presents itself as a clear-cut construction *which no longer depends on time.*

Let us now consider some of the states of mind of our author, whom we shall suppose (for we ought to know something about him) to be extremely lucid.

Our lucid author observes his moments, and notes that he passes quite regularly through two phases, each of which deserves to be examined separately.

There is almost always a first state, an emotional phase tending toward no finite, determinate, organized form, but susceptible of producing partial elements of expression, fragments that will some day—or never—form a *whole*. In this state, there appears a word, a formula, an image, a mechanism, which, recaptured later on, will find its place in a composition, and serve unexpectedly as a germ, a solution. . . . May I venture to call such fragments the *shards of the future*? But the future I have in mind, which may be very far away (as far, sometimes, as maturity from childhood), is not the period marked by the formation of the work as it appears to the public, but rather the period characterized by the living state of the work which, as I have just said, is never final, solidified, separated from its possibilities and chances of transformation, except by an outside intervention.

This first phase belongs, on the whole, to general psychology. The events that take place in it, though essential to the creation whose general substance they supply—in the form of emotional elements, of particularly striking or powerful associations—are far from sufficient for the production of the organized work, which implies a very different order of mental activity. Here the author, whether he suspects it or not, takes an entirely new attitude. At the start he looked only within and saw only himself; but no sooner does he think of producing a *work* than he starts to calculate outward effects. The problem that now arises is one of accommodation: he concerns himself, wittingly or not, with the individuals on whom he wishes his work to act; he forms an idea of those whom he had in mind and considers the means available to him for his action.

I have no need, gentlemen, to tell you that this account is as rough and incomplete as can be. I am only suggesting an outline, whose sole purpose is to bring out the diversity of the independent factors that are combined and intermingled in every work of art.

This sort of combination—like those I have just mentioned —creates almost insurmountable difficulties for aesthetic analysis. It is the aesthetician's duty to know more about the artist than the artist himself knows. He must try to find out how the radically different factors composing the creative mind are adjusted to each other; how, for example, different orders of representation are co-ordinated. I have chosen a theme. I conceive, vaguely or clearly, of a reader. I feel that certain means are available to me. I am tempted by a thousand memories *that might be utilized*, a thousand elements of the emotional substance we were speaking of. . . . The work I shall create will be merely a fitting together, an arrangement, a more or less successful subordination of these independent factors, these "deposits," these energies of diverse kinds.

That is why almost all literary works require a good deal of introduction: expositions, descriptions, preparatory remarks, some serving to define the elements and rules of the game, others to train the unknown reader to the author's sensibility. These are the postulates, the conventions, the premises on the strength of which the work itself can be understood. This brings me to say a few words in passing about a kind of literature that has no need of such precautions. I am speaking of *private* literature, letters between intimates, works intended for a single reader. Here all preambles are superfluous. The reader is well defined. You know how to move him, how to surprise him, what will suffice, what not to mention, and to this reader you can communicate your thought, any thought, almost without . . . formalities, almost in the nascent, immediate state. This special case gives us quite a good idea of the many factors which, in a work intended for the unknown public, the author must introduce artificially, which do not spring from his pure inward experience, or not, at least, from the same source as the free and intimate products of his mind.

To sum up: any speculation on artistic creation must pay ample attention to the "heterogeneous" diversity of the conditions that impose themselves on the workman and are necessarily involved in the work. It is the paradoxical lot of the artist to combine determinate elements with a view to acting upon an indeterminate person.

Perhaps it would be fitting to speak here of all the devices which constitute the technique of art, whose purpose it is to effect the passage from the spiritual to the temporal. But on that subject it is impossible to improvise.

Thus I shall pass by the philosophy of technique and content myself with bringing out one point that strikes me as quite remarkable. In every order of technique the means react upon the ends; *quantum potes, tantum aude*. And quite frequently a knowledge, a sense, of the means engenders the end. I am almost inclined to believe that certain profound ideas have owed their origin to the presence or near-presence in a man's mind of certain forms of language, of certain empty verbal figures whose particular tone called for a particular content.

Let us then put aside these difficult problems, which I am not equipped to deal with. I think it will be of more interest if I give you a few personal impressions about what is called poetic intuition, a subject with which, I am well aware, every philosopher of our time is preoccupied.

Here is a recollection; here is what I find as the origin of a poem I wrote some years ago. One day I was obsessed by a rhythm which suddenly became quite palpable in my mind after a period during which I had been only half-conscious of it as a *lateral* activity. The rhythm asserted itself with a certain authority. I had the feeling that it wanted to be embodied, to attain the perfection of being. But the only way in which it could become clearer in my consciousness was to borrow or assimilate elements of *speech*, syllables, words; and at this stage in their formation, the syllables and words were determined no doubt by their musical value and affinities. This was the preparatory stage of the poem, its infancy, in which form and substance were scarcely distinguishable and rhythmic quality was the sole determinant of what should enter into the poem, of what should be spoken by the poet. This was the second step, the first having been the naked rhythm, the percussion pure and simple. Then, by a sort of awakening of conscious-ness or sudden extension of its domain—I am referring, of course, to a qualitative extension, an increase in the number of its independent demands—substitutions occurred in the syl-lables, words were provisionally summoned up, and a definite *line* made its appearance, which seemed to me not only com-plete but impossible to modify, a product of necessity. But this line in turn demanded a musical and logical continuation. The machine had been set going. Unfortunately for the poet, lucky coincidences are not a continuous process; he must ap-ply effort and artifice in order to *imitate* the man he was for one moment. The reason why spontaneous finds are so inter-mittent is perfectly simple: namely, that in language the link between sound and meaning is supplied only by convention.

In another case a *line* came to me, obviously engendered by its sound, its timbre. The meaning suggested by this un-expected element of a poem, the image it evoked, the syntactical figure it presented (an apposition), acted like a little crystal in a supersaturated solution and led me as though by symmetry to *expect*, and to construct according to my expectation, a beginning before my line, to prepare the way for it and justify its existence, and after it a continuation to round out its effect. Thus from a single line there developed, little by little, all the elements of a poem, the subject, the tone, the type of prosody, etc.

I could not help comparing this proliferation with that observed in nature where, when the environment is favorable, it seems that a bit of stem or leaf belonging to certain plants can reproduce a complete individual. In spite of its differentiation the fragment grows little by little into a complete individual, acquiring leaves, a stem, roots, all that it needs in order to live.

(The analogy is seductive, no doubt; unfortunately, the radical independence of sound and meaning—the constituents of language—forces us to discard it.)

Other cases come to mind. We may say that every work might have been produced in several ways. No objective scrutiny shows us whether a given poem was born of a certain hemistich, of a rhyme, or of an abstractly formulated project. In works of any length the author usually starts with a subject and comes to versification later on. This is the case with the classical epics and dramatic poems, the tragedies and comedies. But these are the poems in which we least clearly discern the specific character of poetry, which consists essentially in a *singular*, an improbable, correspondence between perceptible form and meaning. (Furthermore, there must be an *overabundance* of relations between the successive meanings—more relations than a clear, *linear* understanding requires. This is what leads poets to employ figures, metaphors, etc.)

Epic and dramatic poems have the fault, the antipoetic property, that they can be summarized, narrated; in general, they have an existence, or a kind of existence, that is independent of their value. . . . While in the poetry that is nothing but poetry—I shall not venture to call it *pure*!—the poem cannot be put into prose without perishing entirely. Remember that the poet has made every effort to give the whole of his poem the combined organization of substance and form that chance bestows but charily and seldom.

This pursuit of the improbable, which is far more arduous in poetry than in the other arts, has one very unfortunate consequence: the almost insurmountable difficulty of *composing* in poetry. I know of nothing more rare—in works numbering more than . . . fourteen lines!—than composition in what I shall call the *ornamental* sense of the term. I believe it to be a task almost beyond human powers. Here I am not speaking of logical or chronological composition. I am not speaking of the system which consists in letting oneself be guided by a succession of dated events or by a conceptual order. In lyrical poetry, to be sure, we find numerous examples of a development suggesting a simple figure, a perceptible curve. But the types are always very elementary.

When I speak of composition, I have in mind poems in which an attempt is made to equal the masterly complexity of music by introducing "harmonic" relationships, symmetries, contrasts, correspondences, etc., between their parts.

I own that I have sometimes conceived and even attempted poems of this kind, but my attempts never produced anything—not even anything bad.

This, gentlemen, is all I can tell you.

After the lecture, there were a few questions.

PAUL DESJARDINS: . . . In 1919 you said: "I found, and still find, it unworthy to write out of mere enthusiasm. Enthusiasm is no state of mind for a writer." . . . I should find it hard to believe that the poet who wrote *La Pythie* (which, if I am not mistaken, also dates from 1919) could in composing it have immunized himself to the enthusiasm he communicates and the enthusiasm with which he infects us.

That is the indiscreet question I should like to venture.

VALÉRY: What I had in mind is this: there are two states, one in which the man who practices the writer's trade is traversed by a kind of lightning flash; for, after all, this intellectual, nonpassive life is made up of fragments; it is, in a sense, formed of elements that are very brief and that the writer feels to be very suggestive, which do not illumine his whole mind but on the contrary suggest to him that there are completely new forms that he can be sure of possessing by means of a certain effort. What I have sometimes observed is the occurrence of a mental sensation, a flash that does not illumine but transfixes. It warns, it indicates, more than it enlightens, and in sum, it is itself an enigma which carries with it the assurance that it can be deferred. One says: "I see, and tomorrow I shall see more." Something has happened, a special sensitivity has been produced; soon we shall go into the darkroom and the picture will appear to us.

I cannot guarantee that this is very well described, for it is very hard to describe. I have just mentioned the period spent in the darkroom; no enthusiasm here, or you would spoil your plate. You need your reagents, you have to proceed like your own workman—you are your own foreman. The boss has given you the spark; it is up to you to make something of it. What is very curious is the disappointment that may follow. There are illusory flashes; when he inspects the results, the foreman sees that the flash has not been very rewarding;

but how splendid if it had been true. Sometimes you have a series of judgments that cancel each other out. A state of irritation sets in; you tell yourself that you will never succeed in writing down what has appeared to you.

Here is an important point.

The new element that comes to mind depends on a certain momentary sensibility, which captures or provokes it—it is hard to say which. This sensibility is modified by our mental state or the orientation of our search. I have in mind the phenomenon of sensitization that we observe in biology if not in physics . . . and I wonder whether the effect of intellectual effort is not to favor some sort of increase in sensibility? Effort, then, would not bring about a solution (in the aesthetic order, moreover, neither the problems nor the solutions are usually determinate) but it would increase the chances in favor of the artist's general design; it would, momentarily, turn the artist into a sounding board, highly sensitive to all the incidents of consciousness susceptible of furthering his design.

We do not take the same attitude toward different persons; the value of the words we utter varies according to those we address, and so it is with our attitude toward our inward expectation.

These things are very hard to explain. However, I think we must distinguish—for my part, I distinguish too much—between the different moments of the creative process, and I repeat that these moments of entirely different (and perhaps incommensurable) kinds are necessary to all production.

Once, in a lecture on poetry, I delivered myself of this little quip: "When you ask an engineer to produce a locomotive, you don't ask him to do so at ninety miles an hour; he starts by working quietly in his drafting room." It is at the moment of execution that the poet must keep the closest watch on himself, for that is his best way of knowing the effect he can produce on his reader.

DESJARDINS: Do you believe that the initial impulse you call inspiration is indispensable in poetic creation, or that one can be a poet without being touched by enthusiasm?

VALÉRY: I have answered you already by distinguishing between the author and the reader. The poet depends on the reader. I even maintain that inspiration is what the poet must suggest to the reader. It is up to the reader to provide the energy.

DESJARDINS: Can one inspire without being inspired?

VALÉRY: How can one tell? It would be necessary to reveal the two sides of the phenomenon. Someone would have to say: "I have made this poem," and then you would have to bring him a reader of his poem, who would say: "I am filled with enthusiasm. . . ." You would have to suppose that an entire work might be produced for a single reader.

H. DELACROIX: I should like to ask Paul Valéry a few questions. It is a good opportunity. We psychologists seldom find such a rare case.

I shall not take up what previous speakers have said about the unconscious or the subconscious. It is the duty of the psychologist to elucidate this notion as thoroughly as possible, hence to stress the processes leading from the obscurity of the unconscious to true clarity, to production.

I should therefore like to ask Paul Valéry to enlighten us about this choice before the choice, about those possibilities that are determined before they are invoked. I am familiar with phenomena of the same order, in verbal formulation, for example. Our speech does not consist solely of the words we employ, but resides primarily in the system of relations and oppositions that constitutes language: a whole set of possibilities, of compatibilities and incompatibilities, precedes the spoken word and provides its a priori pattern.

I should now like to ask whether the two processes of invention that you distinguish are as distinct as you say? Does the rhythmical scheme not already contain something of the subject matter, and does not the subject matter contain a beginning of formulation?

VALÉRY: On one occasion a simple rhythm occurred to me. And on another occasion, a distich that represented a part of a sentence and logically demanded a complement to explain it. And since the completed element contained at once the word, the rhythm, and even the rhyme, it had the power to suggest what came before and after. For me, the two cases are distinct. Every work that is produced is governed by these different circumstances. What would be most interesting in a production of this sort would be to impose a priori conditions on a work and to determine it step by step, even down to the execution.

If, for example, we forced ourselves to avoid certain words, we should arrive at some exceedingly curious effects, the mechanism of which would not be suspected by the reader.

DELACROIX: Are you not drawing up a program for poetic action? Are you not setting forth an abstract vision of a certain number of conditions that your poem must meet?

VALÉRY: It is hard to answer your question. I have sometimes imagined constructing a literary work in a completely theoretical way; a work manufactured out of the whole cloth, planned in its most minute details, like a highly complex machine. I never put it into practice, but I have often observed that an actual work may reveal germs of such planned manufacture, in certain groups of facts, in the way we pass from a concrete state to an abstract state while taking all manner of highly delicate conditions into account.

This brings me to a statement that is very close to my heart, namely that the process of manufacture is far more interesting than the work itself. That I tell you frankly.

DESJARDINS: Your answer throws a bright light on the question under discussion, but do not imagine that you have convinced me.

VALÉRY: Everything I say stems from this: at a very tender age I resolved, and made it my personal program, to increase my awareness of the operations of the mind, as applied to poetry. I maintain that this is an interesting experiment, but it would never occur to me to say that I have no esteem for certain works. I have no intention of saying that those works which claim to be more unconscious than they actually are, which attach to a system of spontaneity, are inferior ... everything depends on the reader.

DELACROIX: I should like to go back to the moment of previous choice that you alluded to a moment ago, the moment when you set your machine in motion and leave certain compartments empty for possibilities of development.

VALÉRY: One would have to devise a systematic theory of choice, and I am not up to it. I hold that *choice* is a close relative of *invention*, and that perhaps the difference may be reduced to that between the simple and the complex. There is choice and only choice, when the sum of possibilities is a sum of simple objects or of elements defined by a single quality and susceptible of being registered on a scale, like colors. In this case, we endeavor to put ourselves into such a state that our decision becomes automatic; we try to arrive at a kind of *tropism*. But if the objects are highly complex, there will be an inner effort to construct the sometimes unattainable state which, we hope, will enable us to emit, to draw forth from within us, a decision as immediate as the preceding one. This semiconscious effort is invention.

Reflections on Art

Ladies and Gentlemen:

XAVIER LÉON has asked me to come here today to develop a few ideas on art before this rather intimidating audience, the Philosophical Society.

Art is a vast field, whose range is defined only by our reflections about it; I shall make no attempt to cover it completely here with you today. The great difficulty, in any treatment of so immense a question, is to limit oneself. As I have told MM. Brunschvicg and Lalande, it was only a moment ago (just before entering this hall) that my real subject occurred to me. Circumstances have prevented me from preparing my lecture very thoroughly. However, I shall proceed according to the very cursory preparation that has been possible.

There are of course—almost by definition—a thousand and one ways of thinking and speaking of art. That is the main difficulty. . . .

There is a whole set of disciplines dealing systematically with art; Aesthetics is the generic name for these studies of very divergent matters and of methods that are still more diverse. We have, for example, a classical aesthetics which—and this is what constitutes its special character—was not deduced from observation of artistic phenomena, but arrived at by a dialectic method. It is a set of ideas, a variety of assertions, originating in an analysis of the conceptions of the mind. The remarkable part of it is that our *classical aesthetics might exist without a single work of art*: in a sense it is quite independent of the existence of art. Dialectical in origin, it speculates on language, and if it speaks of observable artistic phenomena and works of art, it takes them as illustrations of rules in the application or breach, not as a point of departure.

We also have what one might call a *historical aesthetics*, which investigates all manner of influences in the arts and concerns itself with the very origins of art.

There is a scientific aesthetics, indeed there are several brands of scientific aesthetics, which analyzes the works themselves (applying, for example, various systems of measurement) or else is concerned with the person who undergoes the effects of the work, to record his reactions. The study of sensations forms a part of this branch. Other investigations concentrate on the producer and try to provide him with practical pointers, with the means of accomplishing his work: for example, all those formulas for proportions (golden section, etc.) which used to be observed—in antiquity or during the Renaissance—and which certain theorists are now trying to reconstitute and revive, pertain to a sort of science of art.

All these varieties of aesthetics are perfectly legitimate— since they exist! But for my part I shall consider the subject in my own way, that is, in the simplest and most positive way imaginable. When I read a work or attend a lecture bearing on the arts, it seems to me that I expect to benefit in one of two ways. Either what I hear will teach me something that will increase my subsequent enjoyment of works of art; I shall be better able to appreciate them, I shall learn how to attune myself more fully to the work in question, and thus

the knowledge that has been communicated to me will en-
large my capacity for enjoyment. However, in saying that a
lecture or a piece of reading matter is likely to increase my
capacity for enjoying a work of art, I am not referring to any
incidental pleasure that I might experience in the absence of the
work; if, in connection with painting, for example, someone
should speak to me about the history of painting, the influences that have affected the painter, about schools, etc.,
such historical remarks may be highly interesting in themselves, but will in no way add to my actual enjoyment, which
can result only from contemplation of the work itself, independently of any notice written under it. I am so convinced
of this that I did not hesitate to say, at the Council of National
Museums, that if I were responsible for the administration of
the museums, I should have all the painters' names removed.
. . . *Let the eye choose for itself!*

Or, on the other hand, and secondly, the communication
of knowledge may serve an entirely different purpose. It may
teach me not to enjoy a work of art but to make one; it
may increase my powers of execution. Here I might remark
that teaching of this sort is extremely rare; though, of course,
there are still art schools where one can learn aspects of technique, it is certain that for a good many reasons instruction in
art as a combination of operations is far less precise today than
it used to be.

There are even branches of art in which technique has
ceased to exist, or virtually so. My personal recollection is
that the last traditional prescriptions concerning poetry to
meet my ears were transmitted by Heredia, who had them
from Leconte de Lisle, who in turn had received them from
some other poet. Young men were taught (quite informally,
I may say) certain very valuable methods applicable to the

composition of verse. I believe that this kind of teaching exists no longer, but it did exist for many centuries—until our own epoch came along, with its concern for originality and contempt for everything that can be learned. A consequence of the modern preoccupation with genius was that everyone felt obliged to invent his own technique.

After all, a work of art is an object, a human product, made with a view to affecting certain individuals in a certain way. Works of art are either objects in the material sense of the term, or sequences of acts, as in the case of drama or the dance, or else summations of successive impressions that are also produced by acts, as in music. We may attempt to define our notion of art by an analysis based on these objects, which may be taken as the only positive elements in our investigations: considering these objects and progressing on the one hand to their authors and on the other hand to those whom they affect, we find that the phenomenon of art can be represented by two quite distinct transformations. (We have here the same relation as that which prevails in economics between production and consumption.)

What is extremely important is to note that these two transformations—the author's modification of the *manufactured object* and the change which the object or work brings about in the consumer—are quite independent. It follows that *we should always consider them separately*.

Any proposition involving all three terms, an author, a work, a spectator or listener, is meaningless—for you will never find all three terms united in observation. Of course you can formulate judgments (there are plenty of them) involving all three, but all you will ever find in observation is either the author and his work, or the work and the observer. The spectator or listener, to be sure, is somehow present in

142

the mind of the author, but only as an ideal personage: consciously or not, the author fashions for himself an ideal audience. Sometimes, on the other hand, the reader conjures up an ideal author. And that in a way bears out my assertion.

I shall go further—and here I come to a point you will no doubt find strange and paradoxical, if you have not come to that conclusion about what I have already said: art as a *value* (for basically, we are studying a problem of value) depends essentially on this nonidentification, this need for an intermediary between producer and consumer. It is essential that there should be something irreducible between them, that there should be no direct communication, and that the work, the medium, should not give the person it affects anything that can be reduced to an idea of the author's person and thinking.

The point I am trying to make is fundamental to the arts. And whenever you hear an artist say despairingly that he has not been able to express himself as he wished, he is under a misapprehension. What he says is essentially an absurdity: I do not deny that such an absurdity may make him do his best to translate his thought into his work, as he puts it, but he will never succeed. All the artist can do is to fashion *some thing* that will produce a certain effect on someone else's mind. There will never be any accurate way of comparing what has happened in the two minds; and moreover, if what has happened in the one were communicated directly to the other, all art would collapse, all the effects of art would disappear. The whole effect of art, the *effort* the author's work demands of the consumer, would be impossible without the interposition, between the author and his audience, of a new and impenetrable element capable of acting upon other men's being. *A creator is one who makes others create.*

Consider how easy it is (in certain cases) to put our finger on what, rather facetiously perhaps, I shall call the *creative misunderstanding*.

In general, the artist maneuvers his material through the intermediary of a host of *conventions*: convention takes a hand in his work. He arouses (or tries to at least) a great number of effects in his audience, and it is implicit in the very nature of man that he need not employ as much energy as he can *release*. The whole process resembles a reflex action in physiology; often it suffices to prick an animal in a certain spot to produce effects that are infinitely more intense than the initial action. In the same way, if we press the button that controls a transformer, the energy so developed is incommensurate, both qualitatively and quantitatively, with that required to press the button. It takes very little effort on the part of a musician to write *"fortissimo"* or *"furioso"* on a staff and so unleash a tempest of a hundred instruments in a concert hall. He need only write one word; and there is no need to reason naïvely and suppose that the author has been obliged to draw from within himself, or even to conceive of, all the energy that seems to have been unleashed in the formidable orchestral storm. Thus there is an intermediate mechanism which enables the author to release considerable effects. It is the same in the arts of language; one can easily write powerful words without taking any more trouble than to write extremely simple or less meaningful ones. I once amused myself by changing two words in a line of La Fontaine, a charming line, remarkable also from other points of view. It is a very successful line, made up of monosyllables and characterized by an almost imitative harmony:

> *Prends ce pic et me romps ce caillou qui me nuit*
> Take this pick and shatter this stone that vexes me

144

In its new form, the line might figure in a cosmogonic poem:

Prends ta foudre et me romps l'univers qui me nuit
Take your thunder and shatter the universe that vexes me

Its whole aspect has changed. An extremely simple alteration suffices to change one line into another. Thus you can see how little the effect of the work of art on the consumer depends on the energy expended by the producer.

I have said that if the maker of the expression communicated directly with the receiver of the impression, a good part of the *effect* would disappear. And that is why all the arts have techniques, some simple, some more complex, by which to produce a wide variety of impressions.

But what is a work of art?

How do we recognize a work of art or an art object? Note that we may discern art in the ugliest of objects; we may say: "It is a monstrosity but it is an art object." We see a good many of this kind. By what distinction do we qualify them as such?

But first we must ask another question. Art object, work of art, these are man-made things. How, in examining an object, do we recognize that it was made by man? One can (as I did long ago) ask oneself this question that seems extremely naïve at first glance: what proves to me that a certain object is man-made? that this inkwell, for example, is not a product of nature? As you might have expected, I developed a *theory* that partly explained the difficulty, or at least gave me a clearer picture of it, and offered me a rough solution. My idea was that a work which is not man-made must embody certain characteristics that contrast with the characteristics of a human work.

In general, if we examine a man-made object, if we consider its form, its *external structure*, and compare it to the *internal structure*, we should find a relation which is not the same as the relation we find between the internal and external structures of a so-called *natural* object, whether geological or organic. I do not claim that the problem can always be solved; there are ambiguous cases, but quite frequently we find—on superficial examination, without the aid of a microscope— that in the human work the structure of the internal parts seems less important than the *form* of the assemblage. Thus the human work, regardless of its material, would seem to be an assemblage whose manipulator takes very little account of the internal structure of the thing he is fashioning. You can make similar things with very different materials; regardless of whether a vase be of glass, metal, or porcelain, it can assume pretty much the same form, but this means that (except during the actual process of manufacture) you have disregarded the *material* of which you have made the vase. Moreover, if you continue to examine the man-made object, you find that the form of the whole is *less complex* than the internal structure of the parts, and this suggests a disarrangement. In this sense, *order* imposes *disorder*. I recall that I once took this example: if you line up a regiment, you obtain a geometric figure composed of elements, each of which is far more complex than the whole, since each one is a man. Similarly, if you make an article of furniture, you disturb the organization of the tree, for you cut it up and reassemble the pieces without concern for its internal structure. The wood provides you with stable elements which you can consider as invariable in relation to the forms and contours you give the assemblage.

But this does not suffice to define a work of art. We have found only a very general characteristic that applies to a multitude of things. We must carry our analysis further.

Simple common sense tells us that an art object is essentially useless. What does that mean? It means that an art object does not answer any physiological need or at least that it does not spring from the physiological functions common to all, whose operation and requirements may be said to be constant. On the contrary, the effects of art arouse or satisfy particular, localized physiological functions, those of the senses. In any case, they are individual and, generally speaking, inconstant; everyone does not react in the same way to a work of art; its "usefulness" to the particular functions I have mentioned varies with the individual and the circumstances. Since it does not satisfy the requirements of any of the physiological functions that I have defined as essential, constant, and general, we may say that it is useless.

Even in the most favorable cases, moreover, even where there is a definite physiological action on the eye, ear, etc., certain *present* conditions must be met if objects are to operate as art objects. Disposed in certain ways, colors or sounds are indifferent to me: I perceive them but disregard them; I pay no attention to the relation of tonalities between this wall and this table. But it exists; I am vaguely affected by it; should the need or occasion arise, my attention would isolate the relation and, from a comparison of tones, I should derive some pictorial intention or suggestion. Thus I can specialize— or be specialized—I can be sensitized to a certain concomitance of colors. And to such specialization we may, provisionally, give the name of artistic or aesthetic attention.

This specialization, like all the successive specializations that make up our life, has its *own* personality, its *own* duration. The art object is not constantly an art object, nor is it an art object for everyone. Hence it is subject to certain restrictive conditions. This useless thing might be said to be an exception with two dimensions.

Lastly, I come to a third characteristic which perhaps it is somewhat rash of me to develop here in your presence. Let me read you a few pages I have written on the subject. I am referring to what I call the *aesthetic infinite*. I hope you will forgive this word "infinite," my intentions are not the least bit dishonorable: it is a conventional term, the use of which in this context struck me as both exact and amusing. Actually, I should be in favor of prohibiting the term "infinite" in all disciplines, since it always creates a certain perplexity, even in mathematics, and of replacing it by an equivalent. The fundamental idea I arrive at in my analysis of the infinite may be reduced to the notion of *independence*. If you are making a pile of stones, the action of adding a stone is independent of the quantity of stones already amassed. This, I should say, is where the *infinite* comes in. Even when you consider a repetitive operation of some sort apart from its practical application to something, the operation in itself leads to an *infinite*. It is this notion of independence between the act and the result of the act which essentially defines our idea of the infinite in this connection. Here is my quotation:

Our perceptions generally arouse in us, when they arouse anything at all, something that annuls or tends to annul them. Sometimes by an act (that may or may not be a reflex), sometimes by a kind of indifference (real or assumed), sometimes out of habit, we do away with them or try to. We have an unfailing tendency, with regard to our perceptions, to get back as quickly as possible to the state we were in before they occurred to us. It would seem as though the main business of our life consisted in turning some sort of index of our sensibility back to *zero*, and in finding the shortest way to restore a *maximum* of freedom or availability to our senses. Our reactions tend always to disappear, we tend to *expedite* them, as they say in the business world. Our reactions that tend to abolish our sensations are as varied as the sensations themselves. Yet we may subsume them under a common name and say that all those reactions that have a *finite aim* constitute the *practical order*. "The practical order" is thus my name for the order in which everything that happens sets in motion a reaction that tends to annul it, and to turn back to zero the act of specialization I have mentioned. But there are other reactions which quite on the contrary arouse desires, needs, and changes of state that tend to preserve, recapture, or reproduce the initial sensations. If a man is hungry, his hunger will make him do whatever must be done to annul it as quickly as possible; but if he finds the food delectable, his delight will *strive in him* to endure, to perpetuate itself, or to be reborn. Hunger impels us to cut the sensation short; pleasure to develop another; and these two tendencies will become so independent of one another that the man soon learns to indulge in delicacies and to eat when he is not hungry.

What I have said about hunger can easily be extended to all kinds of sensation, to every mode of sensibility in which conscious action can interfere to prolong or increase what reflex action in itself seems made to annul. This brings us to the manufacture of the art object that will make it possible to prolong, to restore, the pleasant impression.

Sight, touch, smell, movement, and speech may from time to time cause us to dwell on the impressions they induce—to sustain or renew them. Taken together, those reactions that have an *infinite aim* might be said to constitute the *aesthetic order*—what by way of a shortcut I have called the *aesthetic infinite*.

To justify the word *infinite* and give it a precise meaning, we need only recall that in the aesthetic order *satisfaction* revives *need, response* renews *demand, absence* generates *presence*, and *possession* gives rise to *desire*. Whereas, in the order that I have called *practical*, attainment of the aim dispels the sensory motives of the act (which vanish completely, or at most leave behind them a dim, abstract memory), quite the contrary is true in the *aesthetic order*. In this "universe of sensibility" there is a kind of reciprocity between sensation and the anticipation of it; endlessly one demands the other, just as in the "universe of colors," complementaries alternately replace one another, starting from a powerful impression on the retina.

No phenomenon could be more interesting in connection with our present question, for if we stare at a surface of a given color under an intense light, we perceive a kind of reciprocal action immediately afterward. Interesting as this familiar experiment is, it should not be repeated too often because of the fatigue it involves. Let us suppose, then, that you see a "subjective" green after looking at a red surface; then, in a little while, a new red appears, followed by a new but weaker green, and so on. This process of fading is very slow and may go on for quite a time; I have tested the phenomenon on myself for as much as an hour, with considerable strain to my eyes.

A very curious thing is the kind of pendular movement between the two extremes, starting with either color, the original red or green, and passing to a *corresponding* green or red. The alternating reproduction is not exact; indeed, the way in which our senses produce complementary colors seems to follow the laws of the damped pendulum. In this particular case, an easy one to observe, we see that our sensibility, often regarded as passive, is in reality exceedingly active; though this sort of oscillation, as I have said, follows, or can be represented by, the laws of the damped pendulum, it does not cease of its own accord; an outside factor intervenes, leading us little by little, by way of the pendular motion, back to freedom, the *zero* of which I have spoken. The outside factor that interrupts the process is usually fatigue. One may say that it is not the process itself that stops or breaks off (for it would go on indefinitely), but that the process takes place in an organ which depends on the whole living being: it is in need of a fresh charge that is not forthcoming. In short, this alternating sensation dies down little by little, not because it has attained a point of culmination, but because it has nothing more to feed on.

But fatigue has another effect as well: a reduced sensibility toward the very thing that was at first a delight or a desire. This is where *variety* comes in. In order to revive our sensibility, we are obliged to look for variety or produce it. We demand it to *complement* the excessive continuance of our sensation. It is a remedy for the exhaustion—which we call satiety —of the finite sources of our sensory energy. If we wish to keep on desiring, we have this need for change, which now intervenes. We might call it the *second power* of desire and say that what makes itself felt at this point is a desire for desire. But if the variety does not materialize, if our environment does not offer us an adequate stimulus promptly enough, our sensibility reacts—again as a complementary. But complementaries of this kind can be far more complex than in the realm of colors. Sometimes, when our need has deep roots in life itself, our sensibility produces remarkably precise and powerful images of the object we desire. Thirst engenders images of beverages, hunger of foods, and with such precision and insistence as to produce, in extreme cases, delirious visions or hallucinations.

These very elementary considerations enable us to distinguish and define quite clearly the field of compensatory sensations and sensory reactions that I have assigned to the order of aesthetic things. But to get back to art, we must return to the order of practical things, for art demands an action, the *act of fabrication*, and consequently the order of finite action must combine with the aesthetic order. Thus what we call a work of art is the result of an action whose *finite aim it is to provoke infinite developments in someone*, and from this it may be inferred that the artist must be of a twofold nature: for with a view to producing an effect in the universe of sensory resonance, he devises laws and methods that partake of the world of action.

Many attempts have been made to reduce each of these two tendencies to the other, but I do not think any of them has ever succeeded. In sum, the crucial notion I have been trying to bring out as characteristic of artistic striving is the notion of things that bear within them something which creates the need for them. A work of art is made with a view to producing this effect.

Let us now consider the author. I have spoken of complementaries. I believe that in the production of a work of art we may find an application of the same property. It seems to me that in certain extremely simple and primitive forms of art, such as geometrical ornament, or color combinations in plaited straw, or textile design, ornamentation must be of complementary origin. It seems likely that in the beginning the work of art responds only to a need in the author. There is no public as yet. What interests the maker is action; he is bored. Ornament is the complementary to his horror of the void; his sensibility cannot endure empty time or space, the blank page (for if sensibility has any characteristic property, it is, I believe, instability; sensibility is a kind of aptitude for instability. This we can easily appreciate by observing ourselves: we need only have attended lectures or classes and been engaged in doodling on our pad while listening, or rather not listening, to the lecturer). The need to fill in empty space or time is a very natural one. It is possible that ornament has no other origin.

Let us go back for a moment to the example of the eye and its creative reaction. In primitive decoration employing color, we shall find, I believe, that the choice of colors follows from a kind of alternating principle, from the inventive power of the retina, so to speak. Be that as it may, my contention is fairly self-evident when it comes to lines. For clearly the lines we find on textiles or old vases are very much alike; there are certain varieties of sinusoid or Greek patterns that keep recurring, symmetries which plainly indicate the role of repetition in filling in empty spaces.

But man is an animal who likes to surpass his limits. He did not stop there. He was not satisfied with making spontaneous creations for himself. A social environment set in, techniques were devised; new problems arose, and new pretexts. Man learned to make vases, to turn pottery, to build houses, to fashion furniture; and in each case there cropped up the *complementary* need to decorate the object, that is, to fill in empty spaces. Then the combination of the material component, the technique, with the need for decoration, the need to satisfy the tastes of those for whom the house was built or the piece of furniture made, led to a complex specialization. At this stage mere spontaneous activity, virtually automatic work (comparable to that of the man who hums to himself a monotonous tune, or fills in a space with arbitrary designs) no longer sufficed; something other than pure sensibility took a hand; what we call the intellect, the intelligence, intervened; and with intelligence came conscious foresight. A kind of calculation entered into the work of art. Forms became more complex, the artist tried to make them more interesting.

To abstract ornament the representation of things was added. And so it became necessary to enlist intelligent observation, the intellect with all its resources.

As to the author, the artist, he himself became a more complex being. He had to combine the poet who invents, whose sensibility enriches things, fecundates empty time and space, with the practical man possessing the courage and strength to learn and to combat difficulties by study. He had to have character; and he also had to be a critic in order to predict not only the nature of the work itself but its effects on others as well.

Thus the person of the artist took shape, grew, was enriched. He was not at all the same man as the one who had once produced spontaneously. Yet there remained a kind of prejudice, a magic prejudice one might say, in favor of spontaneous production. A transcendent value was attributed to spontaneity. There was talk of *inspiration*, which was contrasted with intelligence. But the intellect is quite simply the *remainder* of man's being which directs particular activities, which brings all its knowledge, faculties, powers to bear; and its role in the production of works of art increases with culture. The higher the culture, the greater becomes the role of the intellect. It increases with the artist's awareness of the external effect of his work, its effect on the public. It increases also with the physical magnitude of the work: when, like a work of architecture, it is very large and demands considerable time, the co-operation of many men, an advanced technique, the part of the intellect, of knowledge and thought, becomes preponderant.

And there is something else that lessens the role of spontaneity: namely, the external conditions imposed by circumstances. In painting or in sculpture, if you are called upon to fashion someone's portrait, inspiration will not make your portrait a likeness. The painter's individual talent will make his portrait a work of art that *sings* in itself, regardless of any likeness. It will be of value as a picture; when the man who posed for it is dead, it will have no other value than the impression it makes as art; but in so far as a portrait should resemble the model, it is impossible to obtain an exact representation, a resemblance to the model, by a spontaneous act.

Here the artist must take measures requiring a certain precision, he must *rework* his picture; and reworking is a corrective to spontaneous inspiration. Whenever it occurs (and you never know when it does not) a new factor has entered in, which interrupts the spontaneous process and calls on the author's intellectual resources.

Lastly, and this is a very important point (here we are touching on one of the great secrets of art and I really do not know whether I ought to go into it!), a constant and indispensable element of art is the *artist's imitation of himself.* Exactly in proportion as the author has been successful, as he has made the most of his luck, he is obliged, in order to give his work the sustained value he is bound to strive for, to imitate himself, and consequently to study his own method, to manufacture spontaneity.

No one is a better critic of the artist than the artist; no one knows better than he exactly what he is worth, for he has reconstituted by synthesis what has fallen to him from heaven. It is inevitable that he should imitate himself, because he cannot, for the whole duration of a work, sustain the level he has reached at certain points; if he wants his work to be homogeneous in value, he must try to find within himself some way of restoring a certain spontaneity, of constituting a homogeneous whole, by appropriate means, by "tricks."

This is a general rule. A work offering any degree of perfection must have consisted at first of elements of uneven quality. Afterward it was necessary to give these unequal elements an approximately similar value. And here the artist's faculty for criticism, analysis, reasoning, and synthesis is employed to the full.

Composition itself is still another aspect of the question. Composition is extremely rare in certain of the arts, in poetry, for example. I know of very few poems that are really *composed*. Let me explain: I know of very few composed poems, provided in the first place that what we mean by composition is not chronological enumeration. Events follow one another, they are narrated in a temporal order. They begin on a certain day and hour and end on another day and hour. This is a succession of events, but there is no composition, for composition is not the sequence of happenings in someone's life or in the street at such and such a time of day. A work of art that reproduces these events is not a composed work. It is a recording. Secondly, composition in the artist's sense is not the method that consists in following a *plan* (in the logical sense of the word, categories, species, genera, etc.); actually, a plan of this sort provides only a very incomplete cohesion between the different parts of the work, and such cohesion is the essential. It is not brought about by the mere theme of the work, nor by a purely logical dependence of its parts, for the substance and form of the work remain unrelated to the logical order. The composition I have in mind is one which exacts, and sometimes achieves, an indissoluble bond between the matter and form of the work.

I have used the word "matter." I ought to apologize in the presence of philosophers; it is, I believe, a word that should never be employed by itself: we might avoid a good deal of discussion about matter (even in physics) if we agreed, each time we used it, to define it by saying: in relation to a given transformation. We might say: in relation to such and such a transformation or operation, we shall give the name of *matter* to what is conserved (it may be energy or it may be something else). That will enable me to speak of the *matter* of a *work of art*, for outside the plastic arts, in music or in poetry, for example, it would be rather difficult to define the matter of art in the usual sense of the word. If something is conserved in the operation that consists in "undergoing" a piece of music or a poem from beginning to end, we shall call it the matter of the poem or piece.

But let us go back to composition, the striving to create what is so precious, an indissoluble bond between form and substance (I shall explain my choice of words in a moment). It demands that each element be related in a very particular way to some other element. In a poem this will never be accomplished by any logical or chronological tie; a poem or a piece of prose can always be reduced; the reader's mind takes care of that and kills the work by understanding it. Thus we must strive for composition in and through the matter of the poem, which is language: in other words, the substance of the poem must *resist* the immediate transformation of the words into meaning. There must be similarities and correspondences of sound, rhythm, form, etc., which direct the reader's attention to the form. This can be done quite easily in a poem with stanzas. We obtain a kind of unity which comes from the *body* of the poem.

In this connection it should be said (this is a very important parenthesis, particularly for purposes of teaching) that what we call a *poem* exists only in action. When we talk about a poem or poetry or a poet, we must always specify "as I speak it" or "as I understand it." A poem becomes a poem, and the same may be said of a piece of music, only when we hear it resound with its full value. As long as a poem remains on paper, we tend to disregard the essential, the total value, and to judge it by reading it with our eyes. Nothing could be more alien to poetry. Consequently, when we speak of poetry or a poet, we have in mind the poem *in actu*, and there is only one possible definition of verse; it is a "manner of saying."

All the rest is nothing. You are well aware that skillful recitation can easily give the quality of poetry to a piece of poor prose, while there is no poetry so beautiful as to withstand poor recitation. If you are to become aware of a poem, it must ring out from a human mouth. Judgments on paper are beside the point.

Since I have this opportunity to address professors of philosophy, I should like you to give your students this assignment: "Define what is meant in literature and in art by the *subject*." What is the subject of a poem, a play, a picture? There we have something of a riddle. It would be very curious to set it before a body of students. I have my own idea, but I cannot divulge it today; I think it would be interesting to hear what students of letters or philosophy have to say of this familiar notion, and I hope one of you will bring me some answers.

As to the execution of works of art (which may be defined rather grandly as a transition from disorder to order, from the formless to form, or from impurity to purity, accident to necessity, confusion to clarity, etc., or as a change of light to which the eye becomes accustomed), I should have had a good deal to say about it had time permitted. We ought to examine the process in the author, detect its traces in the object, and investigate its effects on the patient who undergoes them.

Execution suggests a great many questions and ideas. For example, there is the problem of facility or of different kinds of difficulty and impossibility; there is the vast problem of conventions and liberties, of the craft itself. Chance plays an enormous role, if one may speak of a role in connection with chance; so does the importance of reasoning and analogies, or of what we might call the *model* or *type* that certain artists seem to have in mind. It is curious to note that in certain cases, in the painting of a portrait, for example, the artist has two models: the person he is trying to portray and the type of work his own nature demands of him.

From an entirely different point of view, the artist's ethics and his related emotional life play an extremely important part in the production of his work. Unfortunately this life is always hidden. It is very difficult to determine the exact part it plays in the work if you have not lived a life of art (or even if you have).

It is clear that the factors we designate by the traditional terms of *pride, vanity, jealousy,* exert an essential influence: how many works owe their birth or miscarriage to effects of the artist's emotional sensibility! And another thing: the artist's conception of his public should also be taken into consideration. A sort of dividing line between works of art might be based on the observation that one class is created by the public, while another creates its public. In this connection, there would be two categories of intentions: (1) to make a work that is "cut to measure" for an audience, a work that will suit its public; (2) or else, to mold an audience that will suit the work.

Lastly, I should like to have spoken of the *idols* in art: we should have had a chapter about the myths, suppositions, beliefs prevailing among artists, and those of the public concerning artists. Here I can only suggest the possibility of such a chapter.

I have often said to myself: Why is the execution of a work of art not in itself a work of art? The thing is conceivable, in certain arts at least. An example comes to mind:

Goncourt tells the story of a Japanese painter on a visit to Paris, who gave a demonstration of his working methods for a few art lovers. After preparing his implements, he took a sponge and moistened his paper, which was stretched on a frame; then he tossed a drop of India ink on the wet paper. When the drop had spread, he rolled some newspaper into a ball and made a fire to dry the paper. When it was dry, he moistened it again, in another corner, and made a second spot, etc. He's a faker, said some of the onlookers. But when he had finished his drying and his tossing of India ink, he went back to his taut paper and put in, here and there, two or three fine brush strokes. The work appeared: a bird with bristling plumage. Not a single operation had gone amiss; the whole thing had been done with a meticulous order, proving that he had done it hundreds of times to achieve this miracle of skill. That man made the execution of a work of art itself a work of art. We can thus imagine a painter or sculptor working rhythmically, in a kind of dance. Execution after all is a kind of miming. If all the movements that went into a picture could be reconstituted, the picture could be explained as a series of co-ordinated acts; the same series could then be repeated or reproduced, and the artist would be comparable to an actor who plays the same role over and over.

This little fantasy is meant to suggest that once the acts of an art are fully mastered, they can, to a certain extent, be repeated, and that the true artist is one who comes, though not exactly in the way I have described, to possess a self-knowledge so considerable that his personality, his *originality*, comes to be applied and practiced *automatically*.

Just a few words more: first, concerning a notion which, like a good many others in art, has been heaped with ridicule. Namely, the notion of Great Art. I believe it might profitably be revived. Great Art is confused with so-called "academic" art: art with big dimensions, tedious and official, has often been called Great Art. I should like to apply the term to an art that requires the artist *to bring to bear all the powers of his mind*: we have seen how the process begins with spontaneity and continues with calculation, reasoning, etc. Let us suppose that an artist finds the strength to go about a work of any kind (regardless of its dimensions) in such a way that this little work will reflect every possible faculty of mind that applies to art, or rather that is applicable in a work of art. There, as far as I am concerned, you have a definition of Great Art, *the work of the whole man*. On the other hand, a work of Great Art must also require the consumer to deploy all his faculties. What an author really wants is a reader who gives him not admiration (which is nothing), but sustained attention. No doubt, such a reader will often find something quite different from what the author wished: conceivably, what the author wanted was less than what the attention of the reader or auditor gives him; but it is certain that an author's desire to awaken all a man's faculties with his work—and hence to exact of his audience an effort of the same quality as his own —defines an art that we may be justified in calling great.

A. LALANDE: We wish to thank M. Paul Valéry for the extremely interesting and personal things he has just told us. We have followed you, M. Valéry, without difficulty and with a pleasure that philosophical disquisitions do not always give us. And now I hope some of the members of the Society will have a few remarks to make or wish to ask a few questions about the ideas you have just expressed. We have a number of writers and aestheticians in our midst. . . . M. André Maurois?

ANDRÉ MAUROIS: I am not an aesthetician, and besides, I am unprepared. . . . Perhaps I might mention a few ideas that M. Valéry's talk has suggested to me. . . . When M. Valéry asked: How do we recognize an art object? I began to wonder whether a natural object can be an art object. And it seems to me that even among natural objects we can distinguish varying degrees of aesthetic value. A painter will choose one subject rather than another, because it is already *ordered*. Often a valley is beautiful because it has a river in the middle that provides it with a kind of axis. A sunset shows us clouds and colors arranged round a center.

But when the order in nature is not so evident, it is up to the artist to discover a hidden order or to create one. Might we not define a work of art as "an order imposed on a disorder"? But the order must be very secret. M. Valéry asked what constitutes the plan of a book. I believe that unity is provided by a constant atmosphere and repeated themes rather than by a rigid plan. The subject of a novel may consist not in the intrigue but in a certain way of looking at life, just as the subject of a painting by Renoir is not a particular nude woman but Renoir's vision. Flaubert said that the idea of his *Sentimental Education* came to him while he was following a funeral at Rouen. It was not so much a subject as a state of mind. But the unity of the state of mind makes the unity and beauty of the book.

Most biographies are mere collections of facts, but a biography by Lytton Strachey is a work of art. Why? Because in dealing with a life, Strachey is able to recognize and isolate the main themes which lend it unity by their recurrence. The end of his biography of Queen Victoria, in which all the themes are summed up and gathered together, is beautiful in the same way as Siegfried's funeral march at the end of the *Ring*. Strachey re-creates history as a great painter re-creates a landscape or a great musician the life of pure sound.

Before aesthetic pleasure can be born, not only must there be order, but this order must dominate an actual disorder. Pure order may have a kind of intellectual beauty, but it does not move us. What we wish is to see the violent universe of the passions, the chaos of color and sound, dominated by a human intelligence. Alain has said—my wording is only approximate—that music is a movement between noise and virtue. Pure noise is mere disorder, without beauty; virtue would be the cold classicism of a purely mathematical music. In great music, the torrent of sound seems always on the point of turning into hurricane and chaos, and always the composer, Beethoven or Wagner, soars over the tempest, reins in the chaos. But it is because the chaos has overwhelmed us that we are moved when it is checked. This, it seems to me, ties in with the idea expressed by M. Valéry that desire must perpetually be re-created. If the need for order is to remain urgent, the artist must everlastingly threaten us with disorder. A work of art that is too well made will be badly made.

CHARLES LALO: I was quite delighted by M. Paul Valéry's talk and I learned a great deal from it. I should only like to emphasize one of the points he raised, which might pass unnoticed or seem to be without importance. Permit me even to exaggerate its importance, in the hope that M. Paul Valéry may express his approval or disapproval of the consequences, which may be very far-reaching. I have in mind the question of *boredom*.

Let me remind you (though it makes me seem a bit of a pedant) that the notion that the need for combating boredom is the source of art is stated quite clearly by the Abbé Dubos at the beginning of the eighteenth century. The same idea reappears, in more philosophical and less directly aesthetic form, in very diverse thinkers, such as Auguste Comte, or in

Kierkegaard and Heidegger, for whom boredom takes on the intensity of anguish.

What I should chiefly like to accomplish by my observation is nothing less than to make M. Valéry admit that aesthetics exists. I remember a certain meeting of the Association for the Study of the Arts, at which I had the good fortune to be seated beside him. After M. Basch had greeted him as the "master of contemporary French aesthetics"— and the title is well deserved—M. Valéry replied that he did not quite understand what it meant to be master of something that did not exist. That was quite a rap on the knuckles. And that is why I am now trying to make him admit that, according to what he has just told us, aesthetics does exist.

For actually, if we pursue the idea I have just mentioned, we shall be led to plot curves of boredom—you yourself came close to suggesting as much. We have experimental curves of attention or fatigue; might we not establish curves of *aesthetic* attention or fatigue? There have already been investigations along these lines. Do you not believe the need for change which you have very aptly called the "aesthetic infinite" to be not an accessory but quite an essential fact of artistic life? I say "very aptly" because, since I am not much of a metaphysician—as I admit to my shame—I like to take the word "change" in the sense of a perpetual renewal—others would say relativity—of values.

If the "aesthetic infinite" reduces itself to a relativism indispensable to the very existence of art, if we are compelled to pass from green to red and red to green, should we not go further and say what you—if I am not mistaken—did not dare to read us from your article in *Pièces sur l'art*, namely, that in the course of the generations we pass from an idealist to a realist phase with the same necessity as the retina passes from red to green and so on?

VALÉRY: I am often unable to remember something I have written, but it does not seem to me that I ever said that; as to the comparison with the alternation of red and green, in any case, I feel almost sure I never made it. If you could show me the passage you refer to. . . . I think I am innocent of it.

LALO: I believe I shall be able to find it. Supposing the passage to be authentic—what rare good fortune to be able to criticize a text in the presence of the author—will you admit that these periodic phases, these rhythms of development through which art passes (which seem to be worth studying and perhaps even formulating as a law) are an essential element of aesthetics? In that case, aesthetics would exist, in this form at least.

VALÉRY: I have not denied aesthetics, not in general at least; I should never have dared to do that. I took a very restricted and practical point of view. My question was: How can aesthetics help us to enjoy a work of art more, or help the artist to fashion one with greater power or ease?

And when I criticize aesthetics, all I am basically trying to do is to withdraw to a very simple point of vantage. Let us suppose that we can find laws of probability, or other laws governing the behavior of living creatures in the presence of works of art. If from these laws we cannot derive a precise relation between the work of art and the consumer or producer, they are without utility or sanction. I strongly suspect that, according to the idea I have already stated and strongly believe to be true concerning the beginnings of aesthetics in antiquity, classical aesthetics was entirely dialectical in origin.

You are aware that in the Latin countries, in Italy or Spain, German philosophy, Hegel's aesthetics, is regarded as fundamental in these matters. I have always found it odd that

Latins should attach so much importance to an aesthetic that is obviously not made for them; it is a beautiful structure, but one that does not apply to Latin minds. May I tell you a quip I once made to a well-known Spanish philosopher: "See here, are you quite sure that Hegel knew how to knot his tie properly?" If his aesthetics is purely natural, there is no possible way of applying it to the creation of works of art; but if it is a personal matter, we may as well say that Hegel is beside the point.

LALO: Permit me to confound the aestheticians you call classical. I believe they derived their ideas from their traditional education, their schooling, rather than from the art of their contemporaries.

VALÉRY: Yes, Hegel knew nothing whatsoever about the art of his time.

H. DELACROIX: There, I am afraid, you are mistaken. A reading of the *Aesthetics* proves that if anyone knew his facts and had a feeling for the concrete, it was Hegel.

VALÉRY: But was he an artist?

DELACROIX: He was extremely familiar with the facts and problems of art. It is a fallacy, I repeat, to regard his aesthetics as a sort of scholastic monster of pure dialectic. I beg M. Brunschvicg's pardon and yours, but Hegel's monumental work is full of concrete richness.

LÉON BRUNSCHVICG: I have never said a word against Hegel's *Aesthetics*.

DELACROIX: It is read, unfortunately, in very poor translations, all of which are abridged. Take the original, you will see how rich it is; a good deal of what you have said here, and so well, particularly about the relation between the author and the work, is admirably stated in it. Read it; learn a bit of German....

VALÉRY: I'll build if I must, but. . . .*

DELACROIX: I once asked my students to consider one of your texts, the passage in which you contrast artistic spontaneity with construction. I showed them two definitions, one yours, the other Hegel's, saying the same thing. You would find a good deal of your own in Hegel, believe me.

RENÉ BERTHELOT: M. Paul Valéry has said that while the artist is fashioning a work of art, one of his preoccupations is to imitate himself. I should like to ask him to clarify those words.

Stravinsky once told a friend of mine that he did not like composers who turned out Stravinsky, that is, who used harmonic methods more or less resembling those he had employed in certain of his works. He said in substance: "If they do that, it means they have no idea what I was trying to do in composing the work. I used such and such a harmonic method because, in composing that particular work, I had a definite aim in mind; but I should not employ the same methods in works where I was trying to do something else. Their way of using them is directly contrary to my own."

Besides, it is clear that for the last ten years or so one of Stravinsky's main preoccupations has been to avoid "turning

---

* The implication is, "I am too old to learn." See end note.—J. M.

out Stravinsky," to avoid imitating himself, to achieve, by new methods, works with an entirely different aim from his earlier ones. I am not offering an objection, but merely asking a question in the hope that you will complete your thought.

VALÉRY: I am not very competent in matters of music. Every artist is concerned with renewing himself, and he also has another preoccupation, running the opposite way and no less important, namely, his desire to capitalize and consolidate the results he has obtained. From the point of view of the audience, he must find something new; in many cases, his problem is exactly the same as that of the artist starting out in life who says: This and this and this has been done: what can I do that is different? He proceeds by elimination. You can see how political this kind of reasoning is—it is artistic politics—and as such how contrary it is to art, how much calculation it demands! Often an artist producing a work is unable to maintain the level, the standard of value he would like; one passage is a bit long, there are awkward explanations; the thing doesn't flow, there are gaps. In the greatest poets there is a good deal of unevenness, inferior passages: it seems likely that the poet has made every effort to be at his best, but to be so by calculation. So you see, the two things are reconcilable: imitation of oneself signifies the will to maintain a certain level of value in a work; and, on the other hand, when, in projecting a new work, the author feels that he is already typed, he wishes to change, curses the imitator, shuns him, and tries his best to throw him off the scent.

It is certain that one of the qualities characteristic of an artist is the ability to imitate himself. Writers who do not know their craft are unable to do so, and their work presents extreme unevenness. All the hard work, the craftsmanship, in literature as in the other arts, is a battle against this. What has value in a work is not so much certain passages as the whole, continuous work. There is too much quoting of fine lines: the beautiful line, if it is too fine and the rest not sufficiently so, becomes a fault that diminishes the work. It seems to me that the striving for continuity is of higher value.

LALO: May I quote the passage I was referring to? It is in "The Triumph of Manet." "Just as the eye replies with a 'green' to a too prolonged and insistent 'red,' so, in the arts, an overindulgence in fantasy is compensated for by a regime of 'truth.' Which is no reason why one side should insult the other; nor why one side should consider itself bolder, and the other consider itself infinitely wiser." It is probably the word "wise" that made me think a philosopher might take a position in the matter.

VALÉRY: When one has seen, as we have, literary fashions that are simply rather naïve retorts to one another—symbolism to Parnassianism, and so on—one tends to explain such phenomena by a kind of fatigue that calls for an opposite reaction.

LALO: Do you find any appreciable difference between the vast fluctuations that are forever taking place in the history of art, and the more limited fluctuations of fashion?

VALÉRY: There is no difference.

LALO: I should also like to make a case, briefly, for keeping the names of painters on their pictures. If you remove them, they will soon be replaced by a curtain which will be another badge of the masterpiece. The public has need of guidance, you know that better than I. In other countries, it is usually a curtain that indicates a masterpiece. The sexton or museum guard draws it solemnly aside.

VALÉRY: The reason why, even in connection with the history of art, the purely external aspect is so much overdone is that in the teaching of art, the study of works themselves gives way to notions about them; some go so far—I have seen it myself—as to teach children the beauties of painting by projecting black and white post cards. Obviously, that is going a little too far.

And so I should like to see more stress laid on the works of art themselves than on the labels attached to them: from the point of view of aesthetic enjoyment, it is no help to know that Manet is a French painter. . . . In this connection I tried an experiment not so long ago. I had not been in Brussels for some time; I went to the Brussels museum, entered a room at random, closed my eyes, turned once round, and opened them again: giving myself the soul of an amoeba, one of those amoebas that are used for experiments on tropism, I moved toward the picture that attracted me. It was one that I never should have noticed on a normal visit, a feminine martyr by a fairly well-forgotten Bolognese painter. I should never have thought of looking at that picture; I should have headed straight for Rembrandt or Rubens. Try it at the Louvre, you'll see.

D. PARODI: I should like to offer an observation on the subject of spontaneity and reflection. Is there really so radical a difference as people seem to say between the "inspired" artist and the one who reflects, starts over a dozen times? Essentially every discovery of a new idea or form, regardless of the labor that leads up to it, is spontaneous; at a given moment something appears that you hadn't thought of before: a new hypothesis, a new connection between hitherto unrelated ideas, an image or phrase you had been searching and searching for, that suddenly turns up at the tip of your pen. Invention is almost always an instantaneous intuition; it is hardly ever the conclusion of a formal process of reasoning, the outcome of a carefully followed plan or of a critical examination of all the possible solutions or combinations, ending with the elimination of the least satisfactory. It is equally certain, on the other hand, that something has always prepared the way for your flash of intuition, that it is preceded by a period of incubation which may consist in meditation on the work in hand, or in a long process of training, experiment, reading, acquisition of experience, the storing up of impressions, etc. The difference between the two families of minds, the "conscientious literary worker" and the "inspired writer," is largely one of measure and degree; but invention in the strict sense, in so far as it comprises an element of novelty and creation, always remains in essence spontaneous and inaccessible to analysis. And indeed, any attempt to explain it would demolish its novelty by requiring us to assume that what invention invents is somehow given in advance.

VALÉRY: Invention does not always lead to a work. I believe that there can be a long psychological interval between the initial germ, the first discovery, and the thing itself. I am by no means certain that the idea which engenders the work is always the idea of the work engendered. It is perfectly possible to arrive at a different work.

PARODI: Is it not conceivable that a work may be at once prepared and spontaneous?

VALÉRY: M. Maurois has cited the example of Flaubert.

MAUROIS: For Wordsworth a work of art is an emotion re-collected in tranquillity. You make use of your emotion later on, at one remove. . . .

VALÉRY: And I say, a profoundly transformed one.

PARODI: The transformation, I believe, consists simply of partial discoveries.

MAUROIS: While you are writing a novel, there is constant invention, since the scene does not exist at the moment when you are creating it. But the emotion that enables the artist to imagine the scene may have occurred long before; it may re-cur only faintly at the moment of writing.

PARODI: The fact remains that in itself invention, novelty, can be nothing other than inspiration, whatever preparation may have taken place. Might we not conceive of a type of artist who, by the method you have so subtly analyzed, the imitation of oneself, succeeds in so fully mastering his tech-nique, in making certain ways of feeling, thinking, or speak-ing so much a part of his nature that he applies them almost instinctively, and perceives as it were automatically the effect to be produced and the means of doing so; so that, at a given moment, under the stress of a favorable emotion, he can at-tain perfection at the first try?

VALÉRY: There are a good many things I have not had time to mention. There are highly important differences between naïve production and production that is not naïve; and the same goes for understanding. The phenomena of production and consumption involve a great many degrees.

RAYMOND LENOIR: The author of *Amphion* has like a magician conjured up all the secrets of art. It is my business as a sociologist to break magic down into its elements. You will forgive me if I apply this technique to what has been said about the origins of art. The way in which the work of art is born in primitive man has been distinguished from the way in which it develops and flowers in civilized societies, where it brings many more important elements and functions into play. Actually, artistic creation is already complex in the so-called primitive societies. Let us consider such true artists as the Melanesians, disregarding their gift for music and dancing and concentrating for the moment on their aptitude for sculpture. They know the art of working clay into graceful, elegant pottery. They have a strong feeling for wood, which they bend into wavy shapes that adorn the prows of their canoes. Their ingenuity suggests that perhaps there is no great difference between the attitudes of primitive and of civilized men. Both show an immediate understanding of form that I shall call plastic intelligence. Both possess an innate sense of rhythm that springs from the organism. There is something muscular and physical about it. This intelligence that emanates from the body meets with the pure forms that nature provides—for the forms provided by the vegetable and animal kingdoms are almost always perfect. It is only in man that deformations become increasingly pronounced, and that is what creates the necessity for style. The artist is always obliged to follow a natural movement, to remain within the limits imposed by nature, content with what it suggests to him within the set conditions of successful birth and growth.

Thus the world as a whole helps the primitive artist to discover the figures whose soul recurs in the watercourses, the winds, and in every movement that may be observed anywhere. It has just been shown very aptly how creation opens up unlimited perspectives that constitute the infinite. Watching the waves at Plougrescan during his childhood vacations, Renan contemplated the divine, but it was the divine in an ephemeral form.

G. BÉNÉZÉ: In contrasting the finite with the infinite, M. Valéry spoke first of utility, which corresponds to finite things, and then of the work of art, which on the contrary corresponds to the infinite need for self-renewal. It seemed to me that in giving these examples he did not draw the distinction that is usual, I believe, between the agreeable and the beautiful in a work of art.

VALÉRY: I did not wish to use those words.

BÉNÉZÉ: It seems to me that between the work of art considered as beautiful and the work of art considered as agreeable, there lies the whole question of freedom. Actually, M. Valéry has spoken of it, calling it independence. We philosophers prefer to speak of freedom. The question leads indirectly to another: a work of art really exists only for certain kinds of sensations, whereas what is agreeable involves other sensations in respect to which one does not think of art. For example, tickling is not a work of art; nor is the object of the sense of taste. We do not speak of art in connection with the sensations that are very close to the body, or with those that we call internal, but only in connection with the eye, the ear. Consequently, we must draw a distinction between the feeling of the dancer while he is dancing and the artistic emotion of the spectator as he watches him dance.

VALÉRY: I did not wish to speak of the "agreeable" or the "beautiful," because I was trying, as far as possible, to limit myself to objective notions. *We* have this distinction between agreeable and beautiful; but conceive of a language in which it did not exist: I am not sure the distinction would then be so clear.

Those who go in for dialectic aesthetics rely on the categories implied in words. But if one is trying to work only with concepts for which one can find a foundation in experience, it is a good idea to keep away from the words I have tried to avoid. I have chosen to restrict myself to two things: the desire, typical of certain cases, for something to begin all over again, and the contrary tendency to get something over with. These have been the point of departure for what I have called the "aesthetic infinite." No attempt has been made to find out whether there is such a thing as the beautiful, the agreeable, the graceful: that would involve me in classical aesthetics.

BÉNÉZÉ: In regard to many sensations, the only possibility of a complete philosophical analysis is a return of some kind to the sensations themselves, which are at the base of everything.

VALÉRY: Sensation does not distinguish between the agreeable and the beautiful. It takes highly advanced language, a civilization with a long past, to arrive at subtle distinctions of that sort. I do not believe that savages have a very clear feeling for them; but as for sensation itself, they have more of it than we do; whether they have the distinction between the agree-

able and the beautiful is something that should be investigated; I do not know.

BÉNÉZÉ: I believe that the freedom you spoke of makes itself
felt more in connection with the beautiful than with the agreeable. Where the agreeable is concerned, we are bound to
things present. When it comes to the beautiful, we are more
free, even in regard to things present.

R. BAYER: I have just two questions about two particular
points in the lecture we have just heard. The first is concerned
with historical circumstances. M. Valéry has said, and he has
just repeated, that they add nothing whatever to the enjoyment of a work of art. But M. Valéry has offered us a theory
that might be called the theory of the fruitfulness of *misconceptions*; he suggests the possibility of a creative misunderstanding between the artist and the various members of his
audience. He has even spoken of a cascade of misunderstandings flowing from one epoch to another. This misunderstanding, you say, is the source of the work's entire value—or
at least a part of it. But I should say that there is a whole
historical perspective based on misconceptions, and that the
knowledge and study of it gives us an aesthetic pleasure of its
own. To take a concrete example: is the whole nature of our
aesthetic enjoyment of Watteau's work not completely
changed by the mere knowledge that this man, who seems so
full of the century of Louis XV, actually lived during the
reign of Louis XIV? I shall therefore ask, in the first place,
whether M. Valéry does not believe that there is a kind of
aesthetic pleasure which might be defined as the enjoyment
of a whole process of exegesis.

The second question has to do with the radical separation

between transmission on the one hand and production and consumption on the other. M. Valéry says: there are three terms—and indeed there are—the artist, the work of art, the audience. He adds that there are two transformations: the one running from the artist to the work, and the other from the work to the audience, and that these are absolutely distinct and mutually independent. I wonder whether there is not, on the contrary, some common factor, something *transitive* passing from our artist to our audience, and whether the place of the work in the scale of artistic values may not be determined by the perpetual transmissibility of this something: I should like to ask, in other words, whether we really have two *independent* series or whether, rather than speak of two transformations, we should not speak of the work of art itself as a special kind of transformer. There is a sort of emotion, of primitive impulse, of rhythmic sentiment (or whatever we may choose to call it) that the artist aims to communicate; the work of art, then, is a kind of relay between the artist and his audience; and it is from this period of gestation, in which he tries to restore contact with a supposed audience, that come all the efforts of which you speak, all the *reworking* and *retouching*. For if I make an effort, it is because I am dissatisfied; and what underlies my dissatisfied strivings if not the need to restore contact: to recapture a particular rhythm, a movement, a curve, an emotional tone in my work and, by fixating them, to relay them to my audience?

I wonder then whether what the work of art accomplishes may not be to fixate, within another system of resistance, the obstacle created by action: to capture in other nets an emotion or a feeling or some rhythm of life, though perhaps not an everyday emotion, but a strictly artistic one. You once spoke, perhaps here in a previous lecture, of a poem that was born in you from a simple rhythmic feeling, a pure form. And then, little by little, you said, expressions adapted to the rhythm came to you, and gradually the poem became a whole in which, as you have just said, you sought inner similarities, in which you sought to recapture the very same rhythm. Here again, it is a primitive emotion that strives to perpetuate itself, though not, of course, an emotion of your personal, lived life, not the great living passion, which in your first lecture you said was one of the two roots from which *Tristan* grew. However, let us get back to this rhythmic emotion of yours, for there is no doubt that that is what you are trying to recapture; it is your never wholly successful effort to come closer to it that prompts all your successive retouchings. Thus—and thus alone—does the work become more perfectly what you want it to be, that is, a communication from *you*, the artist, to *him*, the spectator.

Have we here two transformations? For my part, I see in art a series of relays, wherein misunderstandings can operate as a kind of dynamic that takes hold of a work from generation to generation, to give it new life. But amid all these misunderstandings, there remains in art something of the ideal aimed at, namely a *direct* and *authentic* communication, suspended for a moment, but enduring for all eternity, in the comparative fixity of a created work within the enclosing limits of its perfection as in a strange system of constraints.

VALÉRY: I used the word "relay," or I should have. The problem is to represent this relation of three terms. I think it is more helpful to take two relationships between two terms, because when you try, as you have just done, to take a single relation, you end, in the last analysis, by spiriting away the work, leaving only the author and the audience. What can you say when the communication between author and audience does not take place? If everyone were impressed by the work, that would be splendid; but many people will not be; in this case, the author will be left with his work; there will be no transition from work to audience.

BAYER: When there is no possible transition to an audience, even an enlightened one, I say that there is not, that there cannot be, a work of art. From which I conclude that there must always be something transitive in the work.

VALÉRY: But suppose that nothing is transmitted, that the work is dead—this happens every day—suppose that someone hears a musical composition and gets nothing out of it, or reads a highly obscure poem, or contemplates a work of art that strikes him as affected and uninteresting, then there is no reaction. Consequently, I think it is simpler to consider separately the relation between author and work and the relation between the work and someone who can grasp it, which is not everyone.

I believe that no direct communication is possible. There is the author, his act which impresses form on a piece of matter, and there is someone who sees the matter but not the act—only its result—and experiences something: it may amount to zero, or it may be positive or negative; either the thing does not interest him, or it is beautiful, or it is bad. I find it simpler to express this relation by two transformations that are in a way parallel but not necessarily connected, because a connection is not always established between the realities underlying them. Besides, the whole thing is a matter of opinion.

Part II

Style

STYLE—so pure is the word in sound and aspect, it would be a delightful name for some choice being, a rare bird, a character in a fairy tale. It is one of those names whose musical quality suggests a language whose words would sound out their meaning.

But not at all. *Style* was first of all an engraving tool. In the hands of a Virgil or a Tacitus it incised in thin black wax the illustrious verses, the celebrated prose, a part of which has miraculously come down to us. Later, the stylus became a pen and the wax became paper. But even before the hard, cutting point had given way to the supple tip of a sharpened quill, the name *style* had passed from the instrument to the hand that guides it, and from the hand to the man from whom the hand derives its way of doing, and power to do, whatever it does.

It is these successive transitions of one and the same term from idea to idea that imperceptibly develop the intrinsic poetry of language.

Thus *style* signifies the manner in which a man expresses himself, *regardless of what he expresses*, and it is held to reveal his nature quite apart from his actual thought—for thought has no style. It is in the act of expression that the man distinguishes himself. Here we find his characteristic rhythms, the temperamental constants of his character, his verbal resources which may or may not be very original, his habitual methods, and the enthusiasms or doubts that recur amid the diversity of his written or spoken discourse. All these elements constitute his *style*. But in among them, it should not be forgotten, there slips the curiously insinuating and active faculty of simulation or dissimulation which sometimes becomes dominant.

Thus what makes the style is not merely the mind applied to a particular action; it is the *whole* of a living system expended, imprinted, and made recognizable in expression. It is compounded of consciousness and unconsciousness, of spontaneity and effort; and sometimes calculation enters in. A work of art or an action may be executed with science or skill without disclosing style. A certain negligence does no harm in the matter of style; but neither does care, even excessive care, do away with it. In some men the will breaks through and reveals the sustained energy of their designs; in others indifference is manifest and it too is style; and there are still others who cultivate their carelessness, not unaware that it can take on the value of a style.

But a man's characteristic manner of doing things, *his style*, is not always praiseworthy. There are bad styles. Properly, the word means something more than manner of being or doing, and this "something" is not easily defined. I believe that a good style implies a kind of *organization of originality*, a harmony that excludes the excesses of the imagination. Extravagance and eccentricity burst the bounds of a good style. Untempered caprice is unbecoming to it. Everyone agrees that a tiger has a very different style from a monkey: it has magnificent balance; the monkey is all instability, futile gambols, aimless leaps.

Good style should suggest a very perceptible but indefinable law, which tempers the individual character of acts or works and lends them the dignity of a type or model. A personality then acquires the interest of an original, of a unique specimen which stands out from among the collection of similar beings that is the human race; it becomes a kind of deviation toward the ideal.

Nothing is more devoid of style than a product of mechanical or imitable fabrication. Consequently I deplore (though it is too late) the use of our word to designate an epoch or a school of architecture or of ornamental art, for styles of this kind are definable and imitable; commercial abuse of this verbal abuse has even given us the expression "*meubles de style*" (period furniture), and we know what that means.

A Brief Address to the
Society of Engravers

Gentlemen:

I SHOULD have preferred to address you as colleagues, but what little association I have had with engraving is of the kind one is reluctant to confess; for my efforts in that direction soon made it very clear to me that I was not born to be an engraver.

And now, gentlemen, having admitted my unworthiness, I should like, in thanking you for your hospitality, to say something to make up for it. . . . What better way of showing my gratitude than by trying to tell you, in my own way, of the high esteem in which I hold your noble craft and the special significance I attach to it?

First let me own that I often look on you with envy and wish (though quite without hope) that I might exchange my pen for a point, I dare not say a burin.

But then I compare our two arts; I discover, in engraving as in literary work, an intimate bond between the nascent work and the artist who applies himself to it. The plate (or stone) is quite comparable to the page the writer works on: both fill us with dread; both occupy our zone of *distinct vision*; we take in the whole and the detail in a single glance; the *mind*, the *eye*, and the *hand* concentrate their expectation on this small surface; we stake our destiny on it. . . . Is this not the height of creative kinship, experienced identically by the engraver and the writer, each glued to his desk, where he reveals *all he knows* and *all he is worth?*

But carrying my thought a little further, I find a deeper kinship between us, a rather subtle resemblance which a moment's reflection suggests and a certain trick of thought may render almost acceptable to the mind.

You will forgive me the bit of metaphysics (or fancy, shall we say?) that is needed to explain it.

What we call "nature"—the term is convenient and consecrated by usage—nature makes a good many things, some of which are exceedingly beautiful. But not all. She is an uneven creator, incomparable on her good days, when, for example, she turns out a number of admirably constructed animals. At the Salons of the various seasons, she exhibits remarkable trees, charming flowers, and from time to time she composes sumptuous or sublime backdrops which provide a theater for our actions or marvelous abodes for our thoughts.

But fertile and even prodigal as nature may be, she has not invented everything. She has left us certain realms, certain opportunities for creation; and we for our part have brought forth certain works which are unknown to her, and which, moreover, she is radically incapable of producing. This is the point that interests me.

We feel certain desires that nature is unable to satisfy, and we have certain powers that she has not.

Of course man and his universe might have been exactly in harmony. We can conceive of an Eden, an earthly Paradise, where our eyes and our impulses would find everything they desired and could desire only what they found; a Garden where everything was better than anything we could dream of.

187

But such is not the case. That delectable universe is not ours and, all in all, I think we should be glad of it.

Even children do not relish for very long the lands of candy and gingerbread dripping with syrup that certain fairy tales hold out to them. They prefer an adventure full of marvelous *difficulties*.

For, gentlemen, there is within us something more than a desire for pleasure pure and simple, or even impure and complicated. . . . There is a very special thirst which neither the enjoyment of perfection nor the most blissful possession can quench or appease. The delights of repose in the certainty of a possession do not satisfy us. Passive pleasure wearies and surfeits us; we also need the *pleasure of making* something. It is a strange, complex pleasure, shot through with torments, fraught with hardships; and in our pursuit of it neither obstacles, nor bitterness, nor doubt, nor even despair is lacking. . . .

You and I, gentlemen, are well acquainted with this laborious pleasure, this *pleasure of making*; it is second nature with us, a second nature opposed to the first, immediate nature I was speaking of.

When nature creates, she proceeds in intimate union with herself; for example, she gradually brings her forms into shape by the action of their very matter, which she never allows to become distinct from her energies, nor from herself. When nature produces a plant, she raises it imperceptibly, unfolds it, spreads it out, as though by successive states of balance, so that at every moment the age, the volume, the irregular leafy surface of the plant, and the physical conditions of its environment stand together in an indivisible relation of which the form of our plant is, as it were, the mysteriously exact expression.

188

Quite different is the work of man: man acts; he exerts his forces upon a foreign matter, he distinguishes his acts from the substance on which they operate, he has a distinct consciousness of them; thus he can conceive and combine them before executing them; he can give them the most varied applications, adjust them to the most diverse substances, and it is this power of unifying his undertakings, or of breaking down his designs into distinct acts, that he terms his intelligence. He is not inseparable from the material of his work, but comes and goes between it and his idea, between his mind and his model, and at every moment he exchanges *what he wants* for *what he is capable of* and *what he is capable of* for *what he actually accomplishes.*

Thus operating on beings and objects, on the events and themes that the world and nature offer him, he finally abstracts from them those symbols of his action in which his power of understanding and his power to construct are combined, namely, *line, surface, number, order, form, rhythm,* and all the rest.

But he differs quite clearly from nature by this power of abstraction and composition, for nature neither abstracts nor composes; she neither stops nor reflects; her course is ineluctable. Now we see the extent of the contrast between the human mind and nature, and this, gentlemen, is what I have been leading up to.

I have been leading up to this proposition which concerns us: that art belongs to the province of the mind, whose duration is a tissue of immaterial acts, and that the art that is closest to the mind is the art which, with the *greatest economy* of perceptible means, restores to us a *maximum* of our impressions or intentions. Are you not able with a few lines, a few incisions, not only to give us the likeness of a face, a countryside, but to suggest them so vividly that the color you have not used, and even the richest light, do not seem to be lacking?

And if a writer masters his craft, is he not able in a few words, with a single line of poetry, to awaken in the soul all the qualities of things, even the chords and echoes of a unique remembered moment in life?

That is what brings us together, gentlemen. We communicate in *black and white*, with which nature can do nothing. She can do nothing with a bit of ink. She needs infinite, literally infinite, *material*, whereas we need virtually none, but, if possible, a *great deal of intelligence*.

That's what appeals to me about engravers. I love your work and share your emotion when you take a tiny rectangle of paper, still moist from the press, and holding it delicately between your finger tips, raise it to the light. This proof sheet, this newborn babe, this child of your patient impatience (for the artist's being can be defined only by contradictions) bears upon it that minimum of the universe, that essential trifle which presupposes the intelligence in its entirety.

Intelligenti pauca, they say in Latin. Is that not the proud motto of all who are gathered here today for the greater glory of black and white?

In Praise of Virtuosity

THERE ARE people who are surprised or even indignant at the sight of a playbill or concert poster on which the name of a Molière or a Beethoven figures in characters scarcely larger than a pinhead, while that of an actor or pianist is brilliantly, impressively displayed in letters a foot high.

There are others (and they may well be the same) who deplore and condemn the excess of favor which audiences bestow on the artists who captivate them with their perform-ance on stage or concert platform; they resent the enthusiasm that greets and engulfs them in wave after wave of clamorous, echoing sound, to call them back from the wings a dozen times or more.

We hear murmurs to the effect that the dignity of art is offended by such outbursts directed to the *persons* of its ministrants, whose portraits, signatures, random remarks, and indeed the most trifling details of their private lives, are sought after, as though it were not precisely in order to destroy or ward off the baseness and pettiness of individual existence that the original creators withdrew from the world into the thoughts embodied in their works. The priest, we are told, hides the god, and usurps his place in the eyes of the crowd.

There is a certain ill-concealed jealousy, a certain half-unconscious envy in this bitterness, beneath these uncompromising judgments seasoned with gibes, directed both at the idol and his devotees, disparaging the flowers and epithets heaped on him, the passions he evokes, the prodigious sums with which he is rewarded, and his extraordinary power over so many men and women, whose senses he moves and whose hearts he captures.

It cannot be denied, however, that these unworthy feelings sometimes have a certain substance, that even though unjust they are prompted by real abuses. Yet although the excessive praise and homage, the adulation, often quite intoxicating, that an era lavishes on its favorite artists, may lead certain crotchety observers to protest, to make severe comments on the incongruity between merit and success, nevertheless some of the arguments raised by our rebels are rather specious.

Often they accuse the interpreter of a work of displaying his talents at the expense of its purity, of modifying its proportions, of weighting its effects and even its meaning, in such a way that the author's intentions, as set down in writing, are profoundly distorted. They say he has a gift for perverting the public's taste, for seducing his audience by his mastery of difficulties, by miracles of rapidity, by extraordinary *playing* which shatters our idea of the mechanical limits of human action. Or they accuse him of flattering what is most commonplace or easily touched in the sensibility of his audience, by exaggerating the tenderness of his inflections and modulations, attacking the soul at the weak points that enable him to arouse its desires, its regrets, its memories, and to tap its store of tears.

Virtuosity is, then, a debatable issue.

It arises whenever we can distinguish, to the point of contrasting them, the idea we may form of a work and the *impression* made on us by a certain way of interpreting it. It may come about, for example, that a poem or a melody that we *know* to be very mediocre borrows from a fine voice, skillfully handled, a power and a charm which at first mislead our judgment. The contrary, I believe, is more frequent: there is no masterpiece that has not been massacred a thousand and one times—and that perhaps is how we finally recognize a masterpiece, for only what is alive can be killed.

Interestingly enough, these great exemplary works are the choice victims, sometimes of *too much*, sometimes of *too little* talent.

Having said this, we must banish it from our thoughts, revise our judgments, imitate the magistrate who, when he sits down on the bench, dismisses everything that rumor or the newspapers have told him about the case to be set before him. Once that is done, a moment's reflection will tell us that the case of virtuosity revolves round the essential problem of art, which is the *problem of execution*, for the virtuoso is by definition an executant of unusual abilities, who may now and then, intoxicated by an exaggerated sense of his technical powers, allow himself to abuse them.

Let us look at the matter a little more closely.

It is too often forgotten that art exists only in the act: *art is action*; it is an action whose aim it is to modify man's sensibility and from it to conjure up developments that arouse perpetual desire. This gives rise to needs which may vary in intensity, but which are very different from those that make us slaves to the demands of our organism. They suggest the existence within us of a being—and in a measure they lend form and substance to that being—who lives on rhythms, contrasts, symmetries, similarities, who demands and receives them from himself or from an outside source.

To say that art is action is to say indirectly that a work of art in itself is merely a formula for action. In this state the finest work is merely what it appears, whether we regard it as nothing but a certain number of signs on paper; or else, knowing how to read the signs, we are either unable or unwilling to communicate to our reading the amount of human energy needed to call forth, in the sensibility of a listener, the effects of resonance that I briefly described a moment ago. This work, which for the present is mere writing, has then only a virtual existence. It is a check drawn against the talent of a potential performer. It might also be compared to a machine which, if we neglect to apply the forces its constructor had in mind, is nothing more than an arbitrary assemblage of solid bodies.

A kind of paradox that is no paradox at all, will help you to understand my idea. If someone tells you *Virgil is a great poet*, you will be able to agree with him *in your heart*, and not just in principle, only if someone steps forward who can declaim the *Aeneid* for you after the manner of Virgil, and only if you are able to hear it with the ears of a contemporary and fellow citizen of the author.

It is up to the performer to find within himself the human energy, the intelligently directed forces that the constructor foresaw, the life, the accent, the sonorities that Racine or Mozart found in their being, and to apply them to the mechanism of a score or text. And all this, this essential part of the work, is not written. Nor can it be.

Indeed, texts or scores are only systems of conventional

signs, each one of which, each syllable or note, must arouse a corresponding action. The quality of each one of these acts, the quality of their continuity and mysterious interrelation, depends entirely on the performer who by his *action* transforms the *virtual* work into a *real* work.

But whereas in creating and setting down the virtual work, the creator employs only internal, intermittent, and oddly dispersed forces; whereas the whole of his being participates only irregularly and as it were incidentally in this specialized effort, the public performance of the work requires, on the contrary, the most unstinting expenditure of the whole person, a complete, direct, and sustained *action* in which all the performer's faculties are *present* in the highest degree. The creator counts his measures at leisure, his voice, though feeble or off pitch, suffices to sketch out the most complicated melodies as no more than a murmur hovering on the borderline between dream and form, without concern for high notes or low notes, or for the difficulty of the arabesques, for it will be up to others to sing them aloud and bring out their beauty. But the fate of what he thus composes is dependent on the action that will give the work to the world. A work that has taken years to complete is at the mercy of a performance, successful or not, that takes up scarcely an hour. In these critical moments, the work becomes *real*; it becomes all action, but the action depends on a person, and if the work is a new one, the function of that person becomes all-important. It is the performer who gives the public its first impressions of a work still unknown: it is up to him to see that it is understood or accepted, that it starts on its career with all the advantages it can derive from a performer's talent, taste, devotion, and feeling for, or knowledge of, his audience. And so the performer cannot be denied a certain freedom and initiative, the limits of which are impossible to define.

On this point I should like to make an observation that strikes me as quite interesting: namely, that there is no work, however fine, that is not susceptible of a wide variety of interpretations, all equally plausible. The richness of a work of art consists in the number of meanings or values it can assume, while still remaining itself.

Thus a virtuoso is one who, by definition, gives life and real presence to what was merely a piece of writing at the mercy of all and sundry, and of their ignorance, awkwardness, or inadequate comprehension. The virtuoso makes the work flesh. . . .

Philosophy of the Dance

BEFORE Mme Argentina captivates you and whirls you away into the sphere of lucid, passionate life created by her art; before she demonstrates to you what a folk art, born of an ardent and sensitive race, can become when the intelligence takes hold of it, penetrates it, and transforms it into a sovereign means of expression and invention, you will have to resign yourselves to listening to a few observations on the art of the dance by a man who is no dancer.

You will have to wait a little while for the moment of the miracle. But you are quite aware, I am sure, that I am no less impatient than you are to be carried away by it.

Let me begin at once by telling you without preamble that to my mind the dance is not merely an exercise, an entertainment, an ornamental art, or sometimes a social activity; it is a serious matter and in certain of its aspects most venerable. Every epoch that has understood the human body and experienced at least some sense of its mystery, its resources, its limits, its combinations of energy and sensibility, has cultivated and revered the dance.

It is a fundamental art, as is suggested if not demonstrated by its universality, its immemorial antiquity, the solemn uses to which it has been put, the ideas and reflections it has engendered at all times. For the dance is an art derived from life itself, since it is nothing more nor less than the action of the whole human body; but an action transposed into a world, into a kind of *space-time*, which is no longer quite the same as that of everyday life.

Man perceived that he possessed more vigor, more suppleness, more articular and muscular possibilities, than he needed to satisfy the needs of his existence, and he discovered that certain of these movements, by their frequency, succession, or range, gave him a pleasure equivalent to a kind of intoxication and sometimes so intense that only total exhaustion, an ecstasy of exhaustion, as it were, could interrupt his delirium, his frantic motor expenditure.

We have, then, too much energy for our needs. You can easily observe that most, by far the most, of the impressions we receive from our senses are of no use to us, that they cannot be utilized and play no part in the functioning of the mechanisms essential to the conservation of life. We see too many things and hear too many things that we do nothing and *can* do nothing with: the words of a lecturer, for instance.

The same observation applies to our powers of action: we can perform a multitude of acts that have no chance of being utilized in the indispensable, or important, operations of life. We can trace a circle, give play to our facial muscles, walk in cadence; all these actions, which made it possible to create geometry, the drama, and the military art, are in themselves useless, useless to our vital functioning.

Thus life's instruments of relation, our senses, our articulated members, the images and signs which control our actions and the distribution of our energies, co-ordinating the movements of our puppet, might be employed solely for our physiological needs; they might do nothing more than attack the environment in which we live or defend us against it, and then their sole business would be the preservation of our existence.

We might lead a life strictly limited to the maintenance of our living machine, utterly indifferent or insensitive to everything that plays no part in the cycles of transformation which make up our organic functioning; feeling nothing and doing nothing beyond what is necessary, making no move that is not a limited reaction, a finite response, to some external action. For our useful acts are finite. They carry us from one state to another.

Animals do not seem to perceive or do anything that is useless. A dog's eye sees the stars, no doubt, but his being gives no development to the sight. The dog's ear perceives a sound that makes it prick up in alarm; but of this sound the dog assimilates only what he needs in order to respond with an immediate and uniform act. He does not dwell on the perception. The cow in her pasture jumps at the clatter of the passing Mediterranean Express; the train vanishes; she does not pursue the train in her thoughts; she goes back to her tender grass, and her lovely eyes do not follow the departing train. The index of her brain returns at once to zero.

Yet sometimes animals seem to amuse themselves. Cats obviously play with mice. Monkeys perform pantomimes. Dogs chase each other, spring at the heads of horses; and I can think of nothing that suggests free, happy play more fully than the sporting of porpoises we see off shore, leaping free of the water, diving, outracing a ship, swimming under its keel and reappearing in the foam, livelier than the waves amid which they glisten and change color in the sun. Might we not call this a dance?

But all these animal amusements may be interpreted as useful actions, bursts of impulse, springing from the need to consume excess energy, or to maintain the organs designed for vital offense or defense in a state of suppleness or vigor. And I think I am justified in observing that those species, such as the ants and the bees, that seem to be most exactly constructed, endowed with the most specialized instincts, also seem to be those most saving of their time. Ants do not waste a minute. The spider does not play in its web; it lurks in wait. But what about man?

Man is the singular animal who watches himself live, puts a value on himself, and identifies this value with the importance he attaches to useless perceptions and acts without vital physical consequence.

Pascal situated all our dignity in thought; but the thinking that raises us—in our own eyes—above our sensory condition is precisely the kind of thinking that has no useful purpose. Obviously our meditations about the origin of things, or about death, are of no use to the organism; and indeed, exalted thoughts of this kind tend to be harmful if not fatal to our species. Our deepest thoughts are those that are the most insignificant, the most futile as it were, from the standpoint of self-preservation.

But because our curiosity was greater than it had any need to be, and our activity more intense than any vital aim required, both have developed to the point of inventing the arts, the sciences, universal problems, and of producing objects, forms, actions that we could easily have dispensed with.

And moreover, all this free, gratuitous invention and production, all this play of our senses and faculties, gradually provided itself with a kind of *necessity* and *utility*.

Art and science, each in its own way, tend to build up a kind of utility from the useless, a kind of necessity from the arbitrary. Ultimately, artistic creation is not so much a creation of works as the creation of a *need for works*; for works are products, a supply presupposing a demand, a need.

Quite a bit of philosophy, you may think . . . and I admit that I've given you rather too much of it. But when one is not a dancer; when one would be at a loss not only to perform, but even to explain, the slightest step; when, to deal with the miracles wrought by the legs, one has only the resources of a head, there's no help but in a certain amount of philosophy—in other words, one approaches the matter from far off, in the hope that distance will dispel the difficulties. It is much simpler to construct a universe than to explain how a man stands on his feet—as Aristotle, Descartes, Leibnitz, and quite a few others will tell you.

However, it seems perfectly legitimate for a philosopher to watch a dancer in action, and noting that he takes pleasure in it, to try to derive from his pleasure the secondary pleasure of expressing his impressions in his own language.

But first, he may derive some fine images from it. Philosophers have a great taste for images: there is no trade that requires more of them, although philosophers often hide them under dull-gray words. They have created famous ones: the cave; the sinister river you can never cross twice; or Achilles running breathlessly after a tortoise he can never overtake. The parallel mirrors, runners passing on the torch to one another, down to Nietzsche with his eagle, his serpent, his tight-rope dancer. All in all quite a stock of them, quite a pageant of ideas. Think of the metaphysical ballet that might be composed with all these famous symbols.

My philosopher, however, does not content himself with this performance. What, in the presence of the dance and the dancer, can he do to give himself the illusion of knowing a little more than she about something that she knows best, and he not at all? He is compelled to make up for his technical ignorance and hide his perplexity under some ingenious universal interpretation of this art whose wonders he notes and experiences.

He embarks on the task; he goes about it in his own fashion. . . . The fashion of a philosopher. Everyone knows how his dance begins. . . . His first faint step is a *question*. And as befits a man undertaking a useless, arbitrary act, he throws himself into it without foreseeing the end; he embarks on an unlimited interrogation in the interrogative infinitive. That is his trade.

He plays his game, beginning with its usual beginning. And there he is, asking himself:

"What then is the dance?"

What then is the dance? At once he is perplexed, his wits are paralyzed. He is reminded of a famous question, a famous dilemma—that of St. Augustine.

St. Augustine confesses how he asked himself one day what Time is; and he owns that he perfectly well knew as long as he did not think of asking, but that he lost himself at the crossroads of his mind as soon as he applied himself to the term, as soon as he isolated it from any immediate usage or particular expression. A very profound observation. . . .

That is what my philosopher has come to: he stands hesitant on the forbidding threshold that separates a question from an answer, obsessed by the memory of St. Augustine, dreaming in his penumbra of the great saint's perplexity:

"What is Time? But what is the dance?"

But, he tells himself, the dance after all is merely a form of time, the creation of a kind of time, or of a very distinct and singular species of time.

Already he is less worried: he has wedded two difficulties to each other. Each one, taken separately, left him perplexed and without resources; but now they are linked together. Perhaps their union will be fertile. Perhaps some ideas may be born of it, and that is just what he is after—his vice and his plaything.

Now he watches the dancer with the extraordinary, ultra-lucid eyes that transform everything they see into a prey of the abstract mind. He considers the spectacle and deciphers it in his own way.

It seems to him that this person who is dancing encloses herself as it were in a time that she engenders, a time consisting entirely of immediate energy, of nothing that can last. She is the unstable element, she squanders instability, she goes beyond the impossible and overdoes the improbable; and by denying the ordinary state of things, she creates in men's minds the idea of another, exceptional state—a state that is all action, a permanence built up and consolidated by an incessant effort, comparable to the vibrant pose of a bumblebee or moth exploring the calyx of a flower, charged with motor energy, sustained in virtual immobility by the incredibly swift beat of its wings.

Or our philosopher may just as well compare the dancer to a flame or, for that matter, to any phenomenon that is visibly sustained by the intense consumption of a superior energy.

He also notes that, in the dance, all the sensations of the body, which is both mover and moved, are connected in a certain order—that they call and respond to each other, as though rebounding or being reflected from the invisible wall of a sphere of energy within the living being. Forgive me that outrageously bold expression, I can find no other. But you knew before you came here that I am an obscure and complicated writer. . . .

Confronted by the dance, my philosopher—or a mind afflicted with a mania for interrogation, if you prefer—asks his usual questions. He brings in his *whys* and *hows*, the customary instruments of elucidation, which are the apparatus of his own art; and he tries, as you have just perceived, to replace the immediate and expedient expression of things by rather odd formulas which enable him to relate the graceful phenomenon of the dance to the whole of what he knows, or thinks he knows.

He attempts to fathom the mystery of a body which suddenly, as though by the effect of an internal shock, enters into a kind of life that is at once strangely unstable and strangely regulated, strangely spontaneous, but at the same time strangely contrived and, assuredly, planned.

The body seems to have broken free from its usual states of balance. It seems to be trying to outwit—I should say outrace—its own weight, at every moment evading its pull, not to say its sanction.

In general, it assumes a fairly simple periodicity that seems to maintain itself automatically; it seems endowed with a superior elasticity which retrieves the impulse of every movement and at once renews it. One is reminded of a top, standing on its point and reacting so sensitively to the slightest shock.

But here is an important observation that comes to the mind of our philosopher, who might do better to enjoy himself to the full and abandon himself to what he sees. He observes that the dancing body seems unaware of its surroundings. It seems to be concerned only with itself and one other object, a very important one, from which it breaks free, to which it returns, but only to gather the wherewithal for another flight. . . .

That object is the earth, the ground, the solid place, the plane on which everyday life plods along, the plane of walking, the prose of human movement.

Yes, the dancing body seems unaware of everything else, it seems to know nothing of its surroundings. It seems to hearken to itself and only to itself, to see nothing, as though its eyes were jewels, unknown jewels like those of which Baudelaire speaks, lights that serve no useful purpose.

For the dancer is in another world; no longer the world that takes color from our gaze, but one that she weaves with her steps and builds with her gestures. And in that world acts have no outward aim; there is no object to grasp, to attain, to repulse or run away from, no object which puts a precise end to an action and gives movements first an outward direction and co-ordination, then a clear and definite conclusion.

But that is not all: in this world nothing is unforeseen; though the dancer sometimes seems to be reacting to an unforeseen incident, that too is part of a very evident plan.Everything happens as if. . . . But nothing more.

Thus there is no aim, no real incidents, no outside world. . . .

The philosopher exults. No outside world! For the dancer there is no outside. . . . Nothing exists beyond the system she sets up by her acts—one is reminded of the diametrically contrary and no less closed system constituted by our sleep, whose exactly opposite law is the abolition of all acts, total abstention from action.

He sees the dance as an artificial somnambulism, a group

of sensations which make themselves a dwelling place where certain muscular themes follow one another in an order which creates a special kind of time that is absolutely its own. And with an increasingly *intellectual* delight he contemplates this being who, from her very depths, brings forth these beautiful transformations of her form in space; who now moves, but without really going anywhere; now metamorphoses herself on the spot, displaying herself in every aspect; who sometimes skillfully modulates successive appearances as though in controlled phases; sometimes changes herself brusquely into a whirlwind, spinning faster and faster, then suddenly stops, crystallized into a statue, adorned with an alien smile.

But this detachment from the environment, this absence of aim, this negation of explicable movement, these full turns (which no circumstance of ordinary life demands of our body), even this impersonal smile—all these features are radically opposed to those that characterize our action in the practical world and our relations with it.

In the practical world our being is nothing more than an intermediary between the sensation of a need and the impulse to satisfy the need. In this role, it proceeds always by the most economical, if not always the shortest, path: it wants results. Its guiding principles seem to be the straight line, the least action, and the shortest time. A practical man is a man who has an instinct for such economy of time and effort, and has little difficulty in putting it into effect, because his aim is definite and clearly localized: *an external object.*

As we have said, the dance is the exact opposite. It moves in a self-contained realm of its own and implies no reason, no tendency toward completion. A formula for pure dance should include nothing to suggest that it has an end. It is terminated by outside events; its limits in time are not intrinsic to it; the duration of the dance is limited by the conventional length of the program, by fatigue or loss of interest. But the dance itself has nothing to make it end. It ceases as a dream ceases that might go on indefinitely: it stops, not because an undertaking has been completed, for there is no undertaking, but because something else, something outside it has been exhausted.

And so—permit me to put it rather boldly—might one not—and I have already intimated as much—consider the dance as a kind of *inner life*, allowing that psychological term a new meaning in which physiology is dominant?

An inner life, indeed, but one consisting entirely in sensations of time and energy which respond to one another and form a kind of closed circle of resonance. This resonance, like any other, is communicated: a part of our pleasure as spectators consists in feeling ourselves possessed by the rhythms so that we ourselves are virtually dancing.

Carried a little further, this sort of philosophy of the dance can lead to some rather curious consequences or applications. If, in speaking of this art, I have kept to considerations of a very general nature, it has been somewhat with the intention of guiding you to what we are now coming to. I have tried to communicate a rather abstract idea of the dance and to represent it above all as an action that *derives* from ordinary, useful action, but *breaks away* from it, and finally *opposes* it.

But this very general formulation (and that is why I have adopted it today) covers far more than the dance in the strict sense. All action which does not tend toward utility and which on the other hand can be trained, perfected, developed, may be subsumed under this simplified notion of the dance, and consequently, *all the arts can be considered as particular examples of this general idea*, since by definition all the arts imply an element of action, the *action which produces*, or else manifests, the *work*.

A *poem*, for example, is *action*, because a poem exists only at the moment of being spoken; then it is *in actu*. This act, like the dance, has no other purpose than to create a state of mind; it imposes its own laws; it, too, creates a time and a measurement of time which are appropriate and essential to it: we cannot distinguish it from its form of time. To recite poetry is to enter into a verbal dance.

Or consider a virtuoso at work, a violinist, a pianist. Just watch his hands. Stop your ears if you dare. But concentrate on the hands. Watch them act, racing over the narrow stage that is the keyboard. Are they not dancers who have also been subjected for years to a severe discipline, to endless exercises?

Remember that you can hear nothing. You merely see the hands come and go, stop for a moment, cross, play leapfrog; sometimes one waits, while the five fingers of the other seem to be trying out their paces at the other end of the racecourse of ivory and ebony. You begin to surmise that all this follows certain laws, that the whole ballet is regulated, determined. . . .

Let us note in passing that if you hear nothing and are unfamiliar with the music being played, you have no way of knowing what point in his piece the performer has come to. *What you see* gives you *no indication* of the pianist's progress; yet you are quite certain that the action in which he is engaged is at every moment subject to some rather complex system. . . .

With a little more attention you would discover that this system puts certain restrictions on the freedom of movement of these active hands as they fly over the keyboard. Whatever they do, they seem to have undertaken to respect some sort of continuous order. Cadence, measure, rhythm make themselves felt. I do not wish to enter into these questions which, it seems to me, though familiar and without difficulty in practice, have hitherto lacked any satisfactory theory; but then that is true of all questions in which time is directly involved. We are brought back to the remarks of St. Augustine.

But it is easy to note that all automatic movements corresponding to a state of being, and not to a prefigured localized aim, take on a periodic character; this is true of the walker; of the absent-minded fellow who swings his foot or drums on a windowpane; of the thinker who strokes his chin, etc.

If you will bear with me for a few minutes more, we shall carry our thought a little further: a little further beyond the customary, immediate idea of the dance.

I was just saying that all the arts are extremely varied forms of action and may be analyzed in terms of action. Consider an artist at work, eliminate the brief intervals when he sets it aside; watch him act, stop still, and briskly start in again.

Assume that he is so well trained, so sure of his technique that while you are observing him he is a pure executant whose successive operations tend to take place in commensurable lapses of time, that is to say, with a certain *rhythm*. Then you will be able to conceive that the execution of a work of art, of a work of painting or sculpture, is itself a work of art and that its material object, the product of the artist's fingers, is only a pretext, a stage "prop" or, as it were, the subject of the ballet.

Perhaps this view seems bold to you. But remember that for many great artists a work is never finished; perhaps what they regard as a desire for perfection is simply a form of the inner life I have been speaking of, which consists entirely of energy and sensibility in a reciprocal and, one might say, reversible exchange.

Or think, on the other hand, of those edifices that the ancients built, to the rhythm of the flute commanding the movements of the files of laborers and masons.

I might have told you the curious story related in the *Journal* of the Goncourt brothers, about the Japanese painter who, on a visit to Paris, was asked by them to execute a few works in the presence of a little gathering of art lovers.*

But it is high time to conclude this dance of ideas round the living dance.

I wanted to show you how this art, far from being a futile amusement, far from being a specialty confined to putting on a show now and then for the amusement of the eyes that contemplate it or the bodies that take part in it, is quite simply *a poetry that encompasses the action of living creatures in its entirety*: it isolates and develops, distinguishes and deploys the essential characteristics of this action, and makes the dancer's body into an object whose transformations and successive aspects, whose striving to attain the limits that each instant sets upon the powers of being, inevitably remind us of the task the poet imposes on his mind, the difficulties he sets before it, the metamorphoses he obtains from it, the flights he expects of it— flights which remove him, sometimes too far, from the ground, from reason, from the average notion of logic and common sense.

What is a metaphor if not a kind of pirouette performed

* Valéry tells the story in "Reflections on Art," pp. 159–60 above.—J. M.

by an idea, enabling us to assemble its diverse names or images? And what are all the figures we employ, all those instruments, such as rhyme, inversion, antithesis, if not an exercise of all the possibilities of language, which removes us from the practical world and shapes, for us too, a private universe, a privileged abode of the intellectual dance?

And now let me give you over, weary of words but all the more eager for sensuous enchantment and effortless pleasure, to art itself, to the flame, to the ardent and subtle action of Mme Argentina.

You know what prodigies of comprehension and invention this great artist has achieved, what she has done for Spanish dancing. As for me, who have spoken to you only of the dance in the abstract—and too abundantly at that—I cannot tell you how much I admire the labor of intelligence with which Argentina, in a noble and deeply studied style, has revived a type of folk dance that has been so much cheapened lately, especially outside of Spain.

I think she has achieved her aim, a magnificent aim, since it meant saving an art form and regenerating its nobility and legitimate power, by an infinitely subtle analysis both of the resources of this type of art, and of her own resources. That is something very close to me, that concerns me passionately. I am a man who has never seen a contradiction— indeed, I cannot conceive of one—between intelligence and sensibility, conscious reflection and its raw material, and I salute Argentina, as a man who is precisely as pleased with her as he would like to be with himself.

The Physical Aspects of a Book

A BOOK is a singular object, an open and shut thing which changes its nature completely in that simple act.

I open it: it speaks. I close it and it becomes a thing to be looked at. Thus more than anything else in the world, it resembles a man. At first approach, a man is his form and color; next his voice strikes us, and finally his voice is transformed into a mind that mingles with our own.

Like a man, a book has its physical aspect, its visible and tangible exterior which can be as ordinary or individual, as ugly or pleasing, as insignificant or remarkable as that of any member of our species. As for its voice, which is heard the moment the book opens, does it not reside in the appearance of the page, the paper it is made of, the type face used, the spacing, and the quality of the make-up? Yet this voice like any other is often deceptive: when we begin to read and the spirit of the text is revealed, it may well spoil the favorable impression made by a first glance.

The binder's task is to fashion the physical aspect of a *closed* book. First of all he gives it a body with a system of joints that will withstand the strains resulting from the way a book is likely to be handled. Thus the bookbinder's craft is clearly defined. It consists of mechanical operations quite independent of what I have called the book's spirit and voice. A man can bind a work without knowing what it is; he need not even know how to read. As for the person who makes use of the book, he will be concerned only with its utility, sturdiness, and price. The book, taken as an object, responds to a clear and simple need, concerning which craftsman and purchaser can be in complete agreement; but thus far, hand and eye have only played a subordinate, commonplace role. Yet our senses have their own life and make their own particular demands. As soon as the eye takes an independent interest in the *book as an object*, the art of binding becomes distinct from the craft. It is an art that can be practiced on different levels.

For several years in my youth, I was preoccupied by the problem of ornament. Nothing gave me more food for reflection than the spontaneous appearance, everywhere, of this very primitive form of production, developing like richly diversified vegetation, overgrowing everything—tools, utensils, buildings, weapons, or garments—and changing with climate and race; while concomitantly the mysterious instinct for representing beings and things, no less ancient and inborn, dating in fact from prehistoric times, emerged and asserted itself in wonderful pictures of men and animals.

It would seem that our eye cannot tolerate a bare and empty surface or endure the freedom to wander over an area of uniform color, and that, doing so, it provokes us to an active reaction whose purpose it is to summon into existence, on that too-naked surface, something *our eye would like to see there*. This is a universal phenomenon, and constitutes no doubt a law of our sensibility. A man alone, with nothing to do, reacts against the boredom of idleness. Memories, songs, or a story invented for one's own pleasure, perhaps even a philosophy—such are the products of the freedom from all need to act for practical ends.

But here a marvelous combination sets in. Boredom, leisure, and vacant time on the one hand, and the empty surface on the other beget an action. At first it is monotonous: sheer repetition, simple parallel lines, a sprinkling of dots, serial foliations, the whole of which will transform the surface on which they appear, slyly introducing a sense of richness and abundance by the mere repetition of the same humble motif. In the same way a small plant, sprung up on a vacant ground of gray or tawny dust, multiplies and repeats itself, quickly transforming the landscape, populating it, filling it with color and bloom, making it responsive to winds and hospitable to flocks.

What our eye would like to see. . . .

Such is the pure and simple principle of ornament. The eye knows nothing. It is not the eye that recognizes *objects* and their uses in the blotches of color and light it receives. It is as ignorant, at first, of meanings and acquired knowledge as the ear to the import of a speech in a foreign tongue, whose music alone has a certain power and may or may not command attention. It is by starting from this state of innocence that art becomes creative and, through its need to look on what it loves, discovers a whole world of its own—the world of symmetry, contrast, gradation, chiaroscuro, modulation, and resemblance—a vibrant, self-sufficient world in which desire can create what it lacks, provided only. . . .

There is no certainty that this desire will be satisfied, unless it is content with a moment of reverie: but in that case *the thirst of our senses is not quenched.* To offer the eye that strange and somewhat mystical food that we call enjoyment, action must be brought to bear; the hand and the material it works on, both force and resistance, will be needed to create in its full reality an object or arrangement resembling no other, serving no practical purpose, and explicable only in terms of a pleasure to be produced—that is, if pleasure can be said to explain anything.

Art is an act; but an act of a very special kind, which is far from being completely determined by any given external conditions; nor is it determined by vital utility or necessity. On the one hand, *uselessness* is one of its positive characteristics; on the other, its medium is the arbitrary, and victory over the arbitrary is its triumph. I was trying to express this same idea, which strikes me as essential, when I wrote that the artist's aim and endeavor are to create a *necessity* and a *utility* of a *second kind*. A visible object which makes us aware, first, *that it might not have existed* (since its nonexistence would have meant no vital loss), and secondly, *that it could not have been other than it is*: such an object we declare to be *beautiful*.

Obviously this kind of perception and the creative act that produces it are the two mysterious characteristics that distinguish human from animal nature, and human beings themselves from each other according to their capacity for desiring, perceiving, and creating objects of this distinct class. Animals do nothing useless, even at play. Their play is so closely bound up with their nature that it never gets lost in vain gropings nor ends in mistakes and disappointments, as so often happens with men when they are playing the game of art. Artists are fallible, indeed the most fallible of all makers. Everything that shows a happy result to be an uncertain and even inexplicable thing puts the idea of automatism further from the mind.

This last statement, however, must be reconciled with what we suggested a moment ago, which may be summed up as follows: ornament, we said, is a spontaneous product of the sensibility of one of our senses when it reacts freely to a blank space and tends to a self-induced activity within the field of its own potentialities. In the field of vision, for example, the whole range of colors will develop from complementary to complementary, or else it will run through imperceptible transitions from shade to shade and tone to tone. In the same way, primary rhythms are born in the realm of movement. But all this is automatic. The will is absent. At first that central, dominant authority holds itself aloof. Man creates absent-mindedly, hums a tune of which he is not conscious, weaves strands of color without thinking. Since there is virtually no intermediary between his senses and his organs of action, the operation proceeds without stoppage or delay. But if something calls his attention to the result of this free, mechanical amusement—by which I mean that there is nothing to disturb its organic mechanism—he may reflect on what he was doing and conceive the idea of making something more of it. It is then that the problems of art make their appearance. These problems may be subsumed under two opposed kinds of difficulty: the one resulting from the inalienable *freedom* of the mind as it confronts an undertaking that is far from being fully defined—in which there is no necessity, but rather a multiplicity of possibilities formed and transformed by the excited imagination; the other consisting in the *constraints* imposed by real action and other conditions of a material or conventional order.

Consider a rectangle. This surface, the commonest of all those the decorative mind has to deal with, must be filled. Let us say a door, a wall, a panel, the sides of a chest, a title page, or finally, the *flat cover of a book*. What's to be done? The dimensions (I assume) are given. The material as well. What's to be done? Here is an empty space, which means freedom. Proportions and material—and sometimes certain conventions— are imposed: these are the constraints. This is the moment of perplexity. It is now that freedom becomes the main obstacle. How is this indeterminate state to be overcome? The first obstacle to action is the absence of obstacles.

A simple, immediate idea is to define the rectangle by drawing its principal lines, its diagonals, and the lines bisecting its sides. Possibly this elementary decoration, varyingly emphasized, will be thought sufficient. Or perhaps, in accordance with the same geometrical process, a lozenge will be inscribed within the rectangle; the lozenge may suggest an ellipse, for which it offers the axes.

But so far we have no more than a flight from invention, a confession, as it were, of helplessness or self-distrust. Then a great temptation sets in. Memory intervenes. *What we already know* comes back to us, more or less insidiously, and sometimes very speciously disguised, offering ready-made decorative themes. You cannot do better, whispers the demon of facility, you must follow the masters, don't be afraid of looking up the records. . . . I do not mean that proven values should be ignored; that would be a sort of suicide in advance; to despise is to teach others to despise. Nor should those values be used as a springboard for an ingenious attempt to do the exact opposite—which happens all too often. "Counter-imitation" is worse than imitation. But the true affirmation of a complete artist consists in the penetrating knowledge of earlier works, which can deduce the *ideal* and, in a way, the "moral" from them.

It was necessary to recall all this before approaching the book-binder's art. As I remarked a moment ago, this art in practice has its different levels. These are obviously determined (I am referring not to the technical realization, which I assume to be excellent, but to the *conception* of the task) by the *artist's idea of the scope of his art*. Some pay no attention to what they are decorating, and undeniably there are purely external master-pieces, magnificently decorated covers in vellum, morocco, or calf on books of no particular interest. Such a cover, un-related to its content, can be reproduced indefinitely and used for all manner of books. (Sometimes it may bear its owner's imprint, which, as we know, can give rise to ex-tremely fine or even unique ornamentation: coats of arms, mottoes, symbols, etc. Certain bindings carry the purely his-torical value of having belonged to a famous man. But this has nothing to do with the art in question.) In all the cases I have mentioned, the artist-binder has been concerned solely with the exterior of the book; there is no relation between the body and the soul: once the volume is opened and begins to speak, the binding ceases to exist.

In this connection I might mention a few oddities. I remember seeing and—with a certain horror—daring to handle a ritual of black magic, or perhaps it was the text of a black mass, bound in human skin; a frightful object—there was still a tuft of hair on the back of it. All aesthetic questions apart, there was a very evident kinship between the grisly exterior and the diabolical content of this abominable book.

And now for another and very different example, show-ing the absurd lengths to which even the most distinguished collector may go when the desire for rarity leads him to for-get the basic function of a book and the binding fitted to it.

After having the first editions of his friends' works bound in parchment, Edmond de Goncourt had their portraits painted on the covers by the artists he considered most appropriate to the sitters: for Daudet, Carrière, for Zola, Raffaelli, etc. Since the books could not bear the slightest handling without damage, they were condemned to sit eternally in a glass case. . . . Is that what a real book is meant for? It must be admitted, in any case, that collectors have a penchant for the ridiculous. Books on "handmade paper" with deckle edges are the ugliest and silliest things in the world. This preposterous and unauthentic striving for "authenticity" could only have been thought desirable at a time when taste was corrupt. True taste calls for a kind of balance between *all* the qualities of a book.

The investigations of M. Paul Bonet and their results give the impression of a will to attain that highest point of art to which I have alluded, and which, as I have written (and even taught), resides in the successful participation of *all* of a man's faculties in his work.

M. Bonet has understood and striven to show that the physical aspect of a book should draw its inspiration and its reason for being as it is from what that book will say when it is opened—as though the mind, the style, the inner life which are about to communicate themselves to the eye, the lips, the intellect of the reader, were prefigured in the outward covering.

It should not be supposed that the problem is simple and can be tackled without risk. I own that it admits of facile solutions. And there are grotesque ones as well. The leather can be stamped with emblems, sometimes with actual illustrations relating to the text. Blunders and monstrosities of this kind are by no means rare. But our artist has proceeded along very different paths, the *subtle* paths of analogy.

Between the face and the voice of a book it is not similarities that should be striven for, but rather what Baudelaire (in a somewhat Swedenborgian sense) called "correspondences." While the illustrations for a book (for example) derive from the text by a sort of direct translation, and as though by a clearly defined process, the appropriate ornamentation should spring from the text by a kind of *sympathetic vibration*, requiring of whoever masters this art a highly refined sensibility equipped with all that can respond to the moving power of a text and transpose it into creative action.

From this point of view, the development of M. Bonet's style is most instructive. From one work to the next, we note a certain process of paring down, a transformation of requirements, a reduction in the number of methods in favor of the development of a few and the positive enrichment resulting from a deeper knowledge of their effects. That is the *classical* method par excellence. The approach to perfection in literature is marked, as we know, by a stripping of the vocabulary; the number of words used diminishes, but the number of their different uses increases: and this shrinkage of "material" emphasizes an enlargement of the mind's real resources, of its ability to simplify and combine.

M. Bonet seems today to be turning away from the leather mosaic—not very much to my taste, I confess—which was once in great favor; by the use of gold tooling, fillets, and stippling, whose possibilities one might have thought exhausted, he achieves compositions far more novel and attractive, to my mind, than those involving a variety of colors. Some of his compositions, apparently based on some extremely subtle geometry, seem to me to open up entirely new perspectives in the bookbinder's art. I have long suspected that the decorative arts might find hitherto untapped resources in certain diagrams constructed by physicists; I am thinking particularly of the configurations of "fields of force." There is a highly interesting future in this direction; but whatever the riches offered by the exploitation of this field of mathematics, it must be subjected to and closely assimilated by the laws of taste and creative sensibility.

I must not forget a particular instance of M. Bonet's talent which I have greatly appreciated. Only too often the lettering on the finest of bindings is clumsy, blurred, devoid of style. In my opinion, one of this artist's greatest merits is the care he takes to design characters whose elegance and clarity harmonize with the work as a whole. It is with those words, *the work as a whole*, that I should have liked to conclude these few lines bearing witness to my esteem and admiration for an undertaking and for achievements testifying to the highest ideals. The determination to give a book its fullest value, to give it a form that will be, in a manner of speaking, a visible personality in keeping with its potential personality, is the loftiest aim that the bookbinder can set himself.

But how can I stop without a word for the charming boards designed by M. Bonet for trade editions? The public appears to be very pleased with them. As for myself, some of whose books have been bound in these covers of clear and delicate design, I confess that I am delighted at times to the point of being tempted to reread myself.

Art and Technology

OUR LIFE would be hardly conceivable without a number of minutely subdivided specializations or "techniques," all quite "scientifically" developed. Almost every object we make use of has required the collaboration of several sciences and a good deal of painstaking study; many of them have been perfected by meticulous experiments in laboratories equipped with the most delicate physical and chemical apparatus, and frequently the manufacturing process is checked with the help of precision instruments. The economic function of these objects, the marketing, the display, the pricing, etc., are no less carefully organized, by methods as strict as the nature of the article and the means of statistical forecasting permit.

I wonder if anyone has ever tried to find out how many engineers and specialists of various kinds are now required, at every stage of the process, to produce a kettle or a cooking pot, whereas formerly the whole thing was done by a single artisan.

If a similar curiosity should prompt us to inquire what articles are still made in our time (in the highly "civilized" countries) without the scientific refinements, the co-ordination of multiple effort, the impersonal labor, and the uniform production characteristic of modern technology, we should find first a few unimportant "handicrafts," and then that group of essentially useless, extremely uncertain and anarchic activities which we call the *arts*.

This brings me to the observation I wished to make.

Whereas technology is invading every branch of human activity, substituting its innumerable subdivisions and its objective methods for the personal and complex operations of the individual, making itself felt in sports, pharmacology, cattle breeding, and warfare alike; whereas today technology even enters into men's choice of a career (and tomorrow, no doubt, will play a part in the reproduction of the species)—it would seem that the arts, quite on the contrary, have freed themselves from exact requirements, that they have come to dispense with long preparation, preliminary training, or apprenticeship of any kind; that empiricism, purely impulsive action, production by emotion, have triumphed at the expense of the perfection, duration, and consistency of the finished work. What I call the "consistency" of a work is the sum of the qualities which enable it to stand up to scrutiny and withstand the efforts of a mind determined to analyze it away. To my mind, a work is ruined if it gives the sense that any part of it might be changed without effort or any great damage. Against this destructive agency, that is to say, the "ease of unmaking" suggested by the "*evident ease of the making*," centuries of practice in the various arts had set up defenses: methods, constraints, or conventions, some tending toward the material preservation of the work, others toward the perfecting of its detail or substance, the production of a precious object; still others imposed formal conditions, sometimes arbitrary in themselves, but which, widely accepted and established once and for all, took on the force of law, borrowing from widespread habit, transmitted from generation to generation, its natural power of resistance to change. Moreover, the arts suffered less because of this emphasis on their "techniques" than they do today from value judgments run rampant; from the very first, discussion and criticism had something positive to work with. There were true "masters," a true criticism, true models: none of which exists today. . . .

The Conquest of Ubiquity

OUR FINE ARTS were developed, their types and uses were established, in times very different from the present, by men whose power of action upon things was insignificant in comparison with ours. But the amazing growth of our techniques, the adaptability and precision they have attained, the ideas and habits they are creating, make it a certainty that profound changes are impending in the ancient craft of the Beautiful. In all the arts there is a physical component which can no longer be considered or treated as it used to be, which cannot remain unaffected by our modern knowledge and power. For the last twenty years neither matter nor space nor time has been what it was from time immemorial. We must expect great innovations to transform the entire technique of the arts, thereby affecting artistic invention itself and perhaps even bringing about an amazing change in our very notion of art.

At first, no doubt, only the reproduction and transmission of works of art will be affected. It will be possible to send anywhere or to re-create anywhere a system of sensations, or more precisely a system of stimuli, provoked by some object or event in any given place. Works of art will acquire a kind of ubiquity. We shall only have to summon them and there they will be, either in their living actuality or restored from the past. They will not merely exist in themselves but will exist wherever someone with a certain apparatus happens to be. A work of art will cease to be anything more than a kind of source or point of origin whose benefits will be available—and quite fully so—wherever we wish. Just as water, gas, and electricity are brought into our houses from far off to satisfy our needs in response to a minimal effort, so we shall be supplied with visual or auditory images, which will appear and disappear at a simple movement of the hand, hardly more than a sign. Just as we are accustomed, if not enslaved, to the various forms of energy that pour into our homes, we shall find it perfectly natural to receive the ultrarapid variations or oscillations that our sense organs gather in and integrate to form all we know. I do not know whether a philosopher has ever dreamed of a company engaged in the home delivery of Sensory Reality.

Of all the arts, music is nearest to this transposition into the modern mode. Its very nature and the place it occupies in our world mark it as the first to be transformed in its methods of transmission, reproduction, and even production. It is of all the arts the most in demand, the most involved in social existence, the closest to life, whose organic functioning it animates, accompanies, or imitates. Whether it be a matter of speaking or walking, of meditation or action, of monotony or surprise in the temporal flow of our lives, music can take hold of us, combining and transfiguring the pace and sensory values of them all. It weaves us an artificial span of time by lightly touching the keys of our real life. We become accustomed to it, we give ourselves up to it as voluptuously as one might to the "just, subtle, and mighty" substances praised by Thomas De Quincey. Since it directly attacks the emotional mechanism, which it plays on and maneuvers at will, it is universal in essence; it delights the ear and sets people dancing the world over; like science it becomes an international need and commodity. This circumstance, taken in connection with recent progress in the means of transmission, suggested two technical problems:

I. To make a piece of music instantly audible at any point on the earth, regardless of where it is performed.

II. To reproduce a piece of music at will, anywhere on the globe and at any time.

These problems have been solved. The solutions are being further perfected every day.

We are still far from having controlled visual phenomena to the same degree. Color and relief are still rather resistant. A sunset on the Pacific, a Titian in Madrid cannot yet be enjoyed in our living room with the same force of illusion as a symphony.

That will happen some day. Perhaps they will do still better and find a way of showing us something of what goes on at the bottom of the sea. But as for the worlds of sounds, noises, voices, tonalities, they are already ours. We evoke them when and where we please. Formerly we could not enjoy music at our own time, according to our own mood. We were dependent for our enjoyment on an occasion, a place, a date, and a program. How many coincidences were needed! Today we are liberated from a servitude so contrary to pleasure and, by that same token, to the most sensitive appreciation of works of music. To be able to choose the moment of enjoyment, to savor the pleasure when not only our mind desires it, but our soul and whole being craves and as it were anticipates it, is to give the fullest scope to the composer's intention, for it permits his creatures to live again in a vibrant milieu not very different from that in which they were created. In recorded music the work of composer or performer finds the conditions essential to the most perfect aesthetic returns.

I am reminded here of a fairy play that, as a child, I saw in a foreign theater. Or perhaps I only fancy I saw it. In the Sorcerer's palace the furniture spoke and sang, took a poetic and mischievous part in the action. A door opening set off the piping or solemn tones of a village band. If anyone sat down on a pouf, it would sigh politely. At a touch everything breathed forth a melody.

I sincerely hope we are not moving toward such excesses in the magic of sound. Even now one can no longer eat or drink at a café without being disturbed by a concert. But it will be wonderfully pleasant to be able to transform at will an empty hour, an interminable evening, an endless Sunday, into an enchantment, an expression of tenderness, a flight of the spirit. Days can be gloomy; there are men and women who are very much alone, and many whom age or infirmity confines to their own company with which they are only too familiar. These men and women, reduced to boredom and gloom, can now fill their sad and useless hours with beauty or passion.

Such then are the first fruits offered us by the new intimacy between music and physics, whose immemorial alliance had already given us so much. We shall see many more.

Hypothesis

IN THE FUTURE, when a battle is fought anywhere in the world, it will be a perfectly simple matter for the sound of the cannon to be heard over the whole earth. The thunders of some future Verdun will then be *received* at the antipodes.

It will even be possible to see something of the fighting, to see, at an interval of only three hundredths of a second, men falling six thousand miles away.

But very likely still more powerful and intricate mechanisms will some day make it possible to act from a distance, not only on men's senses but also on the most hidden elements of the human psyche. By stimulating the system and very sources of men's mental and affective life, some remote and unseen operator will impose illusions, impulses, desires, and artificial disorders on their minds. Hitherto we have looked upon our conscious thoughts and powers as springing from a simple, constant origin; we have supposed that to each organism there attaches, from birth to death, a certain something, *indivisible*, autonomous, incomparable, and as some believe, eternal. We used to be under the impression that our deepest substance must be some absolute *activity*, and that in each one of us must reside some strange power to *begin*, a certain quantum of pure independence. But we are living in a prodigious era, an era in which the most widely accredited and seemingly self-evident ideas have been attacked, contra-dicted, undermined, and put to rout by *facts*, so much so that we are witnessing today a kind of bankruptcy of the imagina-tion and corruption of the intellect, for we are no longer capable of forming a self-consistent notion of the world, encompassing all the data, both old and new, of human experience.

This state of affairs permits me to hazard the hypothesis that some day it may be possible, by direct action from out-side, to modify what used to be man's mind and soul.

Perhaps our secret substance is secret only to certain ac-tions from outside; and perhaps it is only partially protected against external influences. Wood is opaque to the light per-ceived by our eyes, but not to more penetrating rays. Once such rays were discovered, our conception of transparency was completely changed. In view of the numerous examples of such transformations in our ideas and expectations, I ven-ture to believe that one day the expression "inner life" will be thought to have had relevance only for the *classical*, or if you prefer, *natural* means of *production* and *reception*.

Perhaps our *self* is insulated from the environment, pre-served from being *everything* or *anything*, in very much the same way as the movement of my watch in my watch pocket.

I presume—I actually *believe*—that it *keeps time* in spite of my comings and goings, my attitudes, the speed of my own movement, and the countless imperceptible circumstances that surround me. But this indifference to other things, this uniformity in its functioning exists only for an observer who does not perceive these other things, who is, accordingly, specialized and superficial. Who can be sure that the same thing is not true of our *identity*? It is useless to speak of memory; it supplies far more evidence of our variations than of our permanence. And yet at any moment we cannot fail to recognize ourselves and to recognize as *ours* the immediate productions of our mental life. *Ours* is what we derive from a certain manner; we need only to be able to reproduce or borrow it, or assume it by some artifice, and it can deceive us about ourselves and induce in us sentiments, thoughts, and desires indistinguishable from our own; which, by their mode of induction, would be just as intimate, just as spontaneous, just as irrefutably natural and personal as our normal thoughts and feelings, and yet would be completely alien in origin. Just as a watch placed in a magnetic field or subjected to rapid motion changes its pace without the observer's being aware of it, if he sees nothing but the watch, so all manner of disorders and alterations might be inflicted on the most conscious consciousness by some remote control impossible to detect.

This, in a manner of speaking, would be *possession synthesized.*

Music sometimes provides a rough idea, a primitive model, of such manipulations of the nervous system. It awakens feelings and puts them to sleep again; it plays with memories and emotions, arousing and mingling, binding and unbinding their secret strings. But it is not impossible that what music achieves through sensibility alone, through sensations that point to a physical *cause* and a clearly separate origin, might be effected with invincible but undetectable force by direct *induction* of the most secret circuits of life. In the last analysis it is a problem in physics. The effect of sound, or more specifically of timbre, including the timbre of the human voice—the extraordinary effect of the voice is a factor of some importance in history—gives us an intimation of the possible action of subtler vibrations attuned to the resonance of our innermost fibers. Moreover, we well know that there are unguarded paths by which the strongholds of the spirit can be breached and captured. There are substances that infiltrate the soul and possess it. And what chemistry can now do, the physics of wave transmission is sure to achieve in its own way.

We know what reactions have been induced in men by the great orators, founders of religions, leaders of nations. An analysis of their methods and a consideration of recent developments in various kinds of action at a distance evoke such daydreams as the following one. I go only slightly beyond what at present is actually being done. Let us try to conceive of a world in which the power to make men live more rapidly or more slowly, to imbue them with tendencies, to make them tremble or smile, to abase or exalt their courage, or if need be, to stop the hearts of an entire people, might be known, defined, and applied! . . . What then would become of the pretensions of the self? At every moment of their lives, men would wonder whether they were the source of their own actions or whether, in their own deepest sense of their existence, they were marionettes.

Is it not even now possible to experience this same doubt? Is not our life, in so far as it depends on what comes to the mind, on what seems to come from the mind and to impose itself first on the mind and then on our whole existence—is not our life governed by an enormous, disorganized mass of *conventions*, most of which are implicit? We should be hard put to it either to express or to define them. Society, languages, laws, *customs*, the arts, politics, in short, everything that is fiduciary in this world, every effect that is unequal to its cause, requires conventions—that is, *relays* or intermediaries, by the indirect means of which a second reality takes hold, blends with the perceptible reality of the moment, covers it over, dominates it—and is itself sometimes torn apart, disclosing the terrifying simplicity of rudimentary life. In our desires, our regrets, our quests, in our emotions and passions, and even in our effort to know ourselves, we are the puppets of nonexistent things—things that need not even exist to affect us.

APPENDIX

Two Early Book Reviews

La Sémantique

TOUTES les transformations que le langage peut subir doivent laisser invariables un certain nombre de propriétés: je le suppose. Ce résidu contiendrait les relations fondamentales du langage avec ce qu'on nomme, par hypothèse, l'esprit.

S'il était obtenu, on pourrait résoudre des problèmes tels que ceux-ci: qu'est-ce qu'un substantif, un verbe, une phrase? —autrement que par des exemples et des définitions plus obscures. On pourrait également construire une loi de toutes les syntaxes qui enfermerait dans une seule expression les nécessités multiples de l'ordre des mots, de leur accord; et qui déterminerait l'unité,—quant à la compréhension,—des phrases.

Tout le monde se doute que ces problèmes sont maintenant inabordables. Mais qui les a abordés? Enfin, on ne les pose même pas. Cette négligence singulière fait que le langage nous appartient beaucoup moins que la plupart des autres phénomènes, en tant que notion définie, et sur laquelle on puisse agir, pour voir ce qu'elle devient après telle tentative. Je veux dire que nous pouvons aujourd'hui encore accepter des idées linguistiques aussi absurdes que celle du mouvement perpétuel en mécanique,—puisque rien ne s'y oppose. Ainsi, il n'est pas rare d'entendre dire que "tout peut s'exprimer," etc.

Semantics

WHATEVER changes language may undergo must leave certain properties intact: this much I assume. The residue will embody the fundamental relations between language and what we hypothetically call the mind.

If we could capture this residue, we should be able to approach such questions as: what is a substantive, a verb, a sentence?—without recourse to examples and definitions more obscure than the question itself. We might likewise be able to build a law governing all syntax, which would comprise in a single statement the many requirements of word order and grammatical agreement, and would determine the unity of sentences from the standpoint of meaning.

Everyone supposes that these questions are for the present inaccessible. But who ever tried to take them up? Actually, they have not even been formulated. The result of this singular negligence is that language, considered as a definite notion on which one might act to see what becomes of it in the process, is much less within our power than most other phenomena. By this I mean that we still accept linguistic ideas as absurd as that of perpetual motion in mechanics—since there is nothing to set up against them. It is not unusual, for example, to hear people say that "everything can be expressed," etc.

Il faut regarder, d'autre part, ceux qui ont pris la charge d'approfondir le difficile du langage et connaître qu'ils en recherchent toutes les curiosités particulières, et qu'ils en notent les états, tantôt à perpétuité, tantôt pour aboutir à des propositions qu'ils appellent des lois, et qui sont ou extrêmement vagues ou extrêmement fausses ou extrêmement inutiles, suivant qu'elles sont plus ou moins éloignées du détail littéral. Les meilleures de ces "lois" ont la valeur de mnémotechniques. Aucune ne montre de construction plus générale et on ne distingue même pas dans leur composition ce qui est constamment supposé connu de ce qui ne l'est pas.

Cette impuissance au delà d'un point, n'est pas étonnante. Elle se déduit toute seule de la nullité de la psychologie. Je ne sais pas exactement ce qu'est la psychologie, mais je donne quand même à un certain ordre de questions cette épithète de *psychologiques*. Par exemple, si je lis et si je me dis: "Je comprends" ou: "Je ne comprends pas," je me demande ensuite ce que cela signifie. Je me demande après s'il y a des degrés entre ces deux états, etc.

Personne n'a répondu à ces questions, d'air si simple. Les psychologues modernes n'ont pas touché, je crains, aux difficultés de ce genre, la résolution desquelles éclairerait presque tout le langage. Ni les purs logiciens eux-mêmes n'ont fabriqué le premier instrument à porter sur la parole : j'entends qu'ils n'ont pas entrepris l'analyse des conditions communes à tous les systèmes de notations, en général : étude dont plus d'un trait précieux se rencontre dans les sciences exactes et y demeure indéfiniment enfermé.

En somme, il faut à peu près admirer les linguistes d'avoir pensé atteindre le langage, à côté de l'esprit peu connu. Leurs œuvres, recueils, myriades de traits, constatations de fréquences, usage libéral de métaphores qui s'évanouissent au

On the other hand, we must consider those who have undertaken to investigate the difficulties of language. We cannot fail to see that their activity consists in seeking out its anomalies and in noting its states. Sometimes they merely move in circles, and sometimes they arrive at propositions they call laws, which are either extremely vague or extremely false, or extremely useless, according to their relative distance from the literal detail. The best of these "laws" are useful as mnemotechnical instruments. None of them discloses a more general construction, and in their formulation it is even impossible to distinguish what is constantly assumed to be *known* from what is not.

There is nothing surprising about this inability to go beyond a certain point. It follows automatically from the nullity of psychology. I do not know exactly what psychology is, but I nevertheless attach the epithet *"psychological"* to a certain order of questions. If, for example, I am reading and I say to myself: "I understand," or "I do not understand," I ask myself later on what that means. I ask myself if there are degrees between these two states of mind, etc.

No one has answered these questions, seemingly so simple. Modern psychologists, I am afraid, have not even touched on difficulties of this kind, the resolution of which would clarify almost everything connected with language. Nor have even the pure logicians fashioned the most elementary instrument with which to approach the word: I mean to say that they have not undertaken an analysis of the conditions common to all systems of notation in general, although more than one precious element of such a study may be found in the exact sciences, where they remain locked up indefinitely.

All in all, one must almost admire the linguists for trying to get at language, while disregarding the mind that is so little

premier essai, n'ouvrent rien. Tel livre est clair, excite à penser: nul n'est le commencement d'une science.

Il arrive alors que M. Michel Bréal,—heureusement, l'un des grands connaisseurs de tout ce que l'on sait et de tout ce qui est en linguistique,—replace justement le langage dans son unique lieu.

La Sémantique nous rappelle que les mots ont des significations; ils constituent un groupe de deux membres, l'un physique, l'autre mental. L'étude du premier a été conduite très loin; l'étude du second est fort peu avancée; l'étude du groupe total n'existe pas, et ce serait l'importante.

La Sémantique retourne à cet ensemble. Elle regarde le langage comme le moyen de la compréhension et le résultat des opérations principales de la pensée. Elle ne dispose malheureusement pas d'une psychologie commode pour correspondre avec cet objet et pour établir son pouvoir. Elle rencontre, dans toutes les théories de l'esprit, des termes trop anciens, débordants, confondus dans leur passé, pleins de querelles, tels que *volonté, intelligence*, etc., qui font incessamment commettre à ceux qui les emploient des jugements synthétiques inconscients. Je trouve désirable que tous les termes destinés à figurer dans une Sémantique soient plus rigoureusement et plus conventionnellement définis que ceux de la géométrie elle-même; puisqu'il s'agit de fixer quelques notions pour y rapporter toutes les autres. . . . Mais la faute des psychologues est infinie.

L'auteur, dès les premières pages, rejette l'usage des métaphores vitalistes, évolutionnistes, qui servent à tout expliquer facilement. J'observe, en passant, qu'il n'y a pas moins de discontinuité logique à faire le langage un être vivant qui évolue, qu'à le considérer, selon de Maistre, un don entier de la divinité. Il y a autant de difficulté à passer analytique-

known. Their works, their compendiums, their thousands of observations, their notations of frequency, their floods of metaphors that evaporate at the first test, reveal nothing. Here and there we run into a book that is clear, that stimulates thought. But none is the beginning of a science.

But now M. Michel Bréal—fortunately one of the great masters of everything that is known and everything that has ever been done in the field of linguistics—has restored language to the one place where it belongs.

La Sémantique reminds us that words have meanings; they constitute a group of two parts, the one physical, the other mental. The study of the first has been carried far; the study of the second has made very little progress; the study of the total group is nonexistent, and that is what would be important.

La Sémantique goes back to the whole. It looks on language as a means of understanding and as a result of the principal operations of thought. Unfortunately, M. Bréal does not have at his disposal a convenient and appropriate system of psychology to serve as a groundwork. In all the theories of the mind, he meets with terms that are too old, that overlap, terms which cannot cast off the confusion of their past, fraught with controversy, such terms as *will, intelligence*, etc., which are forever compelling those who use them to make unconscious synthetic judgments. To me it seems desirable that all the terms destined to figure in a system of semantics should be more rigorously and unmistakably defined than those of geometry itself, since the essential is to establish a few notions to which all others can be related. . . . But the psychologists are infinitely to blame.

In the very first pages, the author rejects the use of the vitalist, evolutionist metaphors which explain everything so easily. I observe in passing that there is no less logical discon-

ment d'une onomatopée au substantif que du pur néant au langage articulé complet: mais, dans le système de l'évolution, cette difficulté est dissimulée par un artifice que la logique désigne aisément, et qui se borne à changer la distribution de ce qui, dans les deux systèmes, est irréductible et inintelligible.

M. Bréal a négligé, avec autant de raison, les mouvantes questions d'origine. En toute matière, l'origine est une illusion. Sa recherche, au delà de notre expérience, est purement verbale. Ce concept est attaché trop fortement à tous les objets de notre connaissance: il nous conduit à les modifier par la pensée, jusqu'à ce qu'ils ne soient plus reconnaissables, c'est-à-dire à les détruire momentanément; et ceci pourrait nous apprendre quelque chose. Mais il nous conduit en même temps à substituer, sans nous en apercevoir, des objets différents de celui qu'on altère, à celui-là même; et ces nouveaux objets sont à la fois contemporains du premier et supposés antérieurs. Cette opération ne nous apprend plus rien; elle nous trompe. . . .

L'auteur expose ensuite par chapitres particuliers les principaux faits sémantiques. Je donnerai l'idée de quelques-uns d'entre eux, bien qu'en réduisant ces remarquables parties, je défigure la méthode originale, inévitablement. C'est qu'elles ne sont guère réductibles; si elles l'étaient, la science à faire serait faite. Chacune de ces parties est construite par la juxtaposition d'exemples choisis avec un sens extrêmement fin de l'état initial de la sémantique. Les lois et les divisions du sujet sont proposées comme provisoires et le livre entier présenté comme une "directive" au monde pensant. Le vœu de l'auteur est de susciter les travaux possibles sur un point: son ouvrage peut supporter des théories différentes: il offre des cadres élastiques, des relations perfectibles, un système défini, solide,

tinuity in making language a living being which evolves, than in regarding it, with de Maistre, as a full-blown gift of God. There is just as much difficulty in passing analytically from an onomatopoeia to the substantive as from pure nothingness to the complete articulated language: but in the evolutionary system this difficulty is dissimulated by an artifice, easily identified by logic, which consists merely in modifying the distribution of what is irreducible and unintelligible in the two systems.

With just as good reason, M. Bréal has disregarded the unsettled questions of origin. In every field, origin is an illusion. The search for it, beyond our experience, is purely verbal. This concept of an origin is too strongly attached to all the objects of our knowledge: it leads us to modify them by thought until they are no longer recognizable, that is, to destroy them for the moment; and this might teach us something. But it leads us at the same time to substitute, unconsciously, objects other than the one we modify, for this object itself; and the new objects are at once contemporaneous with the first and supposedly anterior. This operation teaches us nothing; it merely deludes us. . . .

The author goes on to set forth the principal facts of semantics in a series of specialized chapters. I shall give an idea of some of them, although, in summarizing these remarkable sections, I shall inevitably be disfiguring the original method. For they are not reducible; if they were, the science the author is trying to fashion would be already made. Each of these sections is constructed by a juxtaposition of examples selected with a remarkably fine feeling for the fact that the science of semantics is still in its beginnings. The laws and divisions of the discipline are put forward provisionally, and the whole book is presented as a "directive" to the thinking

de faits tout prêts pour la pensée. J'ai admiré en eux-mêmes ces curieux faisceaux d'observations si unies, et dont pourtant chacune est claire, chacune importante et chacune libre parmi les autres, de sorte que le lecteur en conserve la disposition, et peut, à côté de la sémantique, en composer lui-même un historique concret de notre langage, une grammaire inductive, et maint groupement particulier.

Le lecteur de *La Sémantique* rencontre d'abord la loi de *Spécialité*: un mot susceptible de variation, tel que l'adjectif par ses degrés, le substantif par sa déclinaison, le verbe par sa conjugaison, marque cette variation, à une certaine époque, par la modification de sa partie finale. Peu à peu, dans certains cas, cet indice est abandonné. On le remplace par une série de mots invariables, formant des concepts indépendants. On substitue un moyen général et indépendant à un moyen particulier et dépendant. Enfin, les mots qui deviennent ainsi de purs auxiliaires, perdent dans cet emploi leur signification originale. Ainsi, l'adjectif *fort* donnait au comparatif *forçor* en vieux français; il donne ensuite *plus fort*. En anglais, le verbe *to do*, faire, peut servir à conjuguer tous les autres verbes à titre d'auxiliaire. Dans ce rôle, il dispense peu à peu de connaître les nombreux types de conjugaisons autrefois existants; il porte à lui seul toutes les variations du temps, du mode et de la personne, tandis que le verbe principal, devenant une sorte d'attribut, demeure invariable, à l'infinitif. Cette application de la spécialité n'est pas encore totalement accomplie. On dit: *I go*, je vais, *I went*, etc., et non *I do go*, *I did go*. Mais il est probable que la simplification s'étendra, même aux formes affirmatives, si l'on se rappelle l'extension actuelle de la langue anglaise et ses besoins de toute part.

La loi de *Répartition* s'exerce sur le sens des mots. Si deux mots, à une époque, ont le même sens, ils ne gardent jamais

SEMANTICS

world. The author's wish is to encourage as many works as possible on each of the points he makes. His book is compatible with diverse theories: it offers flexible framework, perfectible relations, a solid, clear-cut system of facts, all ready for thought. I have admired for their own sake these curious collections of observations, so unified and yet each one so clear, meaningful, and independent that the reader is left free to deal with them as he likes, and quite apart from semantics, can compose them into a concrete history of our language, an inductive grammar, or else arrange them in various other ways.

The reader of *La Sémantique* first encounters the law of *Specialization*: a word susceptible of variation, such as the adjective in its comparison, the substantive in its declension, or the verb in its conjugation, marks this variation, during a certain period, by a change of ending. Little by little, in certain instances, the inflection is abandoned, replaced by a set of invariable words, forming independent concepts. A general, independent instrument is substituted for a particular, dependent one. Finally, the words that have become pure auxiliaries in the course of this process lose their original meaning when so employed. Thus in Old French the adjective *fort* had *forçor* as its comparative; later it became *plus fort*. In English the verb "to do" can serve as an auxiliary with which to conjugate all other verbs. In this role, it gradually frees people from the need to know the numerous types of conjugation that used to exist; it attracts to itself all the variations of tense, mood, and person, while the main verb, becoming a kind of attribute, remains invariable, in the infinitive. This process of specialization is not entirely complete. One still says, "I go," "I went," etc., and not "I do go," "I did go." But it seems likely that the simplification will spread even to

longtemps cette synonymie. S'ils proviennent de deux langues dont l'une est regardée comme populaire, le mot populaire prend le sens trivial. "Le Savoyard, dit M. Bréal, emploie les noms de *père* et de *mère* pour ses parents, au lieu qu'il garde pour le bétail les anciens noms de *pâré* et de *mâré.*"

La loi *d'Irradiation* est une des plus surprenantes. Un mot dont je représente le sens par A comporte une désinence ou son final que j'appelle *b*. On forme de nouveaux mots terminés en *b*, tels que C*b*, M*b*; *b* apporte dans ces nouveaux mots quelque chose du sens de A. Ainsi, les adjectifs français en *âtre* qui sont péjoratifs: il y avait, en grec, des substantifs en αστηρ, tels que δικαστήρ, ἐργαστήρ. Quelques-uns de ces mots, qui étaient susceptibles d'interprétations péjoratives ou malignes, passèrent en latin où l'on forma symétriquement une classe de mots péjoratifs en *aster*: *filiaster*, *patraster*, etc. Nous disons aujourd'hui: *marâtre*, *douceâtre*, et nous pouvons amoindrir ou "empirer" le sens d'un adjectif par une semblable désinence. Dans cet exemple, on voit le latin donner arbitrairement un sens à une désinence, parce qu'elle a cohabité avec ce sens dans quelques mots grecs, et transporter ce sens à l'aide de cette désinence. Le français, ensuite, donne à cette désinence une valeur encore plus grande, jusqu'à en faire une modification pour la plupart des adjectifs, une sorte de degré de leur sens.

Sous les titres de Survivance des flexions, Fausses perceptions, Analogies, Acquisitions nouvelles, M. Bréal expose ensuite diverses classes de faits sémantiques qu'il serait trop long de spécifier.

Les autres parties de son livre, "Comment s'est formée la syntaxe," "Comment s'est fixé le sens des mots," doivent être spécialement recommandées à l'attention. Je ne les analyserai pas, je dirai seulement qu'elles conduisent aux

the affirmative forms if we consider the present extension of
the English language and its universal needs.

The law of *Distribution* operates in the meanings of words.
If at a certain epoch two words have the same meaning, they
never keep it for long. If the two words come from two kinds
of speech, one of which is regarded as popular, the popular
word takes the more trivial sense. "A Savoyard," writes M.
Bréal, "employs the words *père* and *mère* for his parents; he
reserves the old local words *pâré* and *mâré* for cattle."

The law of *Radiation* is one of the most surprising. A word
whose meaning I designate as A has a desinence or final sound
that I designate as *b*. New words ending in *b* are formed, such
as C*b*, M*b*; to these new words *b* brings something of the
meaning of A. This accounts for the pejorative sense of
French adjectives ending in *âtre*: there were, in Greek, a number of substantives ending in αστήρ, such as δικαστήρ,
ἐργαστήρ. Some of these words, which were susceptible of pejorative or malicious interpretation, passed into
Latin, where a class of pejorative words in *aster* was formed
by symmetry: *filiaster*, *patraster*, etc. Today we say *marâtre*,
douceâtre, and we can diminish or "worsen" the meaning of
an adjective by a desinence of this kind. In this example, the
Latin arbitrarily gave a meaning to a desinence because it co-
habited with this meaning in a few Greek words, and used the
desinence to extend the meaning to new words. The French,
later on, gave a still stronger meaning to the desinence, to the
point of making it a variant of most adjectives, a kind of
degree of their meaning.

Under the titles "Survival of Inflections," "False Perceptions," "Analogies," "New Acquisitions," M. Bréal goes on
to set forth different classes of semantic facts that it would
take too long to discuss here in detail.

247

problèmes les plus passionnants, ceux que les problèmes peuvent passionner. Et puis, il me serait impossible d'être plus précis ou moins étendu que l'auteur parlant de ces sujets. Je me bornerai maintenant à tâcher de voir dans ce développement de la Sémantique entière quelques caractères généraux.

Il sort de ce livre, feuilleté finalement, revu à travers la roue de ses pages, connu et devenu rapide,—le mélange des idées qui s'y trouvent et de celles qui s'en déduisent, et de celles inventées par le contact d'une première ligne et d'une dernière, brusquement heureux.

Vaguement, d'abord, le langage se montre: proposé comme difficulté; privé de l'accoutumance où il se cache; forcé de parler de lui-même, de se nommer; pourvu, à cette fin, de nouveaux signes. On regarde sa variation, qui peut faire penser aux plus vaines métaphores, si, trop vite, on s'arrête de l'observer. On remarque des sonorités qui paraissent, qui s'étouffent, qui se confondent, qui se détachent; on sent des idées pâlir, bifurquer, s'étendre, être substituées, changer de bruit. Il y a d'inexplicables désuétudes, d'absurdes succès: échanges, altération continuelle, permutations de concepts et d'images, révocations lentes et sûres du dictionnaire de l'entendement.

De ce point philosophique, les formes qui étaient les plus familières, le plus vite comprises paraissent les plus dures à recomprendre consciemment. La logique serait ennemie à la plupart des manières de dire qui s'implantent. Inversement, les formes les plus complètes, c'est-à-dire les plus conformes à l'analyse, celles qui remplissent exactement les catégories du jugement, semblent ne pas tenir contre l'usage, et devoir se dégrader pour pouvoir durer. Leur durée, qu'on penserait garantie par leur perfection rationnelle, est définie par autre chose.

The remaining parts of the book, "How syntax came into being," "How the meanings of words became established," are specially commended to the reader's attention. I shall not analyze them, but only say that they lead anyone capable of a passion for problems to the most exciting problems. And besides, it would be impossible for me, in speaking of these subjects, to be more precise or less diffuse than the author. I shall merely try to distinguish certain general traits in the development of semantics as a whole.

If, after reading this book, we leaf quickly through its pages as though spinning a wheel, we obtain a blend of the ideas it contains with those that may be derived from them, and finally with those created by a sudden lucky encounter between a first line and a last.

Vaguely at first, language reveals itself: introduced as a difficulty; shorn of the familiarity in which it hides; it is forced to speak of itself, to name itself, and equipped, to this end, with new signs. We observe its variations, which may suggest the emptiest of metaphors if we turn away from them too quickly. We note sounds which emerge, which grow muffled and jumbled, and then become distinct again; we see ideas fading, branching out, broadening, changing places, taking on a new ring. We find words falling inexplicably into disuse while others are absurdly successful; we find exchanges, continual adulterations, permutations of concepts and images, slow but sure amendments to the dictionary of the understanding.

From this philosophical angle, the forms that were most familiar, most quickly understood, seem the most inaccessible to our conscious re-understanding. Most of the expressions that become firmly implanted would seem to be

Or, dans cet inattendu, l'individu se dessine.

Il fait tout ce qu'il peut pour *se comprendre*,—lui qui se parle, avant tout, quand il parle. Il a, toujours, à construire, avec des matériaux inflexibles, tirés d'un seul ordre de sensations, un ensemble qui lui redonne la multiplicité et les valeurs, et les variations brusques et les vitesses et les groupements puissants, irréductibles, universels de sa pensée. Il faut qu'il puisse restituer cette pensée en disposant selon des règles, des éléments étrangers à elle. Les éléments peuvent être regardés comme purement conventionnels. Les règles—les indispensables—sont les lois mêmes de la compréhension.

Dans un esprit, toute forme de langage se présente comme une sorte de groupe ou de total, composé de signes fixes et d'idées. Ce groupe doit satisfaire à certaines conditions pour exister,—pour correspondre au sentiment spécial de compréhension: je ne préciserai pas aujourd'hui ces conditions. Les signes qui y entrent demeurant identiques, sa portion idéale peut subir des changements, être remplacée par une autre qui satisfasse également aux conditions d'existence de l'ensemble. Le groupe peut, en général, recevoir *plus* d'une solution psychologique. Cette diversité permet qu'on puisse parler avec contradiction, faire des syllogismes faux,—ou bien justes mais absurdes. Elle explique l'imperfection logique, l'inconstance ou les erreurs formelles qu'on trouve dans les écrits, dans les plus forts ouvrages de construction philosophique et, *régulièrement*, chez le poète. Je dirai, en passant, qu'il n'y a pas de grandes différences intérieures entre le mot, la locution et la phrase. Les locutions deviennent à chaque instant des mots. Les mots sont, pour la plupart, susceptibles d'un développement. La grande affaire de la logique est de fixer un certain développement constant pour un mot: c'est la définition, par exemple. Mais, en réalité,

inimical to logic. Inversely, the most complete forms, those which best lend themselves to analysis, which exactly satisfy the categories of judgment, seem unable to stand up under usage, compelled to degenerate if they are to survive. Their survival, which one would tend to attribute to their rational perfection, is determined by something else.

Now it is in this medium of the unexpected that the individual portrays himself.

He does everything he can to *understand himself*—in speaking, he speaks first of all to himself. He has always to construct, from inflexible materials drawn from a single order of sensation, a totality which gives back to him the multiplicity, the values, the abrupt variations, the velocities, and the powerful, irreducible, universal groupings of his thought. He is compelled to render his thought by disposing, in accordance with rules, elements that are alien to it. The elements may be regarded as purely conventional. The rules—those that are indispensable—are the very laws of comprehension.

Every form of language presents itself to the mind as a kind of group or total, composed of fixed signs and ideas. The group must meet certain conditions in order to exist—in order to comply with our specific sense of understanding: I shall not define these conditions now. The signs that enter into it remain identical; the ideal component can undergo changes, it can be replaced by another that is equally in keeping with the requirements of the whole. Generally speaking, such a group is open to *more* than one psychological solution. This diversity makes it possible to contradict oneself in speaking, to put forward false syllogisms, or sound but absurd ones. It explains the logical imperfection, the inconsistency or formal errors that we find in written works, in the best works of systematic philosophy and *regularly* in poetry. I may say in

l'individu est tout le temps porté à se servir de définitions diverses du même vocable; on peut se figurer comment cela arrive: les signes du langage sont absolument distincts de leur sens: aucun chemin rationnel ou empirique ne peut mener du signe au sens. Ainsi, l'homme n'est jamais incohérent pour lui-même, au même moment qu'il pense, son langage lui appartient; il est forcé de se comprendre.

La recherche de M. Bréal supporte la généralisation qu'elle suggère. Elle attire l'étude sur tous les systèmes symboliques, en masse. L'algèbre, la musique écrite, certains genres d'ornementation, les cryptographies, etc., sont susceptibles d'analyses sémantiques. Regardés du point de vue des significations, tous ces systèmes et le langage doivent, à mon sens, conduire à une distinction capitale parmi les modes dont les états mentaux sont accouplés. Désignons par a et b deux de ces états accouplés, c'est-à-dire tels que si a est donné, b est donné. Il arrivera dans certains cas que l'on pourra trouver une autre relation que celle de séquence entre a et b. Dans ces cas b pourra se construire à l'aide de a, et réciproquement. Il s'ensuivra, en général, que toute variation de l'un des termes déterminera une variation dans l'autre. Mais, dans d'autres cas, il arrivera que les deux termes proposés n'auront entre eux qu'une pure relation de séquence. On pourra dire alors que cette association est symbolique ou conventionnelle. Le langage est formé de relations de cette dernière espèce. La théorie doit rechercher ce que deviennent ces symboles soumis à la répétition, à l'usage, mélangés aux groupements de la première espèce, exposés à l'arbitraire de l'individu et portés par lui à la dernière limite de leur valeur. . . . Le lecteur me trouve obscur; je tâcherai une autre fois d'être plus clair, plus complet, plus long, en formant sous ses yeux, explicitement, les

passing that there is no great internal difference between a word, a phrase, and a sentence. Phrases are perpetually turning into words. Words, for the most part, are susceptible of development. The chief business of logic is to establish a certain constant development for a word: by defining it, for example. But in reality an individual is always being led to employ different definitions of the same word. It is easy to see how this happens: linguistic signs are absolutely distinct from their meaning: no rational or empirical path can lead from sign to meaning. Thus a man is never incoherent to himself, at the moment of thinking; his language is his own; he is compelled to understand himself.

M. Bréal's inquiry bears out the generalization it suggests. It evokes an investigation of all symbolic systems. Algebra, written music, certain types of ornament, cryptographic systems, etc., are all accessible to semantic analyses. Considered from the standpoint of meaning, all these systems and language as well must, it seems to me, lead us to draw an essential distinction between the different ways in which mental states are related. Let us designate as a and b two of these states related in such a way that if a is present, b is also present. In certain cases it will be possible to find a relation other than of sequence between a and b. Here we shall be able to construct b with the help of a and vice versa. It will follow that, in general, any variation in one of these terms will determine a variation in the other. But in other cases, the two suggested terms will have only a relation of sequence between them. Then we may say that the association is symbolic or conventional. Language is made up of relations of this last kind. The theorist must try to find out what happens to these symbols when they are subjected to repetition and use, when they are mixed with

abstractions dont je me sers, et en essayant de déterminer les hypothèses fondamentales du langage.

Regardons encore quelque chose: un texte. L'aspect typographique et la signification générale des phrases nous viennent d'abord. Laissons d'abord passer cent mille idées. Perdons, détruisons même cette complexe signification. Chaque mot semble se détacher de la forme, reprendre une liberté, s'ouvrir, être à lui seul l'entrée de tout l'esprit. Chaque page paraît de suite un système infiniment relié, un incalculable réseau. Imaginons un classement quelconque des mots: apprécions minutieusement leurs différences grammaticales, c'est-à-dire leurs lois de pluralité, d'existence dans la durée, leurs natures psychologiques. Imaginons que nous passons sur un vers, péniblement, percevant toutes ces différences par nos efforts exagérés, travaillant le long de ces contours comme un insecte sur une large feuille. . . . C'est un voyage que l'on peut refaire d'une façon encore différente. Rappelons-nous ce que nous savons d'histoire, de linguistique, d'étymologie. Même si ces connaissances ne sont pas très sûres, elles tiendront lieu des véritables. Passons de nouveau sur notre texte dont la topographie a changé. Les mots, cette fois, seront associés à leur étage historique. Les locutions paraîtront naturelles, mais étranges à cette place. On aura l'impression que donne un monument dont les membres sont antiques, l'ordre barbare; ou bien celle qu'éveille un pauvre, vêtu de quotidiens mangés de prose et qui les a collés pour s'en faire une chemise de fortune.

On sourit alors de remuer tout cela pour écrire la moindre ligne. Une conscience cruelle donne à la moindre ligne la grandeur de Wagram, la difficulté de la théorie de la lune; et l'on en trace des millions sans s'en douter. Que l'écrivain ne s'en doute pas. Je me rappelle cependant de longues conversa-

groupings of the first kind, exposed to an individual caprice which carries them to the extreme limit of their value. . . . The reader may find me obscure; I shall try another time to make myself clearer, to be more thorough, to speak at greater length, giving concrete form to the abstractions I am employing, and trying to define the fundamental hypotheses of language.

There is something else we might consider: a text. What first meets our eye is the typographical aspect and the general meaning of the sentences. But let us dismiss the thousands of ideas that come to us. Let us lose or even go so far as to destroy the complexities of meaning. Each word seems to detach itself from the form, to regain its freedom, to open up, to become in itself a gateway to the whole mind. At once every page seems to be a system of innumerable relations, an incalculable network. Let us consider the words according to any classification we wish: let us examine closely their grammatical differences, that is, their laws of plural formation, of existence in time, their psychological character. Suppose that we go through a line of poetry painstakingly, perceiving all these differences by our exaggerated efforts, working our way along its contours like an insect on a large leaf. . . . We can repeat the journey in still a different way. Let us remember all we know about history, linguistics, etymology. Even if our knowledge is not very sure, it will fulfill the function of real knowledge. Once again we work through our text. Its topography has changed. This time the words will be associated with their stage of historical development. The locutions will seem natural, but strange in this context. We shall have the impression made by a monument whose parts are ancient, but arranged in a barbarous fashion; or the feeling that might be aroused by a poor man clad in daily newspapers corroded

tions avec Marcel Schwob: rien n'était plus amusant que mes surprises—sinon ce dialogue de caractères—quand il tirait je ne sais quel fil d'un mot ou d'une locution pour les rattacher au loin, au diable, à un certain coin d'un certain temps, selon les plus délicates probabilités qui se puissent imaginer. Souvent, une preuve brusque me ravissait. L'argot de tous les brigands, au coin du feu, trié, appelé par lui, me comblait de plaisir enfantin, de jouissance littéraire, de l'extrême bonheur que donne une analyse parfaite. Circonstance d'or: j'avais beau le presser de questions, il n'en laissait pas sans réponse.

with prose that he has pasted together to form a makeshift shirt.

One cannot help smiling at the notion that in order to write the most insignificant line we must stir up all this. We become cruelly aware that the most insignificant of lines is as grand as Wagram, as difficult as the theory of the moon; and we write millions of them without suspecting all this. A writer had better not suspect. And yet I recall long conversations with Marcel Schwob: nothing—except perhaps for the dialogue of our characters—could have been more diverting than my surprise when he drew some sort of thread from a word or phrase by which to attach it, according to the most subtle probabilities that can be imagined, to something far far away, the devil knows where, in a certain niche of a certain epoch. Often I would be delighted by a sudden proof. The argot of all the brigands, as he sifted and conjured it up by the fireside, filled me with childlike pleasure, with literary enjoyment, with the extreme happiness conferred by a perfect analysis. And miraculous to say: I could press him with all the questions I pleased; he left none of them unanswered.

Le Temps

Le roman que l'on a pu lire* ici même, grâce à notre Davray,—précipite son lecteur dans l'absurde; puis, l'arbitraire est exploré.

Ce n'est pas mon rôle de juger cet ouvrage.—Je laisse la fable, je penserai au Temps.

Un lien singulier, un sentiment, une quantité, une catégorie,—*cela*, est présent dans beaucoup d'esprits sous la figure d'une sorte de fluide qui transporte, altère tous les objets, les dissout, les recompose et les analyse, comme le bain chimique ou l'eau mère de tous les événements connaissables. Certains attribuent à la simple durée une action propre qui vieillit les êtres; use les choses; a rongé les roches; améliorera les sociétés, les vins, les livres vraiment bons : et ils se reposent sur l'activité intelligente de ce moteur pour leur amener, souvent, au réveil, l'idée, qu'en se couchant, ils n'auront pas eue.

Ces images sont générales. Elles paraissent grandement dans le langage des hommes quelconques, et elles se cachent dans celui des savants. En vérité, les sciences actuelles ne nous apprennent rien sur le Temps même.

Elles le définissent une quantité continue, à une dimension, mesurable par le déplacement d'un point dans l'espace. On

* *La Machine à explorer le Temps*, par H. G. Wells.

Time

THE NOVEL* which, thanks to our friend Davray, has been made available to you in these same pages† plunges the reader into an absurd, arbitrary world which it then explores.

It is not my role to judge this work. I shall set the story aside and turn my thoughts to time itself.

Many men have looked upon time as a kind of fluid that displaces and transforms all objects, dissolves, recomposes, and analyzes them, like a chemical bath or the mother liquid out of which all knowable events crystallize. And behind this notion they discern a unique bond, a feeling, a quantity, or a category. Some men attribute to sheer duration an intrinsic effect which ages the living and wears out things; which has eroded rocks; which will improve societies, wines, and truly good books: and they rely on the intelligent activity of this force to bring them often, upon waking, the idea they were unable to find before going to bed.

Such images are universal. They are manifest in the language of average men and latent in that of scientists. For the present, the sciences teach us nothing about time itself.

They define it as a continuous one-dimensional quantity,

*H. G. Wells, *The Time Machine.*
†That is, in *Mercure de France.*

suppose qu'à chaque longueur parcourue correspond une quantité de temps, et que, si les longueurs sont égales, les temps correspondants sont égaux.

Mais cette supposition, si utile, n'est qu'un abus de langage destiné à permettre des raisonnements ultérieurs. En effet, des longueurs sont dites *égales* quand on peut, ou les superposer directement, ou leur superposer, suivant une loi uniforme, la même unité. L'égalité résulte alors de la parfaite confusion des deux longueurs, ou, si l'on veut, de l'impossibilité de les distinguer qui se produit à la fin de l'opération. C'est ce qui est impraticable dans le domaine du temps. Deux instants, battements du même pendule, ou trajets, au-dessus de l'horizon, d'un astre, ne peuvent être comparés et enfin confondus. Aucune opération ne peut les faire coïncider, aucune méthode ne peut les substituer l'un à l'autre, ou les transformer l'un dans l'autre ou les altérer de la même façon tous les deux. Chacun, définitivement étranger à l'autre, est inexprimable par l'autre—et quand nous croyons de les confronter, quand nous énumérons dans la même série arithmétique plusieurs battements de pendule, c'est que nous comptons ensemble des objets d'espèce différente et que nous ajoutons des sensations à des souvenirs, comme un écolier additionnerait, sans trouble, des mètres cubes à des mètres carrés. . . .

On va voir que les autres caractères du temps mathématique sont également en opposition avec ceux du temps physique ou psychologique.

Une fois le temps regardé comme une quantité, on l'a employé à ce titre dans les problèmes de la Dynamique et de la Cinématique. Il joue, dans ces domaines, un rôle particulier; il y est considéré comme quantité variable indépendante, de sorte que sa variation détermine celles de toutes les autres quantités qui représentent le fait mécanique à exprimer. Ici,

measurable by the movement of a point in space. We assume that to every distance traversed there corresponds a measure of time, and that if the lengths are equal the times corresponding to them will also be equal.

But useful as it is, this assumption is merely an abuse of language, intended as a basis for further mental operations. Actually two distances are said to be *equal* when we can either superimpose one on the other directly, or superimpose the same unit upon both in accordance with a uniform law. Equality then results from the perfect identification of the two distances or, if we prefer, from the impossibility of distinguishing them when the operation has been completed. But in the realm of time this is not feasible. Two instants, two swings of the same pendulum or passages of a star across the horizon, cannot be compared and in the end identified. No operation can make them coincide, no method can substitute one for the other, transform one into the other, or modify both in the same way. Each one is absolutely alien to the other, and neither can be expressed in terms of the other—when we think we are comparing them, when we enumerate several swings of the pendulum in the same arithmetical series, we are grouping together objects of different species, we are adding sensations to memories, like a schoolboy who has no qualms about adding cubic meters to square meters. . . .

We shall see that the other characteristics of mathematical time are equally in opposition to those of physical or psychological time.

After choosing to consider time as a quantity, we have so used it in problems of dynamics and kinetics. It plays a special role in these fields, where it is considered as an independent variable, so that its variation determines that of all the other quantities representing the mechanical phenomenon to be

on lui attribue implicitement cette action propre dont j'ai parlé, et le savant donne une forme abstraite, analytique, à une opinion vulgaire.

De plus, en tant que variable indépendante, on peut assigner à la quantité *t* toutes les valeurs que l'on veut, — et en particulier, des valeurs décroissantes. . . . La représentation mathématique est donc en défaut. Elle ne conserve presque rien de la notion singulière de temps. Elle ne distingue pas le passé de l'avenir. Elle postule la correspondance complète d'une quantité de temps avec un continu quelconque à une dimension.

Cependant, quelque chose à faire, demeure. Plus riche, plus difficile à représenter, plus singulière me semble être la notion du temps.

La première idée m'en vint en dénouant quelquefois, dans mon esprit, ce vieux et étrange *Principe de Contradiction*. Je le regardais de toutes mes forces comme une prescription arbitraire. Je me disais que la Logique consiste simplement à voir si une chaîne de propositions est, ou non, conforme à certains postulats, tels que ce Principe. — Je pensai ensuite que cette loi absolue: "Une chose ne peut, en même temps. . . . être et ne pas être," ne pouvait avoir été tirée que d'une observation intérieure, et qu'au lieu de la soustraire à tout examen et à tout recommencement, comme le font beaucoup d'auteurs, il convenait, peut-être, de renouveler les antiques tâtonnement et de redescendre dans la région toujours vivante, pareille, presque ineffable, d'où péniblement,* après des siècles de tentatives, les Grecs l'ont extraite.

*Péniblement, car la formule de cette loi, si longtemps élaborée, reste inélégante, inachevée, maladroite, au point que je n'ai pas voulu transcrire ci-dessus le membre de phrase très vague qui s'y intercale: ". . . et sous le même rapport . . ."

expressed. Here the special action of which I have spoken is implicitly attributed to it, and the scientist gives an abstract, analytical form to a vulgar opinion.

Furthermore, if time is taken as an independent variable, we can assign to the quantity *t* any value we wish and, in particular, diminishing values. . . . Thus mathematical representation is at fault. It retains next to nothing of the singular notion of time. It does not distinguish the past from the future. It postulates complete correspondence between a quantity of time and any unidimensional continuum.

Nevertheless, there still remains something to be done. It seems to me that the notion of time is richer, more difficult to represent, more singular than that.

The first idea came to me while I was trying, as I sometimes used to do, to unravel in my mind the strange old *Principle of Contradiction*. All my thought and feeling taught me to regard it as an arbitrary rule. I told myself that Logic consists simply in looking to see whether a chain of propositions does, or does not, conform to certain postulates such as this Principle. Then I reflected that the following absolute law: "A thing cannot, at the same time . . . be and not be," could only have been drawn from an inner observation, and that instead of removing it from all scrutiny, from all reexamination, as many authors do, it might be advisable to renew the old gropings and descend once again into that realm, still living, relatively unchanged, and almost ineffable, whence the Greeks, after centuries of effort, painfully* extracted it.

*Painfully, because the formulation of this law, which it took so long to elaborate, remains inelegant, unfinished, awkward, so much so that, in quoting it above, I have not seen fit to include the extremely vague intercalary phrase: ". . . and in the same respect. . . ." [P. V.]

Tel, le temps m'apparut comme possibilité de contradiction, contact de contradictoires. Mais si je m'écartais du langage, et, par conséquent, du lieu des contradictions, si je n'observais que les phénomènes mentaux eux-mêmes, le Principe s'évanouissant, je croyais en apercevoir un autre dont celui-là n'était que la projection dans le domaine du parler. Il me semblait que certains objets de connaissance étaient incompatibles entre eux,—et, parmi eux, comme une simple catégorie de cette quantité de couples, devaient être ceux qui, une fois nommés et affirmés ensemble, constituent contradiction.

A ce moment de moi, le Principe ne paraissait plus que l'effet admirable, mais incomplet, d'une foule d'expériences de la plus grande délicatesse, tentées sur la pensée même. Ces opérations ayant manqué, le problème, abaissé du degré de la pensée à celui plus accessible du langage, put, à peu près, être résolu. Le Principe était tout ce qu'on avait pu, à une autre époque, dénominer et organiser dans cet ordre de recherches, et il n'était que l'approximation d'une loi bien plus élémentaire ou bien plus étendue, dont existe cette forme vulgaire: On ne pense pas à tout à la fois.

Ainsi, toute connaissance est constamment considérée comme *partielle*, et nécessairement.

Naïve, valable,—ou non,—cette idée me fut le signe de réfléchir indéfiniment. Elle, qui m'inclinait à regarder le temps comme une certaine division de l'ensemble du connaissable, me conduisait de suite à rechercher un procédé de divisibilité, qui, s'il pouvait être inventé, brisant tout objet de pensée en opérations distinctes, indépendantes entre elles et indépendantes de leur contenu, conférerait à son possesseur une méthode neuve et extrêmement uniforme d'analyse. J'illustrerai ce projet par une figure grossière. Qu'on se représente

When I did so, time appeared to me as a possibility of contradiction, a contact between contradictories. But if I withdrew from language, and consequently from the place of contradictions, if I observed only the mental phenomena themselves, the Principle vanished and I thought I caught sight of another, of which the former was only a projection onto the plane of language. It seemed to me that certain objects of knowledge were mutually incompatible, and that one simple category of such incompatible pairs must be composed of those which, once named and affirmed together, constitute contradiction.

To that moment of my mind, the Principle appeared simply the admirable but incomplete outcome of a vast number of extremely delicate experiments on thought itself. Once these attempts had failed, the problem, brought down from the level of thought to the more accessible level of language, could be more or less resolved. The Principle was all that another epoch had been able to identify and organize in this branch of research, and it was merely an approximation of a far more elementary or more inclusive law, which in its popular form says: You can't think of everything at once.

Thus every cognition is constantly considered as *partial*, and necessarily so.

Valid or not, this naïve idea was to me a signal for endless reflection. By inclining me to regard time as a certain division of the knowable as a whole, it led me at once to look for a method of division which, if it could be invented, would break up each object of thought into distinct operations independent of one another and of their content, and so provide its possessor with a new and highly uniform method of analysis. A crude figure may help to illustrate what I have in mind. Consider, if you please, a man who suddenly finds him-

un homme, subitement devant un édifice considérable. Que l'esprit de cet homme soit d'abord infiniment surpassé: il ne lui faut qu'un coup d'œil pour être accablé, anéanti. Ensuite, divisant la masse debout dans sa vue, par celle qu'il imagine pouvoir remuer lui-même, défaisant le monument en opérations successives dont chacune lui est possible, le réduisant en changements qu'il commande, et en éléments invariables définis comme matériaux extérieurs,—il achève par avoir substitué, à un grand étonnement instantané, une certaine suite d'actes simples. . . .

Je tâchais, au même temps, de me préciser ce principe d'incompatibilité que je situais plus profondément que celui de contradiction. J'avoue que je voyais dans la limitation de la connaissance et dans sa partition nécessaire, quelque chose de la nature d'une quantité. Peut-être, les difficultés que je mettais à accepter cette analogie, et qu'il fallait y mettre, ne sont-elles dues qu'à l'insuffisante connaissance que nous avons de la nature des quantités. Quoi qu'il en soit, je supposais mon Principe déjà connu, et je voyais qu'il contenait l'assurance d'une psychologie formelle, venant entourer et situer la Logique formelle. Je crois toujours fermement que si la psychologie peut devenir une science, c'est seulement quand nous connaîtrons comment on ne pense pas tout à la fois. Alors, cette nouvelle science sera, en quelque sorte, la *Géométrie du Temps,*—c'est-à-dire le résumé des lois suivant lesquelles se substituent et se réfléchissent, les uns sur les autres, les états de conscience.

Il est clair que nous sommes faits de choses séparées, parmi lesquelles il en est où l'on peut introduire de nouvelles séparations, ou que l'on peut confondre, et d'autres qui sont indivisibles ou premières. Notre connaissance est A, ou elle est B,

self before an enormous building. His mind is at first over-whelmed: a glance suffices to crush, destroy him. Then, dividing the mass standing before his eyes by the mass he supposes himself capable of moving, taking the monument apart in successive operations each of which is within his capabilities, reducing it to a series of changes under his control, and to invariable elements defined as external materials, he succeeds at length in replacing a vast momentary amazement by a certain sequence of simple acts. . . .

I tried at the same time to define the principle of incompatibility which I held to be more profound than that of contradiction. I confess that in the limitation and necessary division of knowledge I saw something in the nature of a quantity. Perhaps the difficulty I found—and properly so—in accepting such an analogy was due only to our inadequate knowledge of the nature of quantities. Be that as it may, I assumed my Principle to be already known, and saw that it held the promise of a formal psychology which would contain and situate formal Logic. I am still convinced that if psychology can ever become a science, it will only be when we know why we cannot think everything at once. And that new science will be, in a manner of speaking, the *Geometry of Time*—that is to say, a résumé of the laws in accordance with which our states of consciousness follow and reflect one another.

It is evident that we are made of distinct elements, some of which are subject to being either further divided or joined into one, while others are indivisible or primary. Our knowledge is A or it is B, and *in general* there is no path leading from A to B. We know that A and B can be anything at all, as different as we please; nevertheless, we pass immediately

et aucun chemin ne nous conduit, *en général*, de A en B. Nous savons que A et B peuvent être quelconques, aussi différents que l'on voudra ; nous n'en passerons pas moins immédiatement de l'un à l'autre, continuellement enfermés par deux termes tels, comme un être qui serait un point vivant dans une courbe. La question du changement se pose donc, comme la clef de toute psychologie utile, et il est inévitable de se demander comment s'opère la variation de la connaissance, quelle est la règle universelle des altérations ou des transformations d'un état de conscience, soit qu'on le regarde comme comprenant à la fois des données externes et des phénomènes purement mentaux, soit qu'on se borne à l'un de ces mondes. Entre ces deux domaines, uniformément et indifféremment débités en états de conscience, existent des échanges, des correspondances, des actions et réactions, qui, partiellement étudiés et observés, n'ont pas encore pas fait l'objet d'une recherche méthodique. Je conseille au lecteur qui voudrait se donner une idée simple de ces questions, de s'appliquer à concevoir, à titre de fantaisie, un système de notation ou d'écriture de la connaissance. L'éminent professeur F. Klein, dans sa préface aux œuvres de Riemann, dénonce quelque part l'importance du rôle joué dans les Mathématiques modernes "*par la définition des fonctions au moyen de leur mode d'existence dans le domaine infinitésimal . . . .*" Il faut accorder, d'avance, une importance analogue à toute méthode qui permettrait de définir ce que nous appelons une idée, non point, comme on le fait toujours, par un certain développement,—ou signification,—du contenu de cette idée, car ce développement est, d'ordinaire, hasardeux dès ses premiers termes, mais à l'aide d'une combinaison de conditions générales, ou d'un groupement convenable de relations indépendantes, formelles.

Je terminerai ces indications par une sorte de programme.

from one to the other, continually limited by two such terms, as though we were a living point on a curve. Thus the question of change is seen to be the key to any useful psychology, and it is inevitable that we should ask ourselves how the movements of thought occur, what is the universal rule governing the modifications or transformations of a state of consciousness, regardless of whether we consider it as embracing both external data and purely mental phenomena, or whether we limit ourselves to one of these worlds. Between these two realms, uniformly and indifferently transposed into states of consciousness, there exist exchanges, correspondences, influences, and reactions which, though partially studied and observed, have not yet been investigated systematically. I advise the reader who would like to form a simple idea of these matters to attempt, by way of fantasy, to conceive a system of notation or a formula for conscious thought. Somewhere in his preface to the works of Riemann, the eminent professor F. Klein emphasizes the important role played in modern mathematics *"by the definition of functions in terms of their mode of existence in the realm of the infinitesimal. . . ."* A similar importance must be imputed a priori to any method which might make it possible to define what we call an idea, not, as we always do, in terms of a certain development—or meaning—of the content of this idea, for its development, as a rule, is a matter of chance from its earliest stages, but by using a combination of general conditions or a suitable group of independent, formal relations.

I shall conclude these notes with a kind of program. First of all, we must form a precise notion of change. By this I do not mean, of course, that we should define it or take a lofty, metaphysical tone, but that we should characterize its properties. We know them from experience. We posit change as

Il faut, avant tout, se faire une notion précise du changement. Non le définir, sans doute, ni monter au ton métaphysique. Il s'agit de caractériser ses propriétés. Elles résultent de l'expérience. On le posera comme indépendant de ses termes. Puis, considérant un ensemble ou état de conscience sans aucune variation (c'est-à-dire à un *instant* donné), le changement d'une simple portion de cet ensemble sera toujours comparable et, en quelque sorte, équivalent à un changement de toute autre portion ou de la totalité de l'ensemble. De plus, si une sensation suit immédiatement une autre sensation, il y aura toujours entre elles un fait purement mental—un changement. Ces propriétés montrent comment le temps a pu être considéré comme homogène et comme ne comportant qu'une seule dimension. Le temps est l'ensemble des changements. La diversité infinie des choses correspond à cet ensemble, et cet ensemble est composé d'impressions identiques, parfaitement détachées de tout objet.

D'autre part, à un autre point de vue, les changements sont comparables à tous les autres faits de conscience, perceptions, images, etc. On peut rapprocher cette dernière propriété de certaines propriétés des symboles. Ainsi,—dans la notation algébrique, lorsqu'on écrit $a + b$, le signe a et le signe $+$, dont l'un désigne une quantité et l'autre une opération, sont si indifférents comme signes que l'on pourrait, par convention, se servir de l'un au lieu de l'autre, intervertir leur signification. Il y a donc, quelque part, une sorte d'assimilation entre l'opération et les quantités,—ou la possibilité de faire correspondre à deux choses qui ne se peuvent prendre l'une pour l'autre, deux choses dont l'échange est sans influence.

Pour circonvenir davantage la notion de temps, il faudrait adjoindre maintenant à celle du changement quelque chose qui différencierait en antérieur et en postérieur les termes en

independent of its terms. Then, considering a composite state of consciousness without variation (that is, at a given *moment*), a change in one part of this composite will always be comparable, and in a sense equivalent, to a change in any other part or in the whole of the composite. Further, if one sensation immediately follows another, there will always come between them a purely mental occurrence—a change. Such properties show how it has been possible to consider time as homogeneous and possessed of but one dimension. Time is the totality of changes. The infinite diversity of things corresponds to this totality, which is composed of identical impressions, wholly without reference to any object.

From another point of view, change is comparable to the various other phenomena of consciousness—perceptions, images, etc. This last can be likened to certain properties of symbols. Thus, in algebraic notation, when we write $a+b$, the sign a and the sign $+$, the one designating a quantity and the other an operation, are so empty as signs that we might, by convention, invert their meaning and use one instead of the other. There is then, in some respect, a kind of likeness between any operation and the quantities involved in it, so that a correspondence becomes possible between two things that can be interchanged without effect and two other things that cannot be taken one for the other at all.

To circumscribe the notion of time more closely, we should now have to add to the notion of change something that would divide the terms under consideration into anterior and posterior and so would illustrate a striking aspect of temporal things, namely, the fact that we seem to be backing away from them, moving in the opposite direction from the way we are looking. In this connection it will be indispensable, I believe, to define more closely the content of states of

présence, et qui figurerait cet aspect saisissant des choses temporelles dont nous semblons nous éloigner à reculons, nous mouvant dans une direction opposée à celle où nous y voyons. Ici, il sera indispensable, je crois, de préciser davantage le contenu des états de conscience : on observera, par exemple, que la succession d'une sensation et d'un fait purement mental diffère de celle de deux sensations ou de deux faits mentaux. On considérera, de même, les relations, *autres que la succession*, existant entre les états. On trouvera, à ce point de vue, deux grandes classes. Dans l'une, il n'y aura que les couples constitués par la séquence seule, par une substitution pure et simple d'une chose à l'autre. Dans la seconde, les couples reliés plus richement, ceux dans lesquels un terme est donné par une opération de l'esprit sur le premier. Là, encore, la distinction entre phénomènes externes et internes est de première importance. Par exemple : tous les objets peuvent être associés entre eux en général et l'on peut également toujours concevoir que cette association soit renversée, et que le premier succède au deuxième. Mais cette règle tombe, dans la plupart des cas, si l'un des termes est un phénomène externe.

Nous sommes ainsi conduits à parler de la réversibilité ou de l'irréversibilité des états de conscience.

Les transformations que subit un système quelconque sont réversibles lorsque le système peut revenir d'un certain état à un état antérieur, en passant dans ce retour par les mêmes états qu'à l'aller, pris dans l'ordre inverse. Cette définition, quoique d'origine physique, est tellement générale qu'on peut l'essayer à l'esprit et le regarder comme un système de transformations. Il y a des cas où l'application de cette définition est en quelque sorte évidente, quoique la théorie n'en soit pas facile. Par exemple : ce que nous appelons l'ordre des mots dans une phrase, et la relation de cet ordre avec la compréhension de la

consciousness: we shall observe, for example, that a sequence composed of a sensation and a purely mental phenomenon differs from a sequence of two sensations or of two mental phenomena. We shall also consider the relations *other than of sequence* between two states. And here we shall find two main classes. In one there will be pairs constituted by sequence alone, by the pure and simple substitution of one thing for another. In the second we shall find more intricately related pairs, those in which the second term results from a mental operation on the first. Here again the distinction between external and internal phenomena is of the utmost importance. For example: all objects in general can be associated with one another, and similarly, we can always conceive of an inversion of this association, whereby the first term follows the second. But in most cases this rule ceases to operate if one of the terms is an external phenomenon.

Thus we are led to speak of the reversibility or irreversibility of states of consciousness.

The transformations undergone by any system are reversible when the system can return from a certain state to an anterior state, passing, in reverse order, through the same states as in the original sequence. This definition, though physical in origin, is so general that we may apply it to the mind and regard the mind as a system of transformations. There are cases in which the application of this definition is more or less obvious, though the theory governing it is not simple. For example, what we call the word order of a sentence and its relation to the comprehension of the sentence. Similarly it should be possible, on the basis of considerations of reversibility and irreversibility, to study the logical processes of deduction and induction, put back into their psychological condition. In addition let me cite, as a specious case,

phrase. De même, les procédés logiques de déduction et d'induction, replacés dans leurs états psychologiques, doivent pouvoir être étudiés au moyen de considérations de réversion ou d'irréversion. Je citerai, encore, comme un cas spécieux, la répétition d'un phénomène. Il est clair, d'abord, que le système formé par deux états de conscience successifs et n'ayant entre eux que cette relation de séquence, est parfaitement réversible. Mais cette réversibilité n'a plus lieu, si l'on considère le retour final du premier de ces états, comme non absolument identique avec sa première apparition. En conséquence, la répétition d'un phénomène est possible ou non, suivant la définition particulière de la réversibilité qu'on adopte. Ce qui est assez remarquable, c'est que nous croyons, généralement, à la répétition intégrale possible d'un phénomène, conviction qui supporte toute expérience,—et en même temps, nous ne pouvons penser d'une chose qu'elle se répète, qu'en distinguant ses apparitions entre elles et en créant pour chacune un état de conscience irréductible.

A un autre point de vue, une succession qui comprend comme termes des sensations et des faits internes est généralement irréversible. La vue d'un objet me fait penser, mais cette pensée ne peut me faire *voir* l'objet, à moins que, par définition, je n'aie résolu de ne pas distinguer entre la vue d'un objet et sa représentation.

Tout me sollicitant d'achever cette revue précipitée de tentatives, je me borne à signaler finalement une branche de l'étude possible du temps qui nous ramènerait aux conceptions de M. Wells. Je veux parler des symboles. Le symbole est un peu une machine à explorer le temps. C'est un raccourci inconcevable de la durée des opérations de l'esprit, au point que l'on pourrait presque définir le monde mental en disant que c'est le monde où l'on peut symboliser. Un symbole peut

the repetition of a phenomenon. It is clear, first of all, that the system formed by two successive states of consciousness having no other relation than one of sequence is perfectly reversible. But the reversibility ceases if we consider the recurrence of the first of the two states as not absolutely identical with its first occurrence. Consequently, the repetition of a phenomenon is possible or not, according to the particular definition of reversibility that we adopt. It is interesting to note that in general we believe the exact repetition of a phenomenon to be possible—this belief is the basis of all experiment—while at the same time the only way we can believe that a thing repeats itself is by distinguishing its occurrences from one another and creating for each a unique state of consciousness.

Furthermore, a sequence composed of sensations and internal phenomena is generally irreversible. Seeing an object makes me think, but thinking cannot make me *see* the object, unless I have decided, by definition, to make no distinction between the sight and the idea of it.

Since there is every reason why I should bring this hurried review of tentative notions to an end, I shall content myself, in conclusion, with suggesting a possible branch of the study of time that would bring us back to Mr. Wells's conceptions. I am referring to symbols. The symbol is in a sense a time machine. It provides an unparalleled abbreviation of the time required for mental operations, so much so that we might almost define the world of the mind by saying that it is a world in which we can employ symbols. A symbol is capable of representing not only simultaneous images or states, but also groups of states. When we make use of a symbol it is as though we had carried out the operations it replaces—and the necessary condition for a symbol is that it must bear no

représenter non seulement des images ou des états simultanés, mais des groupes d'états. Tout se passe, quand on s'en sert, comme si l'on avait exécuté les opérations qu'il représente, — et sa condition nécessaire est de n'avoir aucun rapport avec la chose représentée. S'il n'en était pas ainsi, il ne pourrait constituer avec elle un couple réversible, c'est-à-dire qu'il ne serait d'aucune utilité.

relation to the thing represented. If this were not so, symbol and thing could not constitute a reversible pair; in other words, the symbol would be useless.

NOTES

NOTES

THESE NOTES are bibliographical and explanatory by turns. The explanatory notes are not meant to supply general information. They are limited, with a few exceptions, to clarifying those allusions and other references which, though a French reader might be expected to catch them, an American or English reader might not. The bibliographical notes indicate for each work the occasion of its composition (when that is known), its first publication, and if republished, one later collection where it may readily be found. The French title of each work is given after the English title. Except where otherwise noted, the place of publication is Paris and the publisher is Gallimard.

3. MAN AND THE SEASHELL: "L'Homme et la coquille," first published, with a dedication to Abel Bonnard, in *La Nouvelle Revue française*, Feb. 1, 1937; separately, with a preface by Valéry and sixteen drawings by Henri Mondor (N.R.F., 1937); see *Œuvres I*, Pléiade (1957).

Henri Mondor: (1885–1962), professor of surgery at the School of Medicine of the University of Paris. Author of the exhaustive documentary *Vie de Mallarmé* and several studies of Valéry and Alain; elected in 1946 to Valéry's chair in the French Academy.

10. *This dissymmetry, to which Pasteur attached so profound*

an importance: One of Pasteur's earliest scientific discoveries proved that the rotation of the plane of polarized light in racemic acid was due to its molecular *dissymetry*. His conviction that this dissymetry was in turn due to the presence of a living organism led eventually to his revolutionary discovery of the principle of fermentation.

15. *I divide myself in order to create*: In his phrase "Je me divise pour créer," Valéry is no doubt playing a variation on the ancient political maxim *divide ut regnes, diviser pour régner*, "divide to rule."

26. *Mr. Einstein would develop an octopus capable of ensnaring and devouring all geometry . . . the all-powerful Mollusk of Reference. This monstrous cephalopod . . .* : The octopus, a cephalopod, is of the highest class of mollusks. There is an amusing consistency in the development of this figure representing the Einsteinian "body of reference" or "system of coordinates."

In his conception of man's relation to the world, Valéry saw each individual consciousness, the *moi*, as the center of its own universe. This idea has more than an accidental formal resemblance to relativity theory, in which space, time, mass, and motion are relative to each observer in his specific universe. Valéry knew Einstein's work as early as 1906. But for more than a decade before that, he had been absorbing the ideas of Faraday, Maxwell, and Poincaré and turning them into the substance of his own thought. Valéry's whole view of the mind and the world was developed in complete contemporaneity with the most advanced work of his time in mathematics and physics.

Miss Judith Robinson has reviewed this aspect of Valéry's thought in her article "Language, Physics and Mathematics in Valéry's Cahiers" (*Modern Language Review*, Oct., 1960,

p. 519). She summarizes his reading in relativity theory in this footnote:

He was well aware of the important contributions made by men other than Einstein—in particular by Fitzgerald, Lorentz and Poincaré, and by non-Euclidean geometers such as Riemann, Gauss and, later, Minkowski. Over the years, he kept in close contact with the development of the theory. As early as 1906, we find him referring in the Cahiers to special relativity theory; in 1919, translating an article from the 14 November issue of the *Athenaeum* on general relativity; in February, 1923, reading Einstein's *Meaning of Relativity* (1922); in November, 1929, attending lectures given by Einstein in Paris. Cahiers VII and VIII (1918–22) show him venturing into the geometry of the subject, and by 1925 he has begun, though tentatively, to explore the tensor calculus (see *Lettres à quelques-uns*, p. 155). Valéry would undoubtedly have learned a great deal from his association with Langevin, who did much to popularize relativity in France.

"*Master of itself and of the Universe*": "maître de soi comme de l'Univers," a variation on a memorable line, "Je suis maître de moi comme de l'Univers," spoken by the Emperor Augustus in Corneille's *Cinna* (V, 3).

31. SOME SIMPLE REFLECTIONS ON THE BODY: "Réflexions simples sur le corps," first published in a special issue, *Médecine et littérature*, of the review *Formes et couleurs* (Lausanne), 1943; in *Variété V* (1944); see *Œuvres I*, Pléiade (1957). "Problème des trois corps" tr. by Louise Varèse as "Problem of the Three Bodies," in *Selected Writings* (New York: New Directions, 1950).

33. "*Eternal returns*": The notion of cyclical repetition in history, life processes, etc. But Valéry is here using the term in the more trivial sense of an *idée fixe*, the obsessive recurrence

of some notion in the mind. (See Collected Works, Vol. 10, p. 254 & n.)

35. *The Problem of the Three Bodies*: A problem in celestial mechanics, also known as the three-body problem and defined in Van Nostrand's *Scientific Encyclopedia*:

> *Three-Body Problem.* If we assume that three or more objects exist in the universe, each of them attracting every other in accordance with the law of *gravitation*, the problem of predicting subsequent positions and motions is commonly referred to as the three-body problem, or the *n*-body problem.
>
> The *two-body problem* has been completely solved and the full solution may be expressed in comparatively few words and symbols. However, if we add one or more other bodies the solution becomes one of exceeding complexity and has never been accomplished in any form which is at all suitable for computational purposes. In fact, only one complete solution has ever been made, in spite of the labors of practically all of the great mathematicians of the past three centuries.

38. *But what would a Descartes, a Newton*: For a longer version of Valéry's fable of the philosophers and the dynamo see "The Outlook for Intelligence," Collected Works, Vol. 10, pp. 133 f.

39. *Relays within relays*: The "relay" was a constant figure in Valéry's thought. He had in mind the broken-circuit relay, the electromagnetic device used to open or close a switch and thus to operate other devices without actually transmitting an electric current to them. This figure expressed the discontinuity he saw between events in the physical world and events in the mind.

For other instances of the term, see herein, pp. 86, 232, and Collected Works, Vol. 12, p. 38 & n.

41. AESTHETICS: "Discours sur l'esthétique," the opening

address at the Second International Congress on Aesthetics and the Science of Art, Paris, Aug. 8, 1937; first published in the minutes of the Congress (Alcan), 1937; in *Variété IV* (1938); see *Œuvres I*, Pléiade (1957).

43. *For this year we must honor and obey Descartes*: Only a week before addressing the Congress on Aesthetics, Valéry had given the formal address in honor of Descartes on the occasion of the celebration at the Sorbonne, July 31, 1937, of the 300th anniversary of the publication of the *Discourse on Method*. (See Collected Works, Vol. 9.)

I shall undertake a "complete enumeration": a paraphrase of the essential sentence in the fourth and last precept of Descartes' method. (See Collected Works, Vol. 10, p. 52 & *n*.)

51. *What, for example, is so sound and satisfying to the mind as the famous rule of the three unities*: The unities of time, place, and action which ruled the French classical theater were stated by Boileau in his *Art poétique* (1674):

> *Un rimeur, sans péril, delà les Pyrénées,*
> *Sur la scène en un jour renferme des années,*
> *Là, souvent, le héros d'un spectacle grossier,*
> *Enfant au premier acte, est barbon au dernier.*
> *Mais nous, que la raison à ses règles engage,*
> *Nous voulons qu'avec art l'action se ménage;*
> *Qu'en un lieu, qu'en un jour, un seul fait accompli*
> *Tienne jusqu'à la fin le Théâtre rempli.*

> A Spanish poet may with good event
> In one day's space whole ages represent;
> There oft the hero of the wandering stage
> Begins a child, and ends the play of age.
> But we, that are by reason's rule confined,
> Will that with art the poem be designed,
> That unity of action, time, and place,
> Keep the stage full, and all our labors grace.

(*Art poétique*, III, tr. by Sir William Soames, 1710, and rev. by Dryden)

53. *Boileau thought he was following reason, and was impervious to the oddness and particularity of his precepts. What could be more capricious than forbidding the hiatus?*:

> *N'offrez rien au lecteur que ce qui peut lui plaire.*
> *Ayez pour la cadence une oreille sévère:*
> *Que toujours, dans vos vers, le sens, coupant les mots,*
> *Suspende l'hémistiche, en marque le repos.*
> *Gardez qu'une voyelle, à courir trop hâtée,*
> *Ne soit d'une voyelle en son chemin heurtée.*

> Write what your reader may be pleased to hear;
> And, for the measure, have a careful ear.
> On easy numbers fix your happy choice;
> Of jarring sounds avoid the odious noise:
> (*Art poétique*, I, tr. and rev. as in note above)

54. *What could be more farfetched than his justification of the advantages of rhyme?*:

> *Quelque sujet qu'on traite, ou plaisant, ou sublime,*
> *Que toujours le bon sens s'accorde avec la rime:*
> *L'un l'autre vainement ils semblent se haïr,*
> *La rime est une esclave, et ne doit qu'obéir,*
> *Lorsqu'à la bien chercher d'abord on s'évertue,*
> *L'esprit à la trouver aisément s'habitue;*
> *Au joug de la raison sans peine elle fléchit;*
> *Et, loin de la gêner, la sert et l'enrichit.*
> *Mais, lorsqu'on la néglige, elle devient rebelle;*
> *Et pour la rattraper le sens court après elle.*
> *Aimez donc la raison. Que toujours, vos écrits*
> *Empruntent d'elle seule et leur lustre et leur prix.*

> Whate'er you write of pleasant or sublime,
> Always let sense accompany your rhyme:

Falsely they seem each other to oppose;
Rhyme must be made with reason's laws to close;
And when to conquer her you bend your force,
The mind will triumph in the noble course;
To reason's yoke she quickly will incline,
Which, far from hurting, renders her divine;
But, if neglected, will as easily stray,
And master reason, which she should obey.
Love reason then; and let whate'er you write
Borrow from her its beauty, force, and light.
(Art poétique, I, tr. and rev. as in note above)

Joseph de Maistre: (1753–1821), political philosopher, diplomat, and historian. Born in Savoy, de Maistre spent 14 years as Italian Ambassador at St. Petersburg, where he was on intimate terms with Czar Alexander I and the Russian aristocracy. A militant royalist, contemptuous of the French Revolution, he wanted the restoration of "God, the Pope, and the King." His most widely read work is *Les Soirées de Saint-Pétersbourg* (1821).

Like Baudelaire, Valéry had a special fondness for this man's high-tempered prose, and cites him often. (See herein, pp. 243 and 54), and Collected Works, Vol. 10, pp. 165 f. & *n.*)

55. *Imperare parendo:* "to rule by obeying."

56. *Secundum artem:* "according to the rules of his art."

63. *Institut Poincaré:* an institute for the study of higher mathematics and physical theory, attached to the Faculty of Sciences at the University of Paris; founded in 1928, with funds from the Rockefeller Foundation and Baron Edmond de Rothschild, and named in honor of the mathematician Henri Poincaré (1854–1912).

66. AESTHETIC INVENTION: "L'Invention esthétique," a

lecture followed by discussion, as part of the 9th annual week
of meetings at the Centre International de Synthèse, Oct. 20,
1937; first published by the Centre in its volume entitled
L'Invention (Alcan), 1938; see *Œuvres I*, Pléiade (1957).

70. THE IDEA OF ART: "Notion générale de l'art," first published in *La Nouvelle Revue française*, Nov. 1, 1935; as introduction to *Arts et littératures dans la société contemporaine*, Vols.
XVI and XVII (1935) of *L'Encyclopédie française*; see *Œuvres I*,
Pléiade (1957).

80. "THE AESTHETIC INFINITE": "'L'Infini esthétique,'"
first published in *Art et médecine*, Feb., 1934; in *Pièces sur
l'art* (1934); see *Œuvres II*, Pléiade (1960).

83. ON THE TEACHING OF POETICS AT THE COLLÈGE DE
FRANCE: "De l'Enseignement de la poétique au Collège de
France," first published separately by the Société Générale
d'Imprimerie et d'Édition, 1937; together with "Première
Leçon du cours de poétique" as *Introduction à la poétique*
(1938); in *Variété V* (1944); see *Œuvres I*, Pléiade (1957).

Collège de France: founded by François I in 1530 to provide
instruction free from the rigid scholasticism of the Sorbonne;
it has preserved its special autonomy ever since, serving as a
kind of national institute of higher learning. Appointment to
its Faculty is considered the highest professorial honor in
France. The professors, not necessarily drawn from the uni-
versities, are nominated by the Faculty, approved by the
French Academy, and appointed by the government. The
lectures are open to the general public.

86. *Which acts largely by relays*: Here again Valéry has in
mind the basic figure of the broken-circuit device which acts

indirectly, not by direct transmission of a current. (See p. 39 & *n.*)

89. THE OPENING LECTURE OF THE COURSE IN POETICS: "Première Leçon du cours de poétique," delivered Dec. 10, 1937, first published separately for the author and the Faculty of the Collège de France, 1938; together with "De l'Enseignement de la poétique au Collège de France" as *Introduction à la poétique* (1938); under the title "Leçon inaugurale du cours de poétique du Collège de France," *Variété V* (1944); see *Œuvres I*, Pléiade (1957); tr. by Jackson Mathews as "A Course in Poetics, First Lesson," *Southern Review* (Winter, 1940); rev. in *The Creative Process*, ed. Brewster Ghiselin (Berkeley: Univ. of Calif. Press, 1952).

Valéry was appointed by government decree of Oct. 19, 1937 to the chair of poetics created for him at the Collège de France. His inaugural lecture two months later was a considerable intellectual-social event.

Mr. Minister: Jean Zay (1904–44), Minister of National Education (1936–40), responsible for democratic reforms still in force in the French educational system. He joined the Resistance in 1940 and was assassinated by the collaborationist militia.

Mr. Rector: Edmond Faral (1882–1958), professor of medieval literature at the Collège de France (1925), Rector (1937).

90. *Joseph Bédier*: (1864–1938), professor of medieval French literature at the Collège de France (1903–29), member of the French Academy (1920). His principal work, *Les Légendes épiques* (1908–13), threw new light on the medieval French epic; he is also widely known for his adaptation in modern French of the story of Tristan and Isolde.

93. *Abel Lefranc*: (1863–1953), professor of French language and literature at the Collège de France (1904–33); known chiefly for his critical editions of Rabelais and Calvin and his studies in the Renaissance.

95. *Internal politics . . . external politics*: In French, *politique intérieure* and *politique extérieure* are normal political terms, and would ordinarily be translated "domestic (or home) policy" and "foreign policy." But in the present context the regular translation would convey little or nothing of the analogy Valéry is drawing between political and intellectual activity. Hence the not altogether happy compromise.

103. "*Odoratus impedit cogitationem*": "A smell interferes with thought," a favorite citation of Valéry's; it expresses not only his sense of the fragility of intellectual structures but the close relation he conceived between sensibility and intellect. (See Collected Works, Vol. 12, p. 126 & *n.*)

112. MY "POETICS": "Ma 'Poétique,' " an article in the *Gazette de Lausanne*, April 26, 1942; see *Œuvres II*, Pléiade (1960), pp. 1604 ff.

Age bids me to step down from a chair to which I was appointed five years ago: Valéry had expected to retire from the Collège de France in the spring of 1941, at the age of 70, but by a decree of May 29, 1941 he was reappointed for one year. In April, 1942, then, when the article "My 'Poetics' " was written, Valéry again thought he was retiring and actually delivered a farewell lecture (unpublished). However, he continued to be reappointed from year to year until his death, July 20, 1945.

Alexandre Moret: (1868–1938), an eminent Egyptologist, professor at the Collège de France.

"*Royal readers*": "Lecteurs royaux," the title of the first professors appointed by the king at the founding of the Collège de France. (See note for p. 83.)

117. THE CREATION OF ART: "La Création artistique," a talk followed by discussion before the Société Française de Philosophie, Jan. 28, 1928; first published in the Society's *Bulletin*, Jan., 1928; in *Vues* (La Table Ronde, 1948).

I am disconcerted and honored to be summoned to appear: Valéry is playfully posing as an outsider, a sort of bad boy of philosophy. In introducing him, Xavier Léon had just said: "I am aware that Paul Valéry claims that he is no philosopher, that he is even the 'anti-philosopher.' But philosophers insist that an antithesis implies a thesis, and that makes Paul Valéry a philosopher in spite of himself" (*Bulletin de la Société Française de Philosophie*, Jan., 1928, p. 2).

Xavier Léon: philosopher, and presiding officer of the Société Française de Philosophie.

123. *M. Brunschvicg*: Léon Brunschvicg (1869–1944), philosopher; professor at the Sorbonne from 1909; he developed from Kantian idealism a philosophy of science and mathematics. (See Collected Works, Vol. 12, p. 72 & *n.*)

129. *Quantum potes, tantum aude*: a line from a great hymn, "Lauda, Sion, Salvatorem" by Thomas Aquinas. Valéry himself, in one of his unpublished lectures on poetics, made this impromptu translation of the line, which he liked to cite: "Ose tant que tu pourras," "Dare to do all you can."

132. *Paul Desjardins*: (1859–1940), philosopher; founder of the series of international summer conferences of writers and artists at the Abbaye de Pontigny, near Auxerre. (See Collected Works, Vol. 10, second note for p. 23.)

"*I found, and still find, it unworthy to write out of mere enthusiasm*": See "Note and Digression" (1919), Collected Works, Vol. 8, or *Œuvres I*, Pléiade (1957).

134. "*When you ask an engineer to produce a locomotive*": Cf. "Poetry and Abstract Thought," Collected Works, Vol. 7, pp. 78 f.

135. *H. Delacroix*: Henri Delacroix (1873–1937), philosopher and psychologist; professor and later dean of the Faculty of Letters at the Sorbonne; wrote extensively on the psychology of mysticism (*Les Grands Mystiques chrétiens*, 1908), and on aesthetics (*La Psychologie de Stendhal*, 1918).

136. *On one occasion a simple rhythm occurred to me*: Valéry discusses the composition of *Le Cimetière Marin* and *La Pythie* in these terms in "Poetry and Abstract Thought," Collected Works, Vol. 7, pp. 80 f.

139. REFLECTIONS ON ART: "Réflexions sur l'art," a lecture followed by discussion before the Société Française de Philosophie, Mar. 2, 1935; first published in the Society's *Bulletin*, March–April, 1935; not republished.

André Lalande: (1867–   ), philosopher of science, member of the Académie des Sciences Morales et Politiques, editor with Xavier Léon of the *Bulletin de la Société Française de Philosophie*, and Secretary General of that Society.

144. *"Prends ce pic et me romps ce caillou qui me nuit"*: Valéry had changed more than "two words." He had a habit of misquoting this line of La Fontaine's, "Prends ton pic, et me romps ce caillou qui te nuit," having long since made it his own. The line is from *Le Chartier embourbé*, "The Cart Driver Stuck in the Mud," Book VI, Fable XVIII. (See Collected Works, Vol. 7, p. 248 & *n*.)

163. *Alain*: pseudonym of Émile-Auguste Chartier (1868–1951), philosopher and moralist; professor at the Lycée Henri IV in Paris. (See Collected Works, Vol. 7, p. 153 & *n*.)

Charles Lalo: (1877–1953), philosopher; he wrote mainly on aesthetics: *Les Sentiments esthétiques* (1910), *L'Art et la vie sociale* (1921), *Les Grandes Évasions esthétiques* (1947).

Abbé Dubos: Jean-Baptiste Dubos (1670–1742), historian, critic, and diplomat; member of the French Academy (1720) and Permanent Secretary of that body (1722); author of *Réflexions critiques sur la poésie et la peinture* (1719).

164. *M. Basch*: Victor Basch (1863–1944), philosopher and political activist; professor of aesthetics at the Sorbonne; founder of the League for the Rights of Man; anti-Fascist; assassinated during the Occupation by the collaborationist militia.

167. *I'll build if I must, but . . .*: In French Valéry cites the first half of a well-known line from La Fontaine: "Passe encor de bâtir; mais planter à cet âge!" (From *Le Vieillard et les trois jeunes hommes*, "The Old Man and the Three Youths," Book XI, Fable VIII; tr. by Edward Marsh):

> *Un octogénaire plantait.*
> *Passe encor de bâtir; mais planter à cet âge!*
> *Disaient trois jouvenceaux, enfants du voisinage;*
> *Assurément il radotait.*

> A man of eighty, planting!
> To build at such an age might be no harm,
> Argued three youngsters from a neighboring farm,
> But to plant trees! the old boy was plainly wanting.

René Berthelot: (1872–1960), philosopher, son of a distinguished scientist; professor at the University of Brussels and member of the Belgian Academy; a "rational idealist," his principal work is on the pragmatism of Nietzsche, Poincaré, and Bergson: *Un Romantisme utilitarien. Étude sur le mouvement pragmatiste* (1911–13).

169. *"The Triumph of Manet"*: For the passage in question, see Collected Works, Vol. 12, p. 107.

170. *D. Parodi*: Dominique Parodi (1870–1955), moral

and political philosopher, editor of the *Revue de métaphysique
et de morale* (1938), member of the Académie des Sciences
Morales et Politiques (1944); author of *Du Positivisme à
l'idéalisme* (1930), *La Conduite humaine et les valeurs idéales*
(1939).

Starts over a dozen times: Valéry's phrase "remet vingt fois
son œuvre sur le métier," is an allusion to Boileau's "Vingt
fois sur le métier remettez votre ouvrage" (*Art poétique*, I).

176. *R. Bayer*: Raymond Bayer (1898–1959), philosopher; professor at the Sorbonne from 1942; editor of the
Corpus des philosophes français, of the *Revue d'esthétique*, of the
Bibliographie de la philosophie, etc.; an organizer of international congresses on philosophy. He called his own philosophy "operational realism."

183. STYLE: "Style," first published in *Arts et style*, Feb.,
1945; in *Vues* (La Table Ronde, 1948).

186. A BRIEF ADDRESS TO THE SOCIETY OF ENGRAVERS:
"Petit Discours aux peintres graveurs," given at a dinner of
the Société des Peintres Graveurs Français, Nov. 29, 1933;
first published by the Society, 1934; in *Pièces sur l'art* (1934);
see *Œuvres II*, Pléiade (1960).

What little association I have had with engraving: Valéry
often made drawings and water color sketches in his notebooks, as part of his early morning spiritual exercises. He was
once awarded the Ambroise Vollard prize for painting (June
15, 1923), and at one point was elected president of the
Société des Peintres Graveurs. He became especially in-
terested in engraving and lithography, and used to work with
Daragnès in his studio. Daragnès has given this account of
Valéry's visits (in his *Paul Valéry vivant*, Cahiers du Sud, Mar-
seilles, 1946, p. 122):

He would often come to my house, his pockets bulging with notebooks full of sketches, his ideas taking shape. . . . With no pretensions at all, he would show me his work and ask my advice, and I was touched to see him follow it without a quibble. Time and again he would spend whole afternoons with me (except Thursdays, which were set aside for the Academy), engraving the copper plates I had prepared for him and keeping up a running conversation, or rather a monologue, to which in turn I listened keenly. That superb thinking machine never stopped. Even while engraving he enjoyed analyzing the act of engraving. . . .

190. *Intelligenti pauca*: "a word to the wise."
For the greater glory of black and white: "Ad majorem gloriam Dei" is the motto of the Jesuit order. The kind of turn Valéry gives to it here has doubtless become usual.

191. IN PRAISE OF VIRTUOSITY: "Esquisse d'un éloge de la virtuosité," first published for the 100th anniversary of the death of Paganini (Nice), May, 1940; in *Vues* (La Table Ronde, 1948).

197. PHILOSOPHY OF THE DANCE: "Philosophie de la danse," a lecture given at the Université des Annales, Mar. 5, 1936; first published in *Conférencia*, Nov. 1, 1936; in *Œuvres*, Vol. K (1939); see *Œuvres I*, Pléiade (1957).
On the Université des Annales and *Conférencia*, see Collected Works, Vol. 10, Notes, pp. 594 f.

205. *Unknown jewels like those of which Baudelaire speaks*: Valéry is probably remembering, inaccurately, the next-to-last stanza of Baudelaire's "Bénédiction":

> *Mais les bijoux perdus de l'antique Palmyre,*
> *Les métaux inconnus, les perles de la mer,*
> *Par votre main montés, ne pourraient pas suffire*
> *À ce beau diadème éblouissant et clair;*

> But the lost jewels of ancient Palmyra,
> Unknown metals, the sea's pearls,
> Mounted by Thy hand, would be unworthy
> Of that marvelous diadem, dazzling and clear;

Everything happens as if: "Tout se passe comme si. . . ." Valéry's phrase is not to be read as if it were simply an incomplete remark. The implication is its actual meaning. It is an idiom of his own which he used to point out the *relativity* of all action whose end is art or faith. In the *Cahiers* (IX, 297 he says:

> Belief—Faith—Relativity.
> Nothing can reveal the God. Everything happens as if—
> The believer pretends that he has performed Michelson's experiment with positive results.

206. *Least action*: a term Valéry adopted from physics and used often. "The principle is displayed where the amount of energy expended in performing a given action is the least required for its execution" (J. R. Newman, *The World of Mathematics*, II, p. 882). (See Collected Works, Vol. 10, p. 8 & *n*.)

212. THE PHYSICAL ASPECTS OF A BOOK: "Le Physique du livre," first published in *Le Physique du livre*, a book on Paul Bonet, by Valéry, Paul Éluard, et al. (Librairie Auguste Blaizot, 1945); see *Œuvres II*, Pléiade (1960), p. 1569.

222. ART AND TECHNOLOGY: "Art et technique," first published in *Revue de synthèse*, July–August, 1937; not republished.

225. THE CONQUEST OF UBIQUITY: "La Conquête de l'ubiquité," first published in *De la Musique avant toute chose*

(Éditions du Tambourinaire), 1928; in *Pièces sur l'art* (1934); see *Œuvres II*, Pléiade (1960); tr. anon as "On Music," *The Commonweal* (Oct. 15, 1930).

226. *"Just, subtle, and mighty" substances*: Valéry says "substances justes, puissantes et subtiles," using Baudelaire's "juste, subtil et puissant opium," but giving the phrase an order and lightness of his own. Valéry probably read De Quincey only in Baudelaire's translation, and that as a very young man.

228. *I am reminded here of a fairy play*: For an elaboration of this childhood memory, see Collected Works, Vol. 10, p. 168 & *n*.

229. HYPOTHESIS: "Hypothèse," first published as one section of an article entitled "Réflexions" in *Revue des vivants*, Mar., 1929; in the same context, in *Remarques extérieures* (Éditions des Cahiers Libres, 1929); see *Œuvres II*, Pléiade (1960); tr. anon. as "Reflections on Commonsense and Personality," *Yale Review* (Autumn, 1929).

232. *Relays*: see p. 39 & *n*.

Appendix

237. SEMANTICS: a review of *La Sémantique* (*Science des Significations*), by Michel Bréal, in *Mercure de France*, Jan., 1898; see *Œuvres II*, Pléiade (1960), pp. 1448 ff.

This is one of three articles by Valéry published under the rubric *Méthodes* in the *Mercure de France* from 1897 to 1899. For the other two, see herein, pp. 259 ff., and Collected Works, Vol. 10, pp. 489 ff. & *n*.

241. *Michel Bréal*: (1832–1915), professor of comparative grammar at the Collège de France (1864); member of the Académie des Inscriptions (1875); author of numerous works

in linguistics, of which *La Sémantique* (1897) is among the last.

247. αστήρ, "a star." δìκαστήρ, "a court of justice." ἐργαστήρ, "a workman, a farmer."

257. *Marcel Schwob*: (1867–1905), symbolist novelist and literary historian; one of Valéry's earliest friends in Paris. (See Collected Works, Vol. 10, p. xii & *n.*)

259. TIME: review of *La Machine à explorer le Temps* ("The Time Machine"), by H. G. Wells, in *Mercure de France*, May, 1899; see *Œuvres II*, Pléiade (1960), pp. 1454 ff.

This is one of three articles by Valéry published under the heading *Méthodes* in the *Mercure de France* from 1897 to 1899. For the other two, see herein, pp. 237 ff., and Collected Works, Vol. 10, pp. 489 ff. & *n.*

Davray: Henry D. Davray reported on English writing in his regular feature, "Lettres Anglaises," in the *Mercure de France*. (See Collected Works, Vol. 10, p. 578.)

INDEX

INDEX

[The subject entries summarize Valéry's basic ideas about aesthetics but do not employ all of the various terms that occur in the text. The letter *n* refers to the textual notes on pp. 281–98; e.g., "3*n*" will be found on p. 281.]

Achilles, 92, 201

accident, *see* creative process, chance in

action(s): of animals, 16–17, 72, 184, 199–200, 215; as basis of explanation, 4, 12, 18, 21; complete human, 4, 46, 61, 67, 161; in fashioning work of art, viii, xii, xiv, 5, 15–17, 66–67, 69, 82, 85, 88, 102, 105, 109–10, 151, 189, 208, 209, 214–15; in interpreting work of art, 66–67, 69, 100–101, 124–25, 142, 157–58, 193–95, 203, 205, 207–8, 210; necessary to survival, 16–17, 31–33, 73–75, 80–81, 148–49, 198–99; unnecessary to survival, as root of art, 33–35, 72–77, 81, 113–14, 149, 152, 198, 200, 208, 215

Aeneid (Virgil), 194

aesthetic infinite, *see* order, aesthetic

aesthetics: aims of, 82, 128, 140–41, 165; combines intellect, sensibility, action, xi, 45, 46–48; distinguishes creator,

work, audience, 96, 98, 106, 124–25, 142–43, 177–79; future role of, 63–64; indefinability of, x, 60, 62, 64; metaphysical, *see next entry;* recommended method in, 60–61; schools of, 139–40, 165–67, 175; self-observation as method in, vii, 59–60, 111, 115, 129

——,metaphysical: flaws in, 48–53, 56–58, 60, 123–24; method in, 43–45, 47–49; subject matter of, 44–48; true role of, 53–55, 60

Aesthetics (Hegel), 166–67

Alain (pseud. of Émile-Auguste Chartier), 3*n*, 163 & *n*

Amphion (Valéry), 173

Aquinas, St. Thomas, 129*n*

arbitrary, the, *see* creative process

architecture, 52

Argentina, Mme (pseud. of Antonia Mercé y Luque), 197, 211

Aristotle, 201

art: aims of, x, xii–xiii, 6, 27, 73, 76, 82, 151–52, 193, 208, 215; fashions in, 169; Great, 160–

ornament: as reaction to va-
cancy, 152, 213–14, 216–17; of
shells, 6, 9, 22

painting(s): a demonstration,
159–60; history of, 84, 141;
labeling of, 141, 169–70;
portraits, 154, 159
Parnassianism, 169
Parodi, Dominique, 170 & *n*,
171, 172
Pascal, Blaise, 200
Pasteur, Louis, 10 & *n*
performance / performer: and
dance, 203–6, 210; effort of,
194–95, 203; freedom and
constraint in, 208–9; and
music, 208–9; and poetry, 69,
100–101, 124–25, 157–58, 193,
194, 208; relation to audience,
175, 191–95; spontaneity and
consciousness in, 204–5; *see
also* virtuosity
philosopher-artists, 60, 117–18,
117*n*
philosophy: analyzes the dance,
202–7; function of, xi, 18, 29,
47; will to power of, x, 47;
see also aesthetics; aesthetics,
metaphysical
physics, 22, 23, 26*n*, 39, 46,
63–64, 221, 231–32
Pièces sur l'art (Valéry), 164
pleasure: aesthetic, x–xi, 45–51,
58–59, 62, 101–2, 107, 163,
176, 215; of dance, 198, 207,
211; of making, 188
Plougrescan, 174
poetics: defined, 86–87, 90–92,
113; program for, 84, 86–88
poetry: composition in, 132,
156–57; creative process of,

67–69, 108–9, 129–31, 136,
178; and dance, 208, 210–11;
language of, 48, 67–69, 108–9,
131–32, 157, 211; recitation
of, 69, 100–101, 124–25, 157–
58, 193, 194, 208; *see also*
literature
poietic(s), 61, 92, 113, 114
Poincaré, Henri, 26*n*, 63*n*, 167*n*
politics, of intellectual life, 95 &
n, 168
producer, *see* creator; economics
psychology, 118, 127, 135, 239,
241, 267–69
Pythie, La (Valéry), 133, 136*n*

"*Quantum potes, tantum aude*,"
129 & *n*

Racine, Jean Baptiste, 53, 194
Raffaelli, Jean François, 219
reality, inner and outer, 28–29,
39*n*, 205, 207
reason, *see* creative process; in-
tellect
relays, 39 & *n*, 86 & *n*, 177–78,
232
Rembrandt, 170
Renaissance, 140
Renan, Ernest, 174
Renoir, Pierre Auguste, 162
Riemann, Georg F. B., 26*n*, 269
Ring of the Nibelungs, The (Wag-
ner), 162
Robinson, Judith, 26*n*
royal readers, 112 & *n*
Rubens, Peter Paul, 170

Schopenhauer, Arthur, 120
Schwob, Marcel, 257*n*, 259
semantics: nonscientific state of,
237–41; and psychology, 239,

This colophon was chosen from a number of drawings by Paul Valéry of his favorite device.